The Truth
Shall Set You Free

The Truth
Shall Set You Free

a memoir

A Family's Passage from Fundamentalism to a New Understanding of Faith, Love, and Sexual Identity

SALLY LOWE WHITEHEAD

HarperSanFrancisco
An Imprint of HarperCollins*Publishers*

HarperCollins Web Site: http://www.harpercollins.com
HarperCollins®, ♠®, and HarperSanFrancisco™ are trademarks of HarperCollins Publishers, Inc.

FIRST EDITION

Library of Congress Cataloging-in-Publication Data
Whitehead, Sally Lowe.
The truth shall set you free : a family's passage from
fundamentalism to a new understanding of faith, love, and
sexual identity / Sally Lowe Whitehead. — 1st ed.
ISBN 0–06–251393–1 (cloth)
1. Whitehead, Sally Lowe. 2. Wives—Georgia—Biography.
3. Wives—Religious life—Georgia—Case studies. 4. Closeted
gays—Georgia—Family relationships—Case studies. 5. Gay
men—Georgia—Family relationships—Case studies.
6. Coming out (Sexual orientation)—Georgia—Case studies.
7. Homosexuality—Religious aspects—Christianity. I. Title.
HQ759.W46 1997
306.872'092—dc21   96–6507

97 98 99 00 01 ❖ RRDH 10 9 8 7 6 5 4 3 2 1

The great Creator of the worlds, the sovereign God of heaven,
his holy and immortal truth to all on earth hath given.
Not to oppress, but summon all their truest life to find
in love God sent His Son to save, not to condemn mankind.

From the 1982 Hymnal, Epistle to Diognetus,
tr. F. Bland Tucker

Suffering comes from resistance, wanting to do something or be something other than who I am.

Diane Mariechild, Open Mind

This legacy is dedicated to the nine very authentic men with whom I am privileged to love and share life:

First and foremost to Mel—my amazing husband, my best friend, and the absolute love of my life.

To Michael—a *real* hero, and at last my *real* and cherished friend. No more suffering, brother.

To Craig—Michael's lifetime companion and now my treasured lifetime friend.

To my six exceptional sons, starting with my very proficient firstborn (and "best-ever" oldest brother) Michael—truly, "on the day that you were born the angels got together and decided to create a dream come true." Daniel—veritable music maker, truth-seeker, and gentle, loving caretaker of souls, including his own. Matthew—a passionate artist of manifold measure who readily returns to the world a medley of gifts, especially the priceless one of real connection. Timothy—truly tenderhearted, immensely creative and knowing, and whose time has finally come to soar! Josiah—a celestial surprise who blesses us all with boundless talent along with keen sensitivity and awareness. Samuel—absolutely sparkling with effervescence and remarkably perceptive—my "baby," whom I simply adore.

Because of each of you, both my life and that of our Mother Earth herself are infinitely inspired and abundantly blessed.

contents

chapter 1

A Safe Place on St. Simons Island

St. Simons Island is one of the three Golden Isles off the Georgia coast. The island had been my second home since I was first brought there, as a baby, by my parents and introduced to its warm gray beaches with matching gray water. We spent every summer there, and a gracious world was mine. As the youngest daughter, I enjoyed an especially free reign, gallivanting all around the otherwise dignified King and Prince Hotel. I had my favorite waiters, knew the room maids by name, drove the desk clerks mad with endless questions, and haunted the gift shop from morning until night. I spent days at the beach or by the pool with my summer friends, and found all manner of boyfriends for my older sisters until they wisely paid me to stop. In the evenings we dressed up to eat in the grand dining room, after which I either played bingo or, if allowed, watched my mother and father glide across the dance floor like Ginger Rogers and Fred Astaire. Sometimes Daddy would take me out onto the floor and, to the oohs and aahs and amiable laughter of friends sipping their drinks by the pool or bar, dance with me. My father, even though sometimes a bit heavy, was a small man, and my mother even smaller, so they seemed a lightsome, adorable couple on the dance floor. *I* imagined them to be the most beautiful and romantic couple on earth. I suppose it was during those magical nights, watching them dance together, that I fell in love with love. Even after, over the years, my family went through various exhausting changes, my fantasies about my parents unraveled, and I simply grew up, the genteel St. Simons Island could restore me.

The first time I saw Michael's lean, tanned body and his broad swimmer's shoulders, golden hair, blue eyes, and killer smile, I was immediately interested and more. Michael's sister Helen, my classmate and friend, had invited me for a week's visit to their family's cottage on Lake Lanier in the North Georgia mountains. It was late afternoon, and the three of us were taking turns water-skiing on the busy lake. I couldn't take my eyes off Michael while he twisted and turned himself magnificently across the choppy water on one ski. I thought dreamily that he reminded me a lot of Troy Donahue in *A Summer Place*. By the end of the day, I had decided: "Helen's *got* to get me a date with him!"

Of course, Helen had been watching me moon over her brother all afternoon. Now she suddenly laughed knowingly and said, "You're pitiful! I'll talk to him, okay?"

"Thanks," I said and gave her knee a squeeze.

That week was special to me. I liked Michael, and I liked his family. My family seemed sparse—with three girls, carefully spaced six and eleven years apart—compared with Michael's, which was definitely teeming, with six spirited children: four boys and two girls. I wondered how Michael's mother managed with so many children; her task seemed overwhelming to me.

And yet I was very taken with the way of life I saw there. The kids all hung out together in the daytime, swimming and skiing on the lake or riding into the nearby small town of Cumming for an ice cream. At night the family played bridge or other games, in which they were sometimes joined by another family with a house on the lake. Theirs was a *real* family, I thought, remembering how I had badgered my mother for years with questions about why she stopped having babies after me. I had always been unhappy that there was no one younger than I in the family. I was sorry that I did not have a brother, something I had romantically imagined as wonderful. Finally my mother told me that there had been a male child, their firstborn, who had died at birth. "Blue babies" they were called then, when the umbilical cord wrapped around their necks. She told me she would have stopped after my two sisters, had her doctor not insisted that she give it one more try, in hopes of providing a son for my father. They got me instead. Her explanation quieted most of my protests concerning the lack of a younger sibling, but it instilled in me an anxiety as to what extent my father, who clearly had yearned for a boy, could enjoy or love a third daughter. Though these concerns complicated my feelings about my parents and my sisters, they never stopped me from wishing that one day I would have a large family of the sort I experienced with Helen and Michael during that summer of 1969.

In the fall Helen and I began our junior year at Lovett, the private coed prep school we attended together in Atlanta, where both of our families lived. Though Helen had suggested to Michael that he ask me out, he asked out another girl instead. I watched them sitting together at Lovett's first football game. Next he asked one of my best friends out, over the phone, while, unbeknownst to him, I stood beside her listening. She said no and, barely controlling her laughter, suggested that he try me. I ran down the street to my house and waited hopefully for his call. It came, and I accepted his invitation for a date.

Years later Michael would love to tell the story of how I chased him until I caught him. Michael was a senior at Marist, a Catholic all-boy military school. Even though he was athletic and an excellent diver on his school's diving team, I saw him as a nice change from the jock-type football players I had known since sixth grade—and from one in particular, a boy I had dated for four years.

Ben was a year older than I, and we had gone steady since I was in the seventh grade and he was in the eighth grade at Lovett, where I was a cheerleader and he was a football player. Our relationship was intense and melodramatic. Whenever the football team lost, he would fall into a macho silence, which I was asked to not disturb. He would then explain that he would emerge from it once he had sufficiently mourned the loss of the game. We would speed out of the football stadium in his baby-blue Mustang, and usually a song, maybe "Hooked on a Feeling" or "Ain't No Mountain High Enough," would come on the radio and lift his gloom.

Ben would play the drums for hours in his basement at home while I happily listened. He was jealous of the time I spent with my girlfriends, while I worried that he would find someone else. Ben and I would frequently and emotionally break up, then urgently reunite. The uncertainty was exciting and held us firmly in its grip. Though I am still not sure how it was possible, as young as we were, we truly loved each other. We never stayed apart for too long.

It was during one of my more lengthy breakups with Ben that Michael finally asked me out. I was correct in thinking that dating Michael would not be so anxiety provoking; we had a terrific and easy time together. Even though I sometimes thought about Ben, and assumed that we would eventually return to each other as we had before, Michael proved to be wonderful. He was playful, and we laughed a lot. Sometimes he would grab me and hold me down on the ground, tickling me until I cried. Ignoring my screams of "Gross! Stop it!" he would proceed to give me what he called a "wet willie," which was in fact a nasty, wet tongue in my ear or, sometimes worse, all over my face. He was so easy to be with, and during those early days he seemed as grateful for me as I was for him.

Even though Mother liked Ben very much, she had understandably grown weary of our volatile relationship. One night, she and I stood talking in her powder room while she performed her nightly ritual of removing her makeup. After coating her face with a thick layer of cold cream, she said, "I'm glad you and Ben broke up, Sally. You look so much happier."

"Yeah, I am," I replied, watching her slowly drag the brown mess off with several tissues, then throw them away. I thought about telling her that I liked her face better without makeup, but I could imagine her taking it the wrong way and telling me, "If you don't have something nice to say, don't say anything at all." It wasn't worth the risk.

Looking at me through her own reflection in the mirror, she suddenly advised, "I hope you wouldn't do anything you shouldn't do with Michael, now that the two of you are going steady."

I knew she meant "do anything sexual," and for a second I looked away from the mirror.

"Michael's family is *Catholic*, Sally!" she said, emphasizing the word *Catholic* as if that would explain everything. Then, to be sure I understood, she added, "I'll just tell you this: if you get pregnant, that boy's family will kill you! They are very well off, Sally."

I knew Michael was Catholic. I also knew his parents owned a chain of fine stores and were part of the "old Atlanta money" scene. But how any of that related to Michael and me I could not imagine.

Shrugging my shoulders, I turned and walked down the hall to my bedroom. Looking back over my shoulder, I lied: "Don't worry, Mama. We're not doing anything." I doubted she believed me, but I also knew that, as vague as it had been, her lecture to me would be the only one I would hear on the subject of my having sex with Michael.

I liked Michael, and I especially liked how well we got along with each other. Besides his sense of humor, I enjoyed his gentle disposition. He was an activist, politically and socially, and he was very much interested in bucking the system. We talked about things that bothered us in our privileged world, such as bigotry and elitism, and about things in the underprivileged world, such as poverty and abuse, that neither of us knew much about but that both of us felt an odd responsibility for. We were against the war in Vietnam, and we thoroughly questioned most of those in authority, especially President Nixon and our parents. Both of our schools had strict requirements for students regarding uniforms and grooming during the school week, so Michael and I played at being "weekend hippies." Michael wore love beads and tight thermal or tie-dyed shirts. We both wore hip-hugging bell-bottom jeans with thick belts. My hair was long and straight, and Michael had grown his sideburns as far down onto his face as was permissible, while still keeping the back of his hair the required military-school length. We were idealistic, zealous young rebels wishing for autonomy, and hungry for a cause that we could believe was worth fighting for. We were ready to change the world "out there," and eager to get away from our parents, whom we perceived to be unjustly dogmatic and intolerant.

Marijuana was then just beginning to become a topic of discussion in our schools; the preppie-type kids at Lovett were not yet smoking pot. However, in the spring of 1970, Michael and I decided that we wanted to try it. We had to secretly cross carefully defined social boundaries just to ask someone in the "freaky" crowd at my school where we could buy marijuana. One Friday afternoon, we sneaked downtown to the forbidden Fourteenth Street area of Atlanta, where all the real, full-time hippies lived and ran paraphernalia shops with names like Onion Dome and Psychedelic Frog. Once we found the street, and then found the person we had been instructed to look for, we nervously bought our first bag of grass. Even though we were scared to smoke much of it, we smoked enough to become mildly stoned, extremely silly, and quite hungry. Laughing all the way, over not much of anything, we drove to my house and ate a huge amount of French toast. The next day we decided we'd better not make smoking pot a regular habit. As carefree and giddy as it made us feel, we were afraid of using a drug that was still such a mystery and possibly carried harmful long-term effects. We decided it was safer to continue with the traditional and acceptable weekend drinking parties we easily enjoyed with each other and our friends.

Soon I was not thinking of anyone but Michael. On school-day afternoons, I stood outside and watched impatiently for him to pull up into my driveway in his Austin Healey Sprite convertible. Then, finely dressed in his ROTC uniform, he would slide out of the sports car, grin, run his fingers through his wavy, blond hair, adjust his hat, and kiss me hello. He was both handsome and beautiful at the same time. Again I would think how unique Michael was, and how lucky I was to have found a boy like him.

Our dating had also given me a newfound courage to explore some ideas and interests in my life that I had not previously believed I could risk considering. In the 1960s, high school cliques were fiercely defined, usually by their activities, and often, too, by a person's degree of physical attractiveness and athletic ability. One did not dare become involved in an activity that might identify one with any group other than one's own. For example, if a cheerleader wanted to maintain her popularity, she did not join the drama club. Football players didn't play chess. In those days, at my school, drama and chess were not on the list of "popular" activities. I began to wonder who had made those lists and began to doubt their importance—both of which were revolutionary notions for a northwest Atlanta girl in a private school in 1970. That kind of thinking would not be helpful when it came time for me to be considered as a Cherokee Club debutante. Even though most of us girls coveted membership in the school's sororities and had been willing to suffer through miserable pledge times and initiations to gain admission to them, the whole experience now seemed a hurtful ordeal that had never really been fun. I wondered if I really fit into these groups anymore, or if I even wanted to.

Throughout the school year, I had become involved in a newly formed Christian organization called the Young Life Club that met each week and offered teenagers a soft, palatable gospel message. Michael shared my interest, and we began to attend the meetings—which were also a great excuse for a midweek date.

The short teachings offered at the Young Life meetings were designed to encourage teenagers to think about the love of Jesus Christ and His death on the cross for the forgiveness of our sins as the only way to salvation. As a child, I had always been interested in God and spirituality. And, although my family were active Episcopalians, I always hungered for something more. It was because of this that the powerful simplicity of these messages touched me in such a profound way.

One weekend I attended a Young Life retreat during which, on the last night, we were all asked to consider responding to the love of Christ by "accepting Him as our Savior," then "living our lives for Him." I could not remember ever having been specifically given this "salvation message" in my Episcopal church. We had dispersed to ponder the message individually, which I did sitting outside on a hill. I thought about Jesus' love, which I understood now to be meant for me personally, and I began to cry. After a few minutes, I looked up at the star-filled sky and prayed: "Thank you, Jesus, for loving me and for dying for me. I want to dedicate my life to you. Amen."

I returned home from the retreat feeling lighter and even freer from worrying about what my peers thought of me—except, of course, for Michael.

The Young Life leaders were also available to teenagers for individual counseling, hoping to help them with the difficult decisions they were having to make while growing up. That spring, Michael and I decided we should talk to one of the Young Life counselors. We set up several appointments, which for various reasons were always canceled by the counselor. We wanted help in dealing with something that was becoming a major issue for us—sex.

The standard accommodation for premarital intimacy in those days was usually the backseat of a car, which in our case was Michael's very small sports car. One warm night, after a Young Life meeting, Michael drove us to our favorite place to "park."

"Turn your headlights off—just in case," I whispered as we turned into the cul-de-sac of empty, newly constructed homes.

Michael parked and quickly shut down the noisy engine. He pushed his car door open because, when he was stretched out in a prone position, he was longer than the sports car was wide. In a matter of seconds, we were lost in unprotected sexual bliss.

So lost, in fact, that we weren't even aware of the car that drove up next to us until its headlights lit up our faces and, I suppose, everything else. With one quick move, Michael jerked his legs back inside, slammed the door, and started the engine; we took off with both of us still scrambling to put ourselves back together.

As we sped away, I glanced back to where we had been parked and burst out laughing.

"What's so funny?!" Michael demanded, straining frantically to look in the rearview mirror.

"Your boxer shorts!" I choked out through my laughter. "They're back there on the road! I sure hope they don't have your name on them!"

"Oh my God," Michael groaned, "they better not." He grinned sheepishly then, to let me know he was joking. We were still laughing when we turned into my driveway and he kissed me good night. "Close call, huh?" he said.

"Yeah, it sure was. I hope it wasn't too close in another way," I said before hurrying into the house.

We were just kids, but we were wild about each other. We were also wild about sex. We spent every possible moment together, and that frequently meant having sex. In those days, girls commonly denied that they were sexually active, even to their friends, and few parents talked about birth control. Couples "did it" and then swore never to "do it" again. Michael and I fell right into that pattern, until the day that we discovered a way to ease our guilt once and for all.

At one of the weekly Young Life meetings, the leader, no doubt in an attempt to discourage premarital sex, instructed the group of teenagers present that night that, in the eyes of God, a couple were already looked upon as married if they were indulging in the forbidden fruits of sexual intercourse. The thought of God watching us having sex disturbed Michael and me. I had just made a commitment to live a life dedicated to God, and Michael had to make daily confessions of any sinful offenses to a priest at his Catholic school. His confessions were growing numerous, and we were beginning to feel guilty. After our unsuccessful attempts to meet with a Young Life counselor, we gave up and decided to look at the teaching we had just heard on sex in a more favorable way. We decided that if we were already considered married in the eyes of God (for clearly we had indulged), there simply was no longer any reason for having guilty feelings, or for confessing what we did. We might just as well accept ourselves as being what God considered us to be—married.

Every day Michael and I wrote long letters to each other, which we exchanged through his sister Helen. Sometimes, after school, I would drive my mother's car over to where his car was parked for a diving meet and leave him a surprise gift on the passenger seat. One spring day I left him a goldfish swimming around in a bowl. He outdid me by giving me a live rabbit as an Easter present. He was a great friend, the brother I had never had; quickly—too quickly—we had become faithful young lovers.

One Saturday morning in May, I got up much earlier than usual. Telling Mother I needed to study for final exams at a friend's house, I asked to borrow her car. Instead of studying, however, I picked up my friend and we hurried to meet our physical-education teacher at her apartment.

The teacher was a large, muscular woman who easily intimidated me with her booming voice. Still, I had heard that she was sympathetic to teenage girls, and earlier in the week I had managed to overcome enough of my fear to tell her about a serious problem I had. She listened with a pained look on her face, then calmly said she would need to make some arrangements but to plan to meet at her place on Saturday.

"So, Sally," she asked me now, as the three of us headed downtown on Peachtree Road, "things still the same with you?"

"Yeah, I'm afraid so. Nothing's changed that I can tell," I said, looking at my girlfriend for moral support. She smiled feebly and squeezed my hand.

"Well, Dr. Hathaway's a really nice guy, and he's not rough. I know you've got to be scared. Just hang in there, okay? Maybe things aren't as bad as you think!" the gym teacher said, trying her best to sound cheerful.

"Okay" was all I could say; for some reason her kind words made me want to cry. This can't be happening, I thought to myself. I can't be on my way to some doctor's office to find out if I'm pregnant.

We drove for a while in silence before the gym teacher asked my friend, "You made cheerleading for your senior year, didn't you?"

"Yes, ma'am," she answered, looking at her lap. Silence again.

I stared at the road ahead and tried hard not to cry.

Dr. Hathaway was every bit as kind to me and as gentle with his examination as my teacher had promised. After it was over, he asked me to dress and come into his office. When I sat down, he pulled his chair up very close to me and said, "Well, my dear, the test was positive."

My hands were freezing; I rubbed them together, close to my face. Suddenly I couldn't think clearly. I wasn't even sure if I had heard what he just said. I asked, "You said the test was positive? And that means . . . "

He interrupted me and, with a little more authority, said, "It means you are indeed pregnant—about four weeks along, I believe. And you told me that you and your boyfriend wanted to get married if that was the case, right?" I heard him clearly that time and nodded affirmatively.

"Okay, then," Dr. Hathaway said. "We've got a lot to talk about. First of all, are you ready to tell your parents?" I could not hold back any longer; he patted me gently on the back while I put my head in my hands and sobbed.

Back in the car, the tough female coach looked at me disappointedly and said, simply, "Damn."

My girlfriend looked at me as if maybe what I had was contagious. She repeated, "I'm sorry, Sally," several times on the way home. As for me, my head felt detached from the rest of me; nothing about any of this seemed real. Maybe it will, I thought to myself, when I tell Michael.

Michael was gone on a long-awaited senior trip to New Orleans, but I had a number for him there. It was early on Monday morning when I called him, between final exams, from a pay phone at school, and I knew I would wake him up. We hadn't spoken since my appointment with Dr. Hathaway on Saturday.

"You're sure you're really pregnant?" he asked in a loud whisper after I had told him our news.

"Yes, I'm sure. Dr. Hathaway says I'm about four weeks along," I answered him, cupping the mouthpiece with my hand. "I wish you were here. I feel awful and I really need you." I knew that in the Atlanta social scene this kind of news would travel fast, so I added, "We've got to tell our parents soon, Michael."

"I'll be home in a few days. It'll be okay, Sally. We'll look for a place to live as soon as I get back; we'll tell our parents, and then we'll get married. Please don't worry." Michael had just graduated and had been accepted at Tulane University as a premed student, and while I knew he had to be stunned with my announcement, it reassured me to hear him say that we would do just what we had always said we would if (we might as well have said *when*) I became pregnant.

"Hurry home. I love you," I said.

"I love you, too," he said. "I'll see you soon."

That night, while drinking with his buddies in a Bourbon Street pub, Michael made a wild announcement. "Guess what?" he shouted over the noise of the pub. "I'm gettin' married when we go home!"

"Yeah, yeah . . . sure you are," a friend answered him back mockingly, thinking he was merely humoring a very intoxicated Michael.

Michael's friends were eighteen years old, finally free from the watchful eyes of ever-present priests and anxious parents. The last thing they had on their minds was losing that freedom. Michael was surely not going to tell them, or me, why he hoped marriage would be a means to freedom rather than an end of it. He fervently hoped it would be a way to divert himself from an alternative future that he had secretly begun to fear.

Together Michael and I began our threefold journey from illusions to truth, from bondage to freedom. It would take us down a long and winding road through twenty-one years of marriage, the birth of six sons, and the adoption of one daughter. It would weave us in and out of several brands of Christianity as we sought to know God. It would include Michael's awakening to himself and my coming to the place of accepting him for who he really was.

While Michael vacationed in New Orleans, I tried to get through the last few days of school without disclosing my situation to anyone else. At least I could stop looking for my missing period every thirty minutes; that verdict was in. Any remorse I had felt earlier had quickly vanished. The thought of getting married and having a baby had begun to sound exciting and terribly adult to me. The need I possessed for emotional and physical love was stronger, at the time, than any regret I felt over missing my senior year and being unable to graduate with my class.

Summer had returned, and during the first week in June, Michael invited me up to the lake house. I was two months pregnant, and it was time to tell his parents. We spent that nervous week water-skiing, lying in the sun, and taking boat rides at night to talk secretly about our future.

Sunday, our day of reckoning, arrived, and we asked Michael's parents to meet us down on the dock. We sat in four lounge chairs facing one another while the water from passing boats steadily lapped up just to the top of the open slats below our feet. I know, because that was where my eyes remained focused during the whole of Michael's confession to them, which went something like this: "Sally and I are going to get married."

His mother gasped. "You are *what?*" his father demanded. "Is she pregnant?" I flinched. It was rare for me to be struck silent, but this was a whole new turn of events. Maybe I would never speak again, I thought. Maybe I could just slide right through those slats and down into the water and fade away. "Riley!" his mother shouted to his father. And then, tentatively to her son, "Well ... *is* she?" Michael, sounding very bold and a little too loud, avowed, "Yes, she is. But that's not the reason we're getting married. We want to." I wondered if that was the truth, but I never asked. I could see that he was at least making a statement against the awful phrase "had to get married," and I appreciated that.

It was clear that Michael's parents were shocked and dismayed at the thought of the changes our announcement would mean for their son, but they kindly kept their thoughts to themselves. Michael's mother is gracious and intelligent. Virginia will speak her mind without hesitation, except for the time it takes to choose her words carefully. That day, she strove to let us know that, while our plight greatly saddened her, she would be with us. His father, on the other hand, sometimes throws his words out too quickly, without always considering where they might fall. A lot of Riley's words are proverbial "barks," but that rarely stops anyone from fearing a potential "bite." That day on the dock we received neither bark nor bite; despite his disappointment, he lent us his support. The supportiveness of Michael's parents gave me a sense of love and gratitude that would remain with me even through some of the more difficult times in our future.

Since things had gone better than we had expected with Michael's mother and father, we headed for Atlanta optimistically to announce our plans to my parents. We took them into the den; this time I spoke. I do not remember what I said, only the look of anger and disgust on my mother's face. At the time I could not quite grasp all of what lay behind her look as she stared at me and did not say a word. I am not sure I ever came to understand it all, but I did later realize some of the bitter disappointment she felt as she instantly envisioned my future as a sickening waste. Both of my older sisters, Eve and Camille, had married young, and she considered me her last hope of having a daughter who would complete college or become a debutante, with her proudly watching me dance with my father at my coming-out ball. All these things mattered so much to her, and she saw the hope of their happening vanish in an instant. At the time, I saw only my life and was not associating it with the lives of my older sisters. She was unable to follow me in that. Lost in her own ire, she left the room. My father spoke then, and his icy words drove deep into me. "You may gain a husband," he said, "but you will have lost a mother."

The rest was a blur until we pulled up into Michael's driveway, where his parents, just returned from the lake, were unpacking their car. I must have looked as though I would not be standing for long, because I was soon being held up firmly by his father. I cried and cried as Michael told them what had happened at my house. We went inside, with them trying to reassure me that my parents would soon calm down and that things would be all right. I always look back on that evening as the point at which Michael's parents became my own. At the time, thinking about my father's words, I was afraid that from then on they might be the only parents I would have.

The next morning I awoke at home and readied myself for summer school, where I was repeating a failed year of algebra. I ate my breakfast in silence, and when my ride came, my mother still had not spoken to me. Her silence continued for a maddening two weeks, broken only once when she erupted in a fiery furor at Dr. Hathaway's refusal to discuss my prognosis with her. In fact, he would not even acknowledge to her that I was his patient. She told me she had called to ask him what he thought the chances of my losing the baby were and then advised me how foolish I was to tell anyone so early, in the event that I might, as she hoped, miscarry. When I attempted to tell her that I was glad to be pregnant and to be marrying Michael, she hushed me and my unsuitable admission away, and her silence immediately resumed.

Silence was one of my mother's frequent means of punishment and had, therefore, become something I loathed and dreaded. Her silent rages were usually directed at my father; this time, however, I was most assuredly responsible for her pain and anger, and therefore the sole object of her silent treatment. I thought it would soon make me crazy.

Daddy was speaking to me, and was actually being kind as he mildly questioned me and, I knew, relayed the essence of our conversations to my mother. Generally speaking, my father was the sort of aloof and detached paterfamilias that was unfortunately common in the 1950s and 1960s. He was a faithful provider for his family's financial needs, but when it came to meeting the emotional needs of teenage daughters, all three of whom desperately wanted his attention, he made a hasty retreat. In a crisis, however, he was the more reasonable one, and it was through his intervention with my mother that at last there was a meeting set between Michael and me and all of our parents.

I heard my mother's voice for the first time in days as she told my future in-laws how sorry she was about "all of this." She said that she wished I would not keep the baby, and I wondered to what extreme she would go if I agreed with her. An abortion? She never suggested such an idea either to Michael's Catholic parents or to me, but still I wondered. Michael's parents did bring up the possibility of my going away, having the baby, and giving it up for adoption. My mother's eyes brightened at the notion, and for a few moments all four parents talked as if Michael and I were not there. At last Michael and I spoke up to tell them we would do no such thing. We wanted our baby, and we were going to get married. Completely determined then, we went on to tell them about the small furnished apartment we had already found and rented for $97.50 a month. Michael had secured a job putting rubber stoppers on the bottoms of table legs. He would also work part-time as a lifeguard at his family's neighborhood pool. In the fall, he would enroll at Georgia State University in downtown Atlanta. We had planned it all out. With that, both sets of parents seemed to give in and finally resign themselves to the fact of our upcoming marriage. It looked as though Mother was the least happy parent of all.

That night our future was set. I went to sleep still under the curse of my mother's silence, but with the assurance that I would soon be married and away. Somehow that comforted me, though not in the way my mother's or my father's arms about me would have. Turning on my radio, as I always did to sleep at night, I wondered if Michael slept with a radio on too. Soon we would be married and know all about each other. It could not be soon enough for me, I thought as I turned over on my tight tummy and slipped into an easy sleep.

I went to summer school every weekday and was surprised one morning to be called from class by the headmaster to speak with him in his office. With unusual tenderness, Dr. Stephens told me what he had heard and asked if it was true. Blushing madly, I told him yes, and added that I would be getting married soon. As kindly as he could, he told me that I would be allowed to complete summer school, but that the school's policy would not allow a student to be married, so I could not return in the fall. He respectfully did not mention the part about my being pregnant, though I knew that a swollen belly was not an appropriate on-campus sight. He wished me well, and I left feeling lonely and strange. I definitely did not fit into Lovett any more than I would fit into my school uniform by fall. I would be glad when summer school was over and I could just leave. I had driven myself to school that day, and as I rounded the school drive to go home, I suddenly braked my car in horrible disbelief. On the crest of the paved hill ahead of me, written in huge and very clear letters, were the words "Sally Lowe Is Getting Married." I sped over the scandalous announcement as fast as I could.

Just a few nights later, when I returned home from a date with Michael, my father took me aside. He told me that he had had a long talk with my mother and in essence had told her that she had better face the inevitability of my marriage to Michael. He had gone on to tell her that she would regret not being involved in planning what they both hoped would be the only wedding I would ever have. Much to my grateful amazement, he said that she had relented and had agreed to making my wedding special, with even a small reception following at our home. When I went into the kitchen to find her, she began to talk to me as though our two weeks of noncommunication had never been. We planned the food, and she insisted we go together the next day to pick out a china and silver pattern. And though at sixteen years of age I didn't particularly care about either of these things, I gladly complied. It felt incredibly good to have my mother with me as I planned my new life with Michael.

In the company of a small number of family and friends, Michael and I were married on July 8, 1970, by his family priest, in the chapel of the Catholic Church of the Holy Spirit. My father, who was long experienced as a writer in advertising, wrote the wedding announcement that appeared in the *Atlanta Journal and Constitution*. Once again I was appalled to see the words "Sally Lowe Is Married." I held my face in my hands and thought that with a headline like that, he might as well have placed it in the gossip column. I knew he had not considered how it would sound, but in my vivid imagination I could see Atlanta matrons running from house to house, newspaper in hand, proclaiming those words aloud.

After the reception at my house, we said good-bye to our well-wishers and headed off not on the usual honeymoon trip, but to our new home on Monroe Drive near downtown Atlanta, in what was in the seventies a questionable neighborhood. As we left my house, my mother made a weak apology, saying she and my father would have sent Michael and me to the Hyatt Regency for the night if we hadn't had work and summer school, respectively, to go to the next morning. I recognized the rebuke hidden in her words and knew that the nice wedding and perfunctory reception were never intended to fully mask her contempt for this marriage, no matter how much I might have wished it to be otherwise. Its only real saving grace for her had been the high social and economic status of Michael's parents. Otherwise, her silence might well have lasted forever.

Our first night together was sweet, even though I ended it with Clearasil acne medicine on my face and my below-shoulder-length hair pulled on top of my head in four giant rollers. I begged Michael to learn to sleep with the radio on, which was not his custom but to which he consented. I lay awake on that first night, and on many nights afterward, listening to the unaccustomed street noises and not feeling very adult or brave.

On our first morning, and on the next three months of mornings, Michael ate his breakfast of either oatmeal or eggs and then, before leaving for work, threw up. I was the pregnant one, but *he* threw up. He was terribly embarrassed and tried to blow it off as nothing. I worried: was it my cooking? (My mother had never allowed me in the kitchen.) Or even worse—was it *me?* Slowly he seemed to get better, and I shifted my worries back to the location of our apartment. We had come to realize that it was not in a safe area, and our parents had wisely urged us to move.

Mother came to visit me more often in our new apartment. On the one hand, her visits helped ease my loneliness; on the other, they added to my angst. A perfectionist at cleaning, she delighted in leaving a dirty ashtray "just to see if it would be washed" when she returned. I thought the poor woman would surely die when one day I pulled out the sofa bed in the living room, showed her the pink satin sheets left there, and then told her that the previous tenants had been two homosexual men. I secretly delighted in her horror, though I did make Michael take the sheets off the bed and throw them away. I refused to touch them myself. I knew little or nothing about homosexuality and had discussed "it" only in hushed giggles. And for all my supposed liberalism, I used the then-popular slang words in a derogatory way. I wondered about those two men and their satin sheets, and though the idea repulsed me, I was curious about what they did together sexually. I was too embarrassed to ask Michael if he had any idea, afraid he might think my interest too strange. He was always so quiet when I brought up the subject of those two men, and I just assumed it made him sick to think about them. Still, it made for an amusing story to tell our friends when they came by.

Michael and I celebrated our first Christmas together and allowed ourselves ten dollars apiece to spend on each other. I bought Michael a wallet, and though I can't remember what he gave me, we would always say that that frugal Christmas was our best. Soon the coldest part of winter was with us, and I dreamed of babies and wished my birthing time would hurry and arrive.

On the snowy evening of January 31, 1971, my dreams became quite real. The pains started slowly and continued to come at long, tiring intervals over the course of the night. I lay on the bed, mostly talking on the phone with Camille, and watched my exhausted and very nervous husband sleep fitfully beside me, fully dressed and shod. A huge book lay across his chest, as he'd fallen asleep studying for an exam that was scheduled for the next day.

When at last the time came, in the early hours of February 1, to take me to the hospital, Michael was as nervous as a father in a situation comedy. Our parents were nervous wrecks too, and stood together outside of Labor and Delivery arguing about what the doctor should do concerning my prolonged labor. Finally Dr. Hathaway came in and told me I had better hurry up and have that baby or he would have to do a C-section to quiet our hysterical parents out in the hall.

Believing he was fairly serious, I guess I willed Michael Jr. to be born. After twenty-four hours of labor, our firstborn was pulled into this world. He weighed seven pounds, five and a half ounces. Michael could not have been more excited about his first son. And, for people who hadn't previously been so excited about this baby, the two sets of grandparents were as in love with their new grandson as any grand-parents could be.

I stayed in the hospital for a week, which was normal in those days. Then I came home with little Michael, and I believe that in caring for my newborn son, what I lacked in wisdom I made up for in love. When it was just the two of us in the apartment, I unabashedly danced around, my little son perched contentedly upon my shoulder, and sang the Carpenters song "Close to You" into his tiny ear. Somehow he sur-vived my neophyte mothering and my singing. Mother would come over and help out some, mostly by bringing much-appreciated food. She could not understand why I chose to breast-feed, why I would re-vert to a way of feeding babies that she had been happy to be liberated from by bottles and formulas. While watching me feed Michael in my favorite rocking chair, she would shudder and say, "I do not see *why* you still do that. Rocking in that chair must make the milk curdle in-side that poor baby's tummy!" Although I loved to see my mother come and visit, I sometimes also loved to see her leave.

When Michael Jr. was about six weeks old, my mother said I had to come over, that her elderly Aunt Josephine wanted to see the baby. I did so less than enthusiastically, and patiently tolerated my great-aunt's pokes and probes as to Michael's well-being. At last she seemed satisfied that I had not yet harmed him, and she and my mother sat down to chat. I needed to feed Michael before I started for home. As I lifted my blouse and placed him squirming hungrily to my breast, I heard her caustic evaluation spoken intentionally loudly to my mother: "Well . . . look at her; it is nothing more than a child with a child." With that I was pronounced unworthy to be a mother and sat undefended by my mother.

When Michael came home that night, he found me angry and upset. I told him what Aunt Josephine had said and added that it was not the first time such a remark had been made to me. I could not understand how people could be so cruel. He picked up his favorite thing in the world now, our son, and held him up high over his face. "Watch out!" I exclaimed. "I just fed him." "Who cares?" he laughed. "And who cares what anyone else thinks, either?" I looked at them both, and though I still hated the thought that it seemed we would never measure up, I knew he was right.

That first year went by fast. We were pleased with our life together and were having so much fun with our firstborn. We moved again, into an apartment complex up the road, where we made friends with some married couples. I went back to get my high school diploma at a nearby public school that allowed married students. My classmates did not believe I had a child, so on the last day of school I brought Michael Jr. to class. The principal had called me into his office earlier that week to discuss my graduating. He had explained that private-school credits differed somewhat from those in public schools, and I had been greatly upset to hear him go on to say that according to the rules I would have to take another year of history to earn my diploma. Then he looked at me and said, "But I think you have been through enough life experience during your senior year to deserve to graduate now." He handed me my diploma. Tears of gratitude welled up in my eyes as I thanked him. I knew it was true that I was a child who had had a child, but this wise man had stopped long enough to notice that I had also grown up some in the process, and I appreciated him for it.

Late in the summer of 1971, Michael and I left our six-month-old son with my parents and took off for a long-overdue honeymoon trip. Instinctively, I had asked him to take me to St. Simons Island. Michael had never been there, and I looked forward to showing him and the island off to each other. My favorite waiters happily greeted me and my husband and hid any surprise they might have felt at our young marriage. Nothing had changed at the King and Prince Hotel. Everything I held dear was there, ready to embrace the both of us. At night we walked the beaches and sat on the swing in front of the hotel as I told him all the stories I could think of about my summers there. Michael fell under the spell of the island easily, and we agreed that as soon as we could afford it, we would begin our own summer tradition there. As we sat and moved slowly back and forth together, I imagined us there with our children, summer after summer after summer.

The island could easily boast of manifesting the best of the South, but it does not seem to have a boastful nature. Like a natural beauty who is totally unaware of her dazzling attraction, it has an astonishingly humble capacity to give to each sojourner according to her or his need. Artists are instinctively drawn to its subliminal mixed message of inspiration and discipline. Creative motivation is simply *there,* whether it drives one to paint, write, lift one's voice in song, run for miles, or make plans to remodel one's home or change one's career. For some, visits to the island result in a decision to enjoy its enchantment daily, in a permanent home.

People come to its beaches to sit quietly and build drip castles on the wet sand or to ride the gentle waves to shore. They take long walks to heal themselves of disease or of the sense of loss brought on by divorce or death. They come to stretch and renew themselves—to adjust to retirement, to grandbabies, or to any new rite of passage in their own journey. The long pier at one end of the island, with its diversity of people who are there either to fish or to walk, is a good place to sort things out, to get perspective. Down the beach a ways from the pier, back in front of the King and Prince, is a wooden two-seater swing. There you can look out over the ocean and think your own private thoughts, or look to either side and see the lights of life on the two other Golden Isles. And the swing is a good place to talk.

There is clearly something there, on those antique, time-honored shores, that provides a safe and compassionate shoulder for tears of grief or joy, for love being made or unmade. And there is the promise, too, that after each wave that breaks, yet another will follow, allowing the permission sometimes needed to release burdens never meant to be carried, to forgive and to begin to go on. It was there, on that swing, in the still-dark early-morning hours of August 1, 1991, that my husband Michael would finally tell me that he was gay. I knew then that with his revelation our world had in a instant stopped, then restarted, and that it would never again be the same. But I also knew a surge of strength and love that broke through the surreal nature of his words and spoke an ancient, insistent hope to my heart.

The author Sue Monk Kidd wrote in her novel *Dance of the Dissident Daughter,* "The truth might set you free, but first it will shatter the safe, sweet world you live in." Michael and I, our family, and our closest friends have known that shattering, after which our small world was opened up to reveal a much larger one. One big enough to contain the new lives that, we would discover, were at last within our reach. Big enough to allow the joy and sorrow that living in the truth brings to finally coexist. For myself, I came to realize that dark secrets, the ones carried deep within a person's being, are the most destructive secrets of all. They do their damage not only to their carrier, but to all lives interwoven with his or hers. For Michael, he came to find that these secrets are more harmful than the feared disclosure of truth could ever be. Together, we learned that courage is always needed to come out of a life of lies, then to move forward and live in truth. Neither Michael nor I was raised with that sort of courage instilled in us, and our journey would have to take us full circle before we would discover it. Courage is needed, too, for others to accept and embrace these new lives of truth. With the awareness of that in mind, it is my hope, and his as well, that our journey will enable another fearful soul to be set free.

chapter 2

I Never Promised You a Rose Garden

Returning home from long stroller walks around our tidy neighborhood or up and down the streets in Buckhead, little Michael and I would be a very tired young mother and son. After climbing the stairs to our second-floor apartment on those hot, muggy afternoons, we'd usually end with a sweet, sweaty nap. I would lie down across our double bed holding little Michael, who would then sprawl out lengthwise across my belly. His tiny hands would slowly slip down in relaxed slumber and come to rest along the sides of my small, seventeen-year-old body. Momentarily I'd close my own eyes and we would be fast asleep.

As soon as Michael arrived home from work he would come and find us asleep together and gently pry little Michael from his "mommy-bed." Sweetly, he would rouse his son into their time of play together while I found my way to the kitchen and attempted to prepare supper for the three of us. The instant Michael put his son down on the hardwood floor, the seven-month-old knew it was his cue to crawl away from his daddy as fast as he could. Michael would immediately begin to crawl on all fours right behind him. "I'm gonna get you!" I would hear, followed by little Michael's squeals as the two of them rounded the corner and headed down the hall, with our son looking like a car on three wheels. I would almost always stop whatever I was doing to watch them, knowing full well that their chase scene would invariably end up with little Michael collapsed spread-eagle on the floor, his head thrown back in out-of-control giggles because his daddy was overhead tickling him. Laughing too, I would finally have to return to the preparation of our evening meal.

The next time I would glance out into the living room, I would be sure to find the two of them sitting quietly together on the sofa, Michael watching the news on TV with little Michael snugly in his lap, chewing intensely on a toy. I knew they looked more like big and little brother than father and son, but I also knew for certain that Michael loved his son as much as any older father could.

Cooking dinner every evening was no small accomplishment for me. The women I came to know during our apartment-living days were usually much older than I was, a fact that had one definite, positive advantage: they knew how to cook, and I could watch them. I asked them all of the questions a young woman would ordinarily ask her mother while she still lived at home, or when she returned home during college breaks, in order for her to be properly primed in the art of pleasing her husband's palate after his hard day at work. Since you wash a chicken, I asked, do you also wash a beef roast or pork chops? What does "Bring to a boil and simmer until done" *mean* exactly? I had to ask them just about everything.

I paid careful attention to those wives, who were on average ten years my senior and whose husbands were, more often than not, much beefier than my thin young mate. Michael was very grateful for whatever I was able to learn, as he had finally grown weary of spaghetti sauce from a packet, and even more so of the one dish his mother had told me he "just loved" and had coached me in making—creamed chipped beef over toast. If he had loved it some time before, he hated it by then and had secretly christened it with a new name—"creamed chipped shit." He shared this fact with me a few years later, when my culinary talents had improved considerably.

Michael was definitely my grand inspiration and my fearless taster as I ventured into the frontiers of cooking. He cheered my first Aunt Fanny's squash casserole, applauded my first milk gravy and *real* mashed potatoes, and managed (with some effort) to be kind when I created my first gooey-in-the-middle pancakes. When I accidentally used baking soda instead of baking powder in my first southern-style biscuits (resulting in a nasty, bitter facsimile of a biscuit that choked all three of us on our first bites), he still spurred me on in my efforts. The man was at once desperate for some good cooking and smart enough to not give up on me.

At last I had one "company" meal I'd practiced enough that I felt comfortable serving it to Michael's parents. I prepared a chicken dish with peaches and a broccoli casserole with Parmesan cheese—all expressly prepared from recipes I had found in *The New Better Homes and Gardens Cookbook* (a gift my mother had sent with me into marriage to serve as my cooking instructor).

After the meal was over, Virginia raved profusely over each dish while I watched Riley unconcernedly pull a bottle of antacid pills from his coat pocket. He got up from the table and headed for the bathroom. He returned to the unfriendly glare of his wife, expertly cast upon her face to ensure that he would immediately be aware of his gauche behavior. Having clearly received her message, he frowned and briskly declared that of course it was not my cooking, how foolish of me to think that such a thing had upset his stomach. End of explanation. End of apology. I looked to my presumed allies, Virginia and Michael, for validation of my hurt feelings, but saw that they both appeared to be satisfied with what I considered to be a puny attempt to make amends. It was the first time I had been treated to Riley's gruff bluntness, and though I answered him by saying it was okay, it certainly wasn't. I could not interpret his crude words, coupled with his abrupt, rude manner, as a sincere apology. Nor did I understand how readily acceptable and satisfactory his behavior was to his wife and son. I thought Michael would fiercely defend me to his father. The thought that I had married a man less valiant than I had believed him to be disturbed me.

Michael and I had kept up with one of the Young Life Club's adult leaders whom we had known in high school and whom everyone called Pearl. We really liked him and were glad that he had taken a sincere interest in our lives and in our spiritual journey even after we had married. He was never overbearing, and though he sometimes disagreed with us, he respected our opinions and took our questions seriously.

"You know? I was thinking about an extraordinary ministry I visited one time in Americus, Georgia," Pearl announced to us one day. "It's a community called Koinonia. A man named Millard Fuller started it by collecting a few volunteers to build a home for a family in need. Then that family helped the next family to build their home and so on. Now quite a few young families—both black and white—have moved there to be a part of Fuller's ministry. It's really shaken up the folks in that South Georgia town. It sounds like something you two would like!"

Michael and I were impressed by what Pearl told us about Koinonia and fascinated by its communal lifestyle. Both racial prejudice and the condition of the underprivileged maddened us. We wanted to do something that would change the way things were in the South about both. The next Sunday, with little Michael in his car seat, we drove around for hours talking about Koinonia and the idea of living in community.

"Do you think we should go down there?" I asked Michael.

"I don't know," Michael said. "Maybe we should stop *talking* about it and just go home, pack our clothes, and go!"

"Maybe so," I said, becoming both excited and nervous at the prospect.

We got on and off the southbound expressway several times that day, but we lacked the nerve to just *go*. Finally we quietly headed home. Yet Michael and I still believed that we had to do something to fight against social injustice. Our personal crusade had grown out of our innate need to fix something we had not actually broken ourselves but nonetheless felt responsible for. We believed we had to do something to help struggling, oppressed people, and the only question in our mind was what that something might be.

Our Lady of Lourdes Catholic Church was small (compared with the huge, imposing Catholic cathedral we normally worshiped in), and the congregation was definitely all black—except for Michael, me, and Father Malone, the priest who had invited us to attend on that Sunday morning. Our own priest, Father Hardy, had excitedly sent us to meet Father Malone after we had shared with him our vision for unity among all God's people. "He will know just how to put the two of you to work!" Father Hardy had assured us.

Only a few heads turned as Michael and I and little Michael took our seats. In fact, the parishioners seemed to have a much bigger reaction to Father Malone's sermon later that morning than they had to a white family attending their church.

"I see absolutely no reason why God, who created the sacrament of marriage—not to mention both love and lovemaking—would then turn around and forbid it to be enjoyed by His priests!" Father Malone defiantly declared to his flock. "This, my friends, is a law imposed on Catholics not by God—but by man. The matter of celibacy should be left up to the personal discernment of each priest." As he spoke, most heads in the church either bobbed up and down or remained perfectly still. A few people leaned over to quietly make a comment to their neighbor. Though there may have been those present who adamantly disagreed with the priest, I saw no one shake his or her head no.

What a liberal-minded church *this* must be, I thought to myself happily. Glancing at Michael, who was smiling and bobbing his head up and down, I knew he was impressed as well.

After several months of attending Our Lady of Lourdes, however, Michael and I had to admit that the blending of colors in friendships that we had imagined was simply not materializing. The notion we had that we would be in the vanguard of blacks and whites coming together freely for worship did not seem to be shared by our fellow parishioners. The fact was, while the parishioners of Our Lady of Lourdes were cordial to us, they did not seem to need our help—or, we felt, even our friendship.

Not many months after we had arrived, we quietly left, disappointed and wondering what had gone wrong with our ardently laid plans. We felt that somehow we had failed the church and, in our own need to be needed, had inadvertently become disillusioned as well. We were too hurt and embarrassed by our aborted mission to explain our departure to Father Malone, much less ask Father Hardy for another suggestion. Still, we wanted to do something positive in our environment.

One day, while driving around the Midtown section of Atlanta, we spotted an old house with a sign outside that read Volunteer Atlanta. It had a good feel about it. We stopped and went in to see what they needed volunteers to do. Michael was disappointed to find that his schedule prevented him from helping at the time but was glad when they quickly found a volunteer job for me.

Soon, several mornings a week I was bundling little Michael up and driving downtown to a building near the old Atlanta stadium. There I placed him in the outstretched arms of a large black woman who sat in a rocker, smiling and rocking crying babies.

"Have a good day," she would sing as I walked out of the workers' day-care facility at Operation Head Start, where I was helping in the newly formed preschool. Head Start served the most underprivileged black and white children in Atlanta. I enjoyed my work, which involved simply shelling a great many hard-boiled eggs, slicing apples, and pouring juice for kids who would probably eat nothing more nutritious all day. I helped keep track of their happy little faces when we took them off to play in city parks that were better kept than many of their homes. They were ecstatic to be set free to run and play.

I was intrigued with the lives of the paid workers, all of them black women, with whom I was working as a volunteer aide. I observed how they worked with the children. They functioned with a sagacity and serenity that I deeply admired and wished for in my life. These nourishing women had a deep-rooted wisdom that even I, in my callowness, recognized and coveted. I eagerly looked forward to every day I was allowed to work with them and the children.

Little Michael, however, was not faring so well. He had begun to suffer cold after cold, and finally I realized that the source of his repeated misery was the day-care center. His health had to come first, which meant I needed to quit. The decision was a difficult one for me since once again I felt I would be letting down the very world I was trying to help. Besides which, I knew that I would greatly miss working with the women and worried that they might think poorly of me for leaving. Still, in the end there was nothing else to do but quit.

Even with all that we had on our plates, it was not long before we became excited about another service project. The wife of a coworker of Michael's worked at the Department of Family and Child Services (DEFACS). She said they had many children who desperately needed foster homes. So desperately, in fact, that they would waive the age requirement and allow Michael and me (then twenty and nineteen years old, respectively) to become foster parents right away.

Michael and I were thrilled at the prospect. Our parents, especially his, were not. They had barely survived our last two social-service escapades, and this was an even less promising notion in their eyes. The idea of bringing "God knows what" kind of influence into the home of their adored little grandson appalled them, and they tried in every way to talk us out of it. But we held firm, believing that our son would benefit from sharing his room and toys with children less favored than he was. We were adamant that he not grow up spoiled and protected from the world's harsh realities.

Ross and Felicia came to us almost overnight. Only four and six years old, the siblings needed a fast, temporary refuge from a negligent mother and her abusive boyfriend. Unfortunately, after a month or so the children were returned to their mother. Shortly after they left, DEFACS sent us a premature infant to care for until he could be permanently placed in his adoptive home. After three weeks the preemie was placed, and within the week we were sent another preadoptive newborn to care for.

Victoria was a difficult and unhappy baby whose formula could never be adjusted to suit her sensitive tummy and who therefore found it impossible to settle down to sleep at night. This made for sleepless nights for me, and as a result, I became an irritable wife and mother. Michael was rarely home, and I secretly resented his freedom to leave home and go to work and school each day.

My exhaustion became evident one night when I woke up on the sofa from a sound sleep to the stares of Michael and the friends we had invited over for dinner. They were amazed to see me asleep, and I was amazed to see them all sitting there staring at me. Until then, I had always been a notorious night owl who stayed up longer than anyone else and still got up early the next morning with no problem. It appeared that there was a problem now, and Michael was concerned enough to call DEFACS the next day to ask that they seriously speed up the process of placing Victoria in her permanent home.

DEFACS said they were sorry, but that because of holdups in their endless paperwork procedures, our care for Victoria would have to continue for at least another week. We had no choice but to comply.

One day soon after, a fine rain was falling while I drove both babies to a sitter so that I could attend a friend's wedding luncheon. It was still falling later that afternoon as I headed back home down Moores Mill Road. Both babies were asleep in the car, and my thoughts had turned to what I might fix for dinner. My head ached, and I was still too full from the luncheon to be enthusiastic about another meal. It would have to be something easy. Maybe ground-beef Stroganoff over noodles and a package of frozen broccoli would do. I decided I really didn't give a damn what we had for supper. I was sick and tired of caring for and giving to . . . everyone. What I wouldn't give just to get a good night's sleep, I thought, or maybe a day to myself. I hoped the babies would stay asleep for a while once we got home.

I was just two miles from our apartment. "Thank God, almost there," I thought.

Then, in what seemed like an instant, I was coming to, squinting up into the lowest branches of a large magnolia tree. I felt exactly as if I had drifted off to sleep while watching a movie and then awakened, amazed that it could have progressed without my knowing about it! Vaguely aware of a crying baby, I fought hard to pull my mind out of its fog. I looked over to check on Victoria and was shocked to see that her child seat had toppled over onto the floor from its place on the seat beside me.

In the rearview mirror I could see that little Michael was unhurt, had quit crying, and was quietly gazing out of the car window at the man approaching us, whose yard we were somehow in and on top of whose chain-link fence I suddenly realized we were poised. I looked to see if there were any other cars involved. I could see none behind or around me. Slowly, I let myself and Victoria out of the car. Her crying stopped as soon as I stood up with her, and mine began. I was absolutely terrified. What had I done?!

The kind man whose yard I had dreadfully torn up could offer me little clarification as to what had happened. He could say only that from his chair beside the picture window he had first heard and then seen us slowly drive right over the fence and come to rest in the giant arms of the magnolia tree. He was just glad we were all okay.

I was promptly sent to Virginia and Riley's internist, one of the best in Atlanta. After seven hours of glucose-tolerance tests, he determined that I had suffered a one-time attack of hypoglycemia. He explained that the attack had been brought on by just the right circumstances occurring simultaneously: a high-carbohydrate lunch, a temporary drop in my blood-sugar level, extreme fatigue—and, he pointedly added, some amount of depression. What he wanted to know was what I thought was causing the depression. I really could not tell him. "Think about it," he encouraged me, "and if you want to talk to someone, let me know."

After making me promise to eat right and get some rest, he dismissed me. DEFACS immediately relieved us of our duties as foster parents. We were sad, but thankful to be just our little family again.

Still, I needed to answer the question of why I had been feeling so blue of late. I thought about how bored and restless I sometimes became at home. My female friends in the apartment complex had begun to seem depressing to me with their day-in, day-out routines. I resented Michael's exhausting schedule and longed for the fun times I had assumed we would have as a married couple, free from the restrictions imposed by our parents. I thought about what it was like the few times Michael and I had most recently been together. It seemed like we seldom really talked with each other as we used to. Then I thought about how his touch barely excited me when we made love and how seldom I even wanted to be intimate with him. Although thinking about these things made me feel extremely guilty, I nevertheless had to recognize that I found our life together dull.

Michael had changed, I decided. He was too quiet, too passive, no longer the radical hippie I had found so refreshing and exciting in high school. Maybe it was time to change boyfriends, I thought acidly.

Meanwhile, I watched one girlfriend after another make a trip to Europe, then take off to college, where, I imagined, she found the perfect man, the one she was meant to marry. Finally, her father would indulge his baby girl in a beautiful and extravagant wedding. I attended several such weddings. Remembering my own rushed-through chapel wedding, I was jealous and resentful of them all.

Soon I began to wonder if I had done the right thing by marrying Michael, and sometimes I felt that maybe I had missed the one who was really meant for me. What should I do? I wondered despairingly. One day I leaned toward the good and faithful husband I had in Michael, the next day toward the fantasy spreading inside me like wildfire that I knew would mean the end of our marriage. Finally my dissatisfaction broke loose from its restraints and powerfully pushed its way to the surface of my mind, where its presence became impossible to ignore or hide from and insisted upon being dealt with.

We had been happy at first, I reminded myself, and had been so determined to prove everyone who had predicted our doom to be wrong. I thought about how Michael had always preferred doing things together, just the two of us, whereas I usually wanted friends to join us in our social activities. I knew I should feel complimented that he preferred to be alone with me, and I felt guilty that I needed to have people other than him in my life. I suddenly realized that I was feeling trapped.

Our lives suddenly seemed terribly predetermined, which panicked me. I knew that I was destined to stay at home and that, though I might take a few noncredit courses, I would never go to college or have a career. Because of the long years of study and the high cost involved, Michael had already abandoned his plans for a medical career and had opted instead for a business degree. I hated seeing him give up on his dreams. There never seemed to be much choice in any of our decisions. More often than not we resembled lambs being passively led to the slaughter with no idea that they could resist following the path before them.

Although during those days I wondered if Michael was struggling with some of the same feelings I was, he never indicated as much to me. Looking across the room at him while he was studying one of his college textbooks, I thought to myself that he certainly seemed happy enough. He went to work and school without complaint, came home tired but wanting to make love as much as ever, and in general seemed perfectly content with our life. If he was not happier than I was, he was at least more resigned to our future, that was for sure. *All* of which infuriated me! What was wrong with me that I was not more content? I wondered. My marriage fantasy was fading rapidly, and a nightmare seemed to be taking shape in its place.

Finally, the thought occurred to me that our marriage needed a fast-drying cement to hold it together. It was then that I thought that maybe we should try to have another baby. Perhaps that would settle my confusion. Michael had no problem agreeing to hasten our efforts to conceive. In no time I was pregnant again and trying hard to ignore any wild fancy that might penetrate through to the surface of my thoughts. Still, in spite of these efforts and the pregnancy, my questions persisted and my restlessness grew.

Even though I was pregnant, Michael and I foolishly kept up an occasional weekend party life. Sometimes we went to fraternity parties at Georgia Tech with some of our old high school buddies. Leaving one night from one such event late, I lost my questionable balance and bottomed down a short flight of stairs. I did not feel much pain at the time, but later that night, when the bleeding began, I knew I might be suffering a miscarriage. Sick with guilt and fearful of losing our baby, I called my doctor, who ordered me to stay in bed. Luckily for me, in a few days the bleeding stopped; I assumed the baby was safe.

One month later I was happy to still be pregnant but was unhappy with the fact that my attempt to ignore my persistent feelings of discontent had not driven them away. Instead, they had escalated to the point of becoming a large, overshadowing distraction.

When I went for my three-month prenatal checkup, the doctor quietly sat me down in his office with disturbing news. He explained that during my examination, he had listened for a long time, in vain, for a heartbeat and had finally come to the conclusion that at some time during the last month, the baby had almost certainly died. It was too early in fetal development for a safe x-ray, however, and since sonograms were still in the future, my only choice was to wait. He explained that if the fetus was dead, I would probably self-abort—preferably, soon. By law he could not even consider inducing labor until he had absolute proof of the baby's death. I was extremely upset over the possible loss of the baby and terrified that I might carry a dead baby inside of me for months before x-rays could confirm what the doctor felt was all but certain.

While I was driving home from his office, an idea struck me regarding an omen: I decided that if the baby had truly died inside of me and I did abort, it would be a sign that my marriage to Michael was meant to end. If the doctor was wrong and the baby was alive, I would absolutely stop flirting with any thoughts of ending our marriage. I would know then that it was meant to be. This divine sort of gambling somehow made sense to me and provided at least temporary relief from the weight of the decision I felt falling on me. I would let fate have its way; then I could not be to blame for its whims.

We had taken little Michael to the petting zoo when I felt the first freakish labor pains begin and then the sudden rush of fluids. Michael hurried us all home and then hurried me to the hospital just in time for the delivery of a stillborn three-month-old fetus so terribly shrunken in size that the doctor was unable to tell us the sex for certain. He thought that it was most likely a boy. I cried and opted not to see the tiny infant.

So far, I had not said one word to Michael about how I was feeling. He had no idea that I was questioning our life together and that, unjustly, I resented him and blamed him for my growing unhappiness. We did not have loud arguments; in fact, we rarely quarreled at all. I dreaded the inevitable talk that loomed before us.

One night I finally sat down with him. " I'm not happy, Michael," I began without much delicacy. "I think you and I are just too different to be married. We hardly ever talk to each other anymore, and I'm afraid that if we did, we wouldn't have anything to say."

Michael was astounded. "You're wrong!" he protested emphatically. "None of that's true for me. I *am* happy, and I thought you were too."

"We never have any fun together anymore, Michael. In fact, I hardly ever see you!"

"That's not fair," he answered. "If you'll think about it, you'll see that we *do* have fun. It's just that, because of my school and work, we don't have as much time to do stuff together as we used to. I can't help that. But I still believe we have a good life together."

I sat there quietly frowning, wanting to tell him that I had thought about it for months, but for some reason I couldn't. We sat together in silence for a few more minutes before we went to bed.

"I don't think I ever really loved you!" I blurted out at dinner a few nights later. My longing for a life apart from Michael, and the sense of bondage I now felt in our marriage, had become so strong in me and had gained so in propulsion that I had finally exploded. I saw that my words had shocked Michael and had struck him deeply.

"I don't believe you," he said, tears beginning to come into his eyes. I could tell, however, that he was losing the heart to argue with me, so I pushed even harder.

"We're not right for each other, Michael. We should divorce now, while we're both still so young, and each find the person we should be with."

"I can't believe you're saying that. You can't really mean it."

I cried then, but I continued what I had begun. "I don't want us to stay together and be miserable like my parents have done all these years. I can't believe you would want that either."

"No," he agreed sadly, "I don't want that. But I don't think we're *like* your parents, Sally. We can't suddenly decide to get a divorce! Let's give it a rest, please? Can't we just think about this some more?"

I heard him, but because I was grossly impatient and completely positive that I knew what should happen, I walked out of the kitchen without answering him.

"What are you doing?" Michael demanded.

Overwrought and angry, I did not answer him. Instead I threw on a halter top and jeans, and left him for the night. Furious with me, he just let me go. I drove and drove, finally ending up staying overnight at a motel just three miles from home.

I came back the next morning, picked little Michael up from his play group, and silently resumed my daily routine as mother and wife. On the inside, I was seething with a more panicky determination than ever. Michael's anger was the painful, hurt kind, and I had to fight back any compassion that seeing him so wounded might possibly create in me. I had made up my mind, and I feared that if I wavered at all, I could easily fold. We talked very little to one another, and not at all about what had happened.

During those days when I was fervently planning my escape from my marriage (which by then had become only a matter of how and when), Mother and Daddy decided to rent the Whiteside Cottage on St. Simons Island for a two-week vacation. The rambling old house called to everyone who came by with soothing ocean sounds and potent ocean smells, making it so popular with island visitors that we had not managed to rent it since Camille and I were young children. Michael and I were invited—along with Camille; her husband, Richard; and their son—to join Mother and Daddy for a week. Excited at returning to the Whiteside Cottage, and never being able to resist time away in St. Simons, I agreed to go. I doubted that it would be such a good time for Michael and me to be together for a week; as things had gotten pretty chilly between us; and, too, I did not want to give him any false hopes. But we all needed a vacation, and I did want to enjoy little Michael on the beach.

It was not a restful or fun week. The house had fleas; the two-year-old cousins were as mischievous and rambunctious as two little boys could be; and my parents were more tense than usual. As for Michael and me, our marriage was plainly a mess—a fact my parents tried to pretend not to notice. We were not getting along at the beach any better than we were at home.

One afternoon, while Camille and I sunbathed luxuriously on the warm sand, the background music of the waves lulling us into a false sense of peace and harmony, my sister suddenly began pleading with me: "Sally, I know you're not happy now, but you can't tell me that you *never* loved Michael, because I remember when you did! And do you mean to tell me that you honestly cannot remember how happy the two of you were at first—and how much fun you were together?"

I buried my face in my towel, deeply inhaling the heat and the smell of suntan lotion until I could inhale no more. Slowly I let it all out as Camille's words softened my heart and touched memories I had carefully avoided dealing with for months. I thought to myself: Don't do this to me, Camille. I don't want to remember the days that you're talking about. I can't turn back, the way things are going . . . not now.

Finally, with total determination in my voice, I answered her. "*No* . . . I did not really love him; I only thought I did. It was all a mistake. I won't ever be happy with Michael and you know it! I need someone stronger, someone who really excites me. Michael and I are just *boring* together. I hate being married to him. Please don't make it any harder for me, Camille."

I knew she was not convinced, but she remained silent. When I looked at her face, I saw such sadness and hopelessness that it made me realize our breakup was breaking her heart. I thought about how she and Richard and Michael and I had grown to be such close friends and how our two feisty little boys, although absolutely incorrigible together, loved each other madly and had become delightfully inseparable. The thought of it all made me suddenly feel sick and, just as I had feared, weak. My head ached with the pain of my sudden confrontation with the reality of separation.

On the beach, my reasoning sounded as shallow and lame to me as I knew it did to my sister. I looked out to my beloved ocean, wishing for it to speak strengthening words—to tell me that I was right to leave Michael and begin a new life. That I *could* do it. Yet instead of providing the soothing balm of assurance, my old sea-friend seemed far removed from me, just as unreal and remote as the lifeless photos of it plastered on postcards that hung on the gift-shop rack at the King and Prince Hotel. Though I still lacked the steadiness I sought, I was determined not to let my mind be diverted any longer and rejected the thoughts that nudged at me, threatening to disturb my plans. Soon the waves began to bear down harder in front of us, and we watched quietly as each retreat left puddles closer to our place on the sand. We had to move quickly then, before our towels and magazines were soaked. The tide was coming in on us whether we were ready or not.

"Over here, Sally!" Riley waved to me from the table in the Lenox Mall restaurant. "Glad you could meet me," he said, rising to seat me. "How are you, and how's my grandson?"

"I'm okay, and little Michael's great. We'll bring him over to see y'all on Sunday."

As soon as we ordered lunch, Riley got right to the point. "What's this Virginia tells me about you and Michael having problems? Tell me what's going on; I think I have some advice for you that will help."

I noted the presumption that our "problems" were solvable and mentally began to hold on to my seat and get myself ready for a rough ride.

"Well, Riley, I know that you had serious doubts about Michael and me getting married in the first place. It's just that I think you were right—that we made a big mistake. Michael and I were too young to really be in love. We just thought we were, you know?" I looked at him, foolishly thinking he might consider my judgment to be sound if it was lined up with his. However, he was moving in a direction I had not thought of.

"Okay, Sally, I agree that your marriage was not made under the best of circumstances and maybe you weren't 'in love' with Michael. Maybe Michael wasn't in love with you, either. But so what? A lot is to be said for companionship. A number of fine marriages are based on it," Riley expounded.

Balking furiously, I shot back at him: "I'm sorry, but I'm not about to settle for companionship! Why should I, Riley?"

His smile was smug and his tone condescending as he answered me with a canny question: "Sally, have you ever heard the song [and he sang it to me without waiting for my answer] . . . . 'I beg your pardon, I never promised you a rose garden . . .'"

When he was finished singing, his wily look of self-satisfaction summed up his message to me: by getting pregnant and marrying Michael, I had asked for it, and I got it. Now I had only one choice, and that was to live with it.

As far as Riley was concerned, that was that, and if I had any sense at all I would take his advice, stop all of this silly stuff, and let Michael get back to work. Bottom line: grow up, Sally. The real problem was that I didn't want to, and definitely not in his or in my parents' style. I wanted so badly for someone to hear and understand that I was not ready for the life I was trapped in.

As I drove home, several of Riley's other not-so-endearing adages came back to me. After we had shared the news with Michael's parents that I was pregnant and that we planned to be married, Riley had remarked coarsely to Michael, "Well, you got your ox in a ditch and now you have to get it out." Then I thought about something he had said during a prenuptial talk with his son—that one day Michael and I would wake up and each would begin to blame the other for our predicament. The words he advised his son to have on hand when that day came were: "You made your bed; now you have to lie in it." It sounded like the same counsel he had just tried to pass on to me, and it made me furious.

I shook Riley's brutish admonishments off as fast as I could. When Michael wanted to know how my lunch with his dad had gone, I rudely informed him that I would rather die than have a marriage of the sort that Riley wanted for us. I quoted to Michael his father's latest words to the wise and sarcastically sang him the song Riley had sung to me at lunch. Michael's face fell in embarrassed disappointment, and I wondered if maybe he was beginning to see my point. Perhaps he too felt the fear of being trapped in a passionless marriage. I do know that, after that, he knew there was no further possibility of stopping me from leaving.

In just a few days, I announced to Michael my plans to take little Michael and temporarily stay with mutual friends in Athens, Georgia. After a while I would get a job and we would get a place of our own. Michael was clearly angry but had resigned himself to the inevitable and agreed to drive us up there on Labor Day. From then until I left with little Michael, a sadness befell our home that was almost tangible. Our third summer together had come to a hapless end.

On the day we left, everything seemed strange. As though on a casual family outing, we stopped to have lunch along the way, and

Michael stayed for a while to play with little Michael outside our friends' apartment. When the time came to say our good-byes and I saw his tears, I could no longer hold back my own. I think he was both shocked and glad to see that I was still able to cry. I thought, as I watched him drive away, that it had hurt so much more to say good-bye than I had told myself it would.

We were like a snapshot suddenly ripped apart: one minute a whole, lovely family photograph, then a picture torn down the middle, barely hanging together at one ragged edge. On one side of the picture was Michael standing alone, and on the other side were Sally and the baby. I was the one who had torn it apart, and I knew that if I concentrated on that image for much longer, I would not survive away from Michael for one single day. Later that night, my sadness subsided a bit and I began to think about what lay ahead.

The friends whose apartment little Michael and I now shared were away at work or at school most of the time, leaving the place pretty much to us. I pretended that it was ours and imagined what it would be like to actually live in a place of our own.

Toward the end of the week, I took little Michael home for one night, by Greyhound bus. Michael and I were to attend a previously agreed-upon marriage-counseling session, and he also wanted some time with his son. Since I had made the move to separate from Michael, I hoped that the counselor would consider our case ready to be closed.

A strained-faced Michael stood waiting for us at the bus terminal in Atlanta, but his face quickly softened into a smile when he saw little Michael rush merrily up to greet him. Gathering him up into his arms, he turned and abruptly walked toward the car. Not a hello to me, and not even an offer to help with the bags. It was clear that this was not going to be an easy visit.

Michael did not have a lot to say in our counseling session, and neither did I. It was clear that he was no longer interested in trying either. The counselor dismissed us, but I could tell it was with much hesitation and regret on her part. She urged us to come back should we ever need her, either together, she added without much hope, or individually. We thanked her and left.

In the car, Michael was unusually silent. When he finally spoke, it was to make a very straightforward announcement: "I'm not going to make it easy on you if you go through with a divorce." When I asked exactly what he meant, he answered that he was not saying he would challenge the divorce itself. However, he promised with a voice full of no-nonsense vengeance, he would make it *very* difficult for me. I knew that he meant he would not be magnanimous with me financially. After the brief job search I had made, that was a matter of concern. But what sent a hot rush of panic through me was the definite feeling I got that he was also referring to his rights as a father.

I wondered: Would Michael fight me for custody of our son? Suddenly overwhelmed with the thought that he might try to prove himself the more fit parent, and wondering if his parents were urging such a move, I did not push the issue any further. I was suddenly intimidated by his unusual behavior. What had happened to my meek husband? After a minute I also wondered why I was finding his new demeanor to be somewhat enticing. I didn't say much to Michael for the remainder of the ride. My brain was too busy trying to process the differences between the man I had left a week before and the one now sitting beside me.

Michael was in fact very angry and resentful. His sense of pride had been brutally shaken by what he saw as my thankless out-of-the-blue decision to end our marriage. Since my leaving, he had experienced his own share of anger. What about the ambitious plans and dreams he had abandoned to marry me and be a responsible father to our child? And what about the persistent thoughts and curiosities he had had since well before he met me about a different kind of life that, had he not married me but instead gone far away to college, he would no doubt have checked out?

That evening, little Michael and I returned to Athens, where we remained for one more week. Back in Susan and Paul's apartment, nothing seemed right, and single life began to feel more like a millstone around my neck than like freedom. As I looked around me, I thought despondently: freedom to do what? Sit around at night and eat TV dinners with a very bored two-year-old (who had told me many times all evening how sad he was because he missed his daddy)?

Late that night, I called an ex-boyfriend whom I had run into earlier in the summer and who was now back at a college several hours away from Athens. I thought he might come down the next weekend and "rescue" me from my doldrums. Before he had left for school, I had told him of my plans to leave Michael. He had told me to call if it ever got too tough.

"Can you come this weekend?" I asked when he finally came to the phone. Occasionally he responded to the dorm noise behind him, letting me know that I did not have his undivided attention.

"Sorry—but, I can't. I just got back to school, you know? And there's a lot of stuff going on this weekend. Another time soon, okay? Listen, I've really got to go."

For several more minutes I hung pathetically on the phone before I slowly said good-bye and burrowed myself into the sofa cushions. I may have overreacted to what I was positive was his rejection, but it marked a real turning point for me.

I could feel a great alarm beginning to rise inside of me, and I stood up, trying quickly to think of something that would calm me down. I could fix myself a drink . . . or even get some pot if I wanted to. That's a stupid idea, I said to myself as I began pacing the apartment floors. I suddenly realized that I felt more trapped there than I ever had at home. I checked on little Michael, who was still fast asleep. The sight of him curled up in his sweet innocence made me cry. I thought about his daddy and grew even sadder.

I went into the tiny bathroom, where I stared at my tired and unhappy face in the mirror. I didn't look at the reflection for long before I let myself slump down onto the cold floor, where I sat in total despair for a long time. I let my thoughts go. My life seemed so ill-fated. No matter which direction I chose, it seemed to be the wrong one. Having reduced myself to such hopeless, dead-end thoughts, I had no idea where to go next. I had brief thoughts of ending my life, but as my next thoughts were of little Michael, I knew I could never leave him like that. Suddenly feeling extremely frantic, I put my face in my hands and cried out loud, "I know that whatever I decide to do will just be the wrong thing again!"

From a place deep in my soul, an anguished sob of desperation pushed its way up and out. I was so lost . . . and so terrified that I would not see my way out of the place I had come to all by myself. I lay on the dirty floor and sobbed until I was completely exhausted.

When at last I pulled myself up, I was dizzy. Gripping the sink for balance, I cried out to God with the perpetual prayer that many anguished souls before me had spoken to implore Him. Looking into the mirror, I cried, "God! If you're out there, *please* do something with my life. I have made a terrible mess out of everything. Don't let me screw it up anymore. Tell me what to do." Leaning across the sink, I rested my forehead on the cool, polished reflector. Within a few minutes everything inside seemed to quiet down, and slowly the desperation let go its tight grip on me.

I returned to the living-room sofa, much calmer now. For a while I sat very still. A little later, I had a plan. I searched for a piece of paper, and when I found one, I began composing a list.

At the top of the page I wrote "Michael." On one side I listed every reason I could think of why I should return to him (and the life I had so adamantly rejected). On the other side I listed all the reasons why I should not. It didn't take long at all to see that the pros greatly outweighed the cons. I felt foolish and giddy with the sudden realization of what it meant. I would be going home.

I went to bed with the happy image of myself calling Michael first thing in the morning and telling him that we were coming home. He would be thrilled! I felt sure about my decision. Only a slight ache remained when I thought about all the possibilities I might be shutting the door on. The sense of security I felt when I imagined returning to Michael was like a magnet to my soul. I was ready to go.

The next morning I told Paul and Susan my news, and they replied simply that they were glad I had finally come to my senses. I understood then that they had never been pleased with my decision to leave Michael but were good enough friends to let me flounder and find my way without interference.

After they left for classes, I grabbed the phone to call Michael at work. When he answered, he did not sound glad to hear my voice. That was okay, I thought; he would be ecstatic just as soon as I told him my reason for calling.

As I exploded with the news that I wanted to come home, there was a pause on the other end of the line, then a long, drawn-out "Well . . . what made you change your mind?"

Feeling very foolish, I nonetheless quickly made my confession. "I miss you, Michael, and I miss our life together. I really want to come home."

He answered me carefully but firmly: "I need to think about it." I was stunned at his response. It sounded as though he was not sure whether he wanted me to come back or not. Panic was spreading inside of me again, fast, and I had no idea what to say.

"How can I be sure that you won't leave again?" Michael asked.

He had every reason and right to ask that question, and I answered him carefully. "Let me come home and prove it to you. I made an awful mistake; I know that now. I promise you can trust me. I won't ever leave again."

After a minute he answered me, but his tone was cautious. "All right. Get bus tickets for this afternoon. Call me back and tell me what time to meet you at the station."

Allowing me to come back to him had not been an easy decision for Michael to make. He had come very close to deciding that he might live more happily without me. Too, if only in his mind, he had allowed himself to explore another life—one that a woman would not even be a part of. He had, however, decided to let me come back, and he found, after the news had sunk in, that he was actually relieved.

After we hung up that morning, I felt another strange sense of enticement that was close to being arousing. Michael was different, I thought to myself, and I liked it. It seemed that I was going home to a stronger, more virile man. I packed our things as fast as I could, and we caught the first bus out of Athens to Atlanta.

I was relieved to see that Michael seemed to hurry us home from the bus station. Once we got home, little Michael's timing for a nap was perfect. We would have at least an hour or two to be alone. We closed the door to our bedroom and came together in an explosion of the most powerful lovemaking we had ever experienced. We had never made love like that, not even when we were dating and the "forbidden fruit" of our random times together had invariably proved to be an arousing aphrodisiac. Both of us were amazed by, and even a little shy about, its intensity. And afterward I could tell that Michael had been reassured of my faithfulness, and I was completely convinced that I had made the right decision in coming back to my husband.

chapter 3

The Dance of Discipline

It was fall, my favorite season, and with it came air so cool and crisp that your lungs felt purged with each breath. It always came as a blessed relief in the South, after the insufferably hot, humid days of summer. When Michael and I took little Michael out for a Sunday drive, the spectacular colors on the magnificent old trees that stretched themselves out along West Paces Ferry Road, in northwest Atlanta, seemed to be even more brilliant that year than usual. I was more intensely aware of *everything,* and I could only attribute that awareness to my gratefulness for our being back home and a complete family again.

My sole aim was to make a comfortable home for Michael, and to be the best mother I could be. The only thing I wanted at all was another baby, which we agreed to begin trying for right away. Still seeking to somehow seal my commitment to Michael forever, I felt an urgent need for us to add to our family as soon as possible. If ever I doubted my decision to return to my marriage, which occasionally I did, I quickly reminded myself of that dreadful, lonely night in Athens when I had wanted to give up, and of how close I had come to losing Michael. Every time, I shuddered.

It was then that I began to think of Michael as "good" and myself as "bad." I often found myself thinking about how committed Michael had been to our marriage, even when I had been ready to give it all up. I vowed, then, to do all I could for the rest of my life to redeem myself. I loathed myself for my stupid foolishness and wished so much that I could erase all that had happened. I knew I could never equal Michael—who, in my eyes, was now above reproach—but I did hold out the hope that maybe I could make it up to him by being the good wife.

One day, while talking about our time of separation, Michael shocked me by confessing how close he had come to deciding that he did not want me to come back to him. "I went out to a few bars one night," he began, "and I have to tell you, I *liked* the feeling of freedom and wondered if maybe a divorce would not be such a bad idea. I liked the *possibilities,* you know?" Seeing my startled look, he quickly added, "Nothing happened! I just liked the thought, that's all—I promise."

I calmed down, but the mere mention of bars was enough to get my mind going. I wildly imagined girls (women!) trying to seduce my husband—and him starting to enjoy it. The mental picture made me crazy and only increased the desire I had felt for him since our reunion.

I naively presumed that Michael's desires were for other women. And he did not tell me otherwise; this was his first sin of omission.

One night, Michael and I sat together and listened intently to an audiotape given to us by our marriage counselor, on what she referred to as "Christian principles of marriage." The speaker on the tape was Dr. Paul Walker, the pastor of Mount Paran Church of God, a well-known church on Mount Paran Road in Atlanta. The concepts that he taught his congregation about marriage seemed to be sensible.

Suddenly Michael pushed Stop, and then Rewind. "*What* was that?" he asked.

"I'm not sure," I answered, "but whatever it was, it sure sounded weird."

After listening carefully to the tape again, we distinctly heard a woman's high-pitched voice shouting something that interrupted the service. She spoke very fast, in a language that neither of us could seem to recognize.

"I still don't know what that was. Do you think maybe she had some kind of fit or something?" Michael asked.

"I don't know," I said. "I bet somebody had to take her out of the church and calm her down. She sounded wild! Poor woman, she must be a complete mess."

"Yeah, I guess so," Michael agreed.

Puzzled, we moved the tape ahead to where Dr. Walker was speaking. "Husbands, you have been ordained by God to be the spiritual head of the household. Your wife, therefore, is to be tenderly kept under your protection." While I liked the sound of the latter, having always longed for some sort of masculine protection in my life, to Michael the thought of his being in charge of our home sounded good. Though we had little idea of what these Christian principles actually meant, we were interested in anything that might prevent us from falling into disunity again.

While listening to the tapes, I also thought about the time when, only a few nights before we separated, Michael had said to me, "You know what's wrong with us? We don't have any faith." It was unlike Michael to say something like that, and though he had caught me off guard, I knew he meant faith in God. It was true that we had stopped going to church consistently, as we had when we were first married. On that particular night, however, I had not wanted to hear anything that might suggest hope for our relationship and so had easily shrugged off his words. Now I began to wonder whether Michael had indeed been onto something.

Earlier in our marriage, when we had gone to church it had always been a problem deciding which of our family churches we ought to attend. If we went to the Episcopal church, in which I had grown up, Michael did not feel that he had officially *been* to church. If we went to his Catholic church, I was not allowed to take Communion because I was not Catholic—a fact that I greatly resented. We discussed the problem for nearly a year. Finally I decided—partly to make my husband happy, partly to impress his parents, and also partly because I was seeking God for myself—to take instructions to become a Catholic.

Michael was touched and his parents were thrilled, immediately setting me up with private instruction sessions with their family priest. Monsignor McNeil was a statuesque man of about fifty-five years, with a face bearing a classic Roman nose, and he struck an elegant pose in his priestly garb. He was the same priest who had married us (after I had signed the required document promising to raise our children as Catholics) and had christened little Michael. So far, our son had not been raised nearly as "Catholic" as had been promised, and for that reason, too, I eagerly, and with much enthusiasm, began my weekly classes with the monsignor.

I was fascinated, listening to Monsignor McNeil's explanation of Catholic rites, sacraments, and liturgy. While I loved the mystery surrounding Communion and the ritual and formality in the Catholic Mass, I still had questions I was eager to ask.

"Michael says that Catholics are obligated to make their weekly confession with a priest or else remain, and possibly even *die,* in sin. Why," I asked, "is it necessary to have a priest as one's mediator with God?"

"First of all, Catholic priests are in a direct descent from Christ's apostles. Secondly, a layperson cannot possibly fully understand either the mysteries of faith or the significance of spiritual obligations, such as confession. Therefore, it is necessary to have a priest to speak to God on their behalf."

"Oh," I said. "Well, can you also explain why is it that the Catholic faith claims to be the only true faith?"

The priest leaned back in his chair and thought a moment before he answered me. "God specifically gave Saint Paul the Apostle the authority to begin the Catholic Church, Sally. Consequently, it is impossible to come to God by any other means except through the Catholic Church." Then, anticipating my next question, he added with a smile, "God will supernaturally provide an opportunity for every person on earth to come to know Him—through the Catholic Church—just as He has for you."

Though I continued to struggle with what I considered to be dubious concepts, I remained faithful to the monsignor's weekly instructions and to my decision to join my husband's church.

Early the following summer, I received a letter that surprised me and would drastically alter our lives. It was from old high school friends of ours, Mary and Ricky, who now lived in Montgomery, Alabama. Mary and Ricky were evangelical Christians, and in the letter they wrote how much they loved us and missed us. I had missed them, too, and impulsively called Mary to ask if she and Ricky could come for dinner the next time they visited Atlanta. She was so happy to hear my voice; they would be in Atlanta the next week, and they would love to come for dinner.

After dinner, the four of us caught up on the last two years. Michael and I told Mary and Ricky a little about the bad time we had gone through in our marriage the summer before.

"We even separated for a little while," I said, giving Michael a weak smile.

Awkwardly, Mary and Ricky admitted that they had heard about it. Michael and I looked at each other, embarrassed to hear that gossip about us had found its way from Atlanta to Montgomery. I wondered if they had heard that it was I who had left Michael.

"We're just glad things worked out for y'all," Mary said sweetly.

"Marriage is hard," Ricky added. "We've had our problems too. There have been times when I know we've both been tempted to give up."

"But you stayed together," Michael said. "What kept you both so strong?"

"The glue that's held us together has been Jesus," said Ricky. "Having Him as the Lord of our lives is what gave us the power to hang in there. Mary and I ask His direction about every decision we make." They quietly waited for our response.

It was Michael who finally spoke. "How can we have assurance like that in our marriage?"

"All you have to do is ask Jesus into your hearts!" Ricky said. "If you're interested, Mary and I will pray the 'sinner's prayer' with you. You'll be saved from spending eternity in hell, plus He'll show you the plan He has for your lives now. Do you want to pray with us?"

Michael and I wanted a strong marriage more than anything. Looking at each other, we nodded our heads yes, and we followed them word for word in prayer: "Dear Jesus, we confess our sins to you and ask that you please forgive them. Come into our hearts, Jesus, and be the Lord of our lives. In Jesus' name, amen." Smiling and hugging us, Mary and Ricky pronounced us born-again Christians.

Michael and I looked at each other timidly. We had never prayed together before.

"Now we're brothers and sisters in Christ!" Ricky announced. "Our lives are bound together for all eternity." By then it was very late, and they promised to return the next day to begin what they called "discipleship" with us. "Great things are getting ready to happen in your lives," Ricky shouted as he shut the kitchen door behind him.

Alone now Michael and I undressed for bed. As I slipped under the covers beside him, I admitted that I did *feel* different. Michael said he did too. It was impossible to explain what had happened to us, but we agreed that there was an excitement in the room and the feeling of a fresh start. I tried to lie still next to Michael while he peacefully slept, but I felt euphoric. I knew we had taken a step that would change our lives forever.

Later in the week, I took little Michael and drove out to the house of one of Mary's friends to spend the day. Mary had suggested that Carla might be willing to "disciple" me on a weekly basis about such things as how to parent children in a Christian way and how to be a godly wife. "Sally," she had told me, "I know how much you and Michael want to be good Christian parents. I've noticed, however, that sometimes you are firm with little Michael and sometimes you let things slide. You and Michael need to learn to discipline in the way God has instructed us. Listen carefully to Carla; you'll get a lot of helpful advice."

Mary was right about our parenting skills. Having been so young when we became parents, we had no idea how to correctly discipline a sweet but strong-willed three-year-old boy. "What do you mean by 'the way God has instructed us'?" I had asked.

"What I mean is teaching little Michael God's rules as they are given for our instruction in His Word, and disciplining him *promptly*, according to God's Word, whenever he disobeys the rules."

"Okay, but how does someone 'discipline according to God's Word'?"

Mary had answered my last question simply: "With the rod of correction."

Carla was a fairly attractive young woman of about twenty-eight. She wore no makeup, and her shiny brown hair was tied carefully back with a kerchief, with not one strand out of place. Though she didn't strike me as very friendly, or even very happy, I had still been grateful when she agreed to disciple me.

Now, while we all had lunch at the kitchen table, Carla fed her seven-month-old baby, Bethany, seated in a highchair. As I watched Carla place a bowl of baby food in the middle of the highchair tray, I thought it a daring thing to do with a baby of that age. Every time the baby put an inquisitive finger into the bowl, Carla reacted by giving the baby's hand one sharp whack with a wooden spoon and speaking a stern "No, no."

I sat staring wide-eyed at Carla, the spoon still poised tightly in her hand; my own hand flinched as though it had actually suffered the blow. I glanced over to see that little Michael's eyes were wide too; a bite of a peanut-butter-and-jelly sandwich hung unchewed in his open mouth. I gently reached over and moved his chin up and down a few times while we watched in silent alarm as the scene with the baby girl, the bowl of food, and the wooden spoon inconceivably repeated itself several more times. With each whack, Bethany would cry for a few minutes, then, still sniffling, resume eating from the spoon her mother held out to her. In a while she would inevitably forget and reach those. tiny soft fingers out again, to explore the food that was still tempting her on the tray. *Whack!* the spoon would crack across her fist again, each time accompanied by Carla's forbidding "No, no." I began to worry that her tiny bones might break. This went on until the poor infant finally finished every bite of her lunch and, in hiccups of miserable exhaustion, confusion, and pain, was set down by her mother for a nap. We could hear Carla's parting words as she put her to sleep: "Shhh . . . No more crying. Go to sleep."

Returning to the kitchen, she was quick to instruct me: "A child is never too young to learn obedience."

While Carla had been out of the room, I had realized that I was near tears from the lunch ordeal. Little Michael had pressed himself close to my side, clearly uninterested in going back outside to play. As soon as I could tactfully manage it, I excused little Michael and me to our hostess and we left for the long, and welcome, drive home. Little Michael was asleep before we hit the freeway, and I finally allowed myself to cry over what we had seen that day.

"Tell your child only one time," Carla had strongly admonished me on the way to the kitchen table for lunch. "When he disobeys, first have him tell you what it was that he did wrong, to make sure he knows what he is being disciplined for. Then use the rod of correction, as the Bible teaches—never your hand. Spank him until he is genuinely crying and showing true remorse. Let him cry only for a minute or two. Then tell him he must stop or the discipline will be repeated. Have him tell you that he is sorry for his offense, to which you respond by telling him you forgive him, and not to sin again.

"In doing all of this, Sally, your children will learn to obey God instantly. Which," she added sternly, "is God's will for *all* of His disciples, both children and adults alike. Do you understand?"

I had nodded my head unenthusiastically.

As I drove home with my sleeping son, all the new information Carla had exposed me to that day churned inside of me, trying to find a place to settle. The "Christian life" was so different from the life we had previously led. Though I wanted so badly to do it right, it seemed terribly difficult. I felt completely overwhelmed and exhausted.

Once we arrived back home, I wanted to just sit quietly and hold little Michael close and watch *Sesame Street* with him until his daddy came home. Little Michael was unusually sedate while Bert and Ernie clowned around on the show he loved best. I watched his face, wondering what unpleasant thoughts might be going through his mind, but I didn't yet have the sagacity to talk to him about it.

Michael grimaced when I told him what had occurred at lunch. "Still," I said, "I have to admit, little Michael does need more discipline. Do you think we should try spanking him?"

"I'm sure we are doing little Michael more harm than good by being so inconsistent," Michael admitted halfheartedly. "I guess we really should give it a try. But, that 'Do it the first time or else get spanked' rule seems a little overboard to me."

Relieved, I told him I agreed. In fact, as we continued to talk, Michael and I decided that Carla and her husband were altogether too rigid for us; we did not want to be discipled by them. We called Mary and Ricky in Montgomery to explain how we felt. We were relieved when they said they understood. What they felt we should do instead was look for a solid, Bible-teaching Baptist church. We said we would, right away.

Michael and I sat mesmerized by the colorful antics of the visiting evangelist Rob Holy, of the Rob Holy Evangelistic Crusade, as he preached a vivid hellfire-and-damnation message during our first visit to the Atlanta Baptist Tabernacle. We were amazed to see how many "souls were saved" and how many others "rededicated their lives to Christ." Each night concluded with testimonies from those whose lives had been "completely changed by Jesus." Then everyone newly saved was invited by the church's pastor, Ed Miller, to return for baptism there as soon as possible.

We found ourselves smiling and nodding our heads in agreement as we listened, night after night, to the new converts testify as to how Jesus had changed their lives. We stopped drinking alcohol, which put an end to weekend partying. I quit smoking, much to Michael's pleasure. I surprised myself by catching each curse word before it came out of my mouth, which, "before the Lord," I would never have given a second thought to. Michael and I studied our Bibles faithfully and took each passage literally, and to heart. We were completely enthralled with—and "sold out" (Christian idiom for "committed") to—Jesus.

Having just learned about the Second Coming of Christ being imminent, we were suddenly caught up in an excited panic much like what Atlantans experience when half an inch of snow is expected—a mixture of thrill and horror at likely disaster. Upon His return, those who had accepted Christ into their hearts would instantly be caught up in the sky with Him in what we had been told was called the Rapture. Thus they would escape the horrible time of tribulation, complete with torture and famine, that awaited those who refused salvation. One might get a second chance to repent during that time—if one didn't die first. It was so clear to us what a person should do once that person was made aware of God's plan.

One night Michael and his father became embroiled in a terrible argument that began when Michael chose to inform Riley of his need to get saved in order to ready himself and his family for the impending Second Coming.

Riley was heated. "Christ came once and that was it! Where did you come up with this ridiculous nonsense about him coming again? I have never heard a priest say anything about a Second Coming in a sermon, and not one damn thing about whatever you called it—a Rapture!"

Michael proudly proclaimed, "It's all in the Bible, Dad, which you ought to read *for yourself.*"

Riley shouted, "Catholics don't *need* to read the Bible! The priests read it and tell us whatever we need to know. That's enough."

Michael shook his head in dismay, but before he could protest any further, Virginia put a temporary halt to their arguing with a timely call to dinner.

When we got into our car to go home that evening, we shared with each other the first of many self-righteous assessments of his parents. Poor Virginia and Riley, we concluded—so spiritually lost.

"We've got to keep witnessing to them, Michael," I stated emphatically. "We can't just let them go to hell!"

To our amazement, Virginia and Riley agreed to accompany us to one of the nightly evangelical meetings at the Baptist tabernacle. We were excited, sure that their coming with us was a miraculous sign that they would simply hear the gospel message preached that night and immediately get saved.

Well, it didn't go exactly the way we thought it would. Michael's father used the twenty-minute drive to the church to come up with as many sarcastic remarks as he could about evangelism and to chide us heartily for having gotten ourselves involved in a *Baptist* church.

"You are Catholics, for Christ's sake!" he retorted to us along the way to church that night. "Or at least *you* are, Michael. And aren't you taking instructions to join the church? What about that?" He had turned his attention to me.

I guessed it was time to tell them that, several weeks before, I had ended my classes with Monsignor McNeil. The last time I had gone to the priest, I had been anxious to tell him all about my "born-again" experience. However, Monsignor McNeil had treated my testimony like an annoying fly and simply waved it away with his hand. Taking a deep breath for confidence, I proudly declared to my in-laws, "The priest's instructions ended up conflicting terribly with my salvation experience." Glancing at Michael for his concurrence, I continued, "So we decided that I should stop." Virginia looked sadly disappointed; Riley looked disgusted.

Suddenly, I felt distinctly uncomfortable. The look on Riley's face as he stared at me then let me know clearly that he now believed just one thing: *I* was the one responsible for the absurd religious mess Michael and I were involved in.

Much to our dismay, Virginia and Riley easily resisted every appeal Rob Holy made to "receive Christ." The ride back home was somber, but before Riley got out of the car, he summed up the preacher's message on the Beatitudes that night with a parting thought he was sure I would not forget: "Sally, I just want to tell you one thing: if the *meek* are going to inherit the earth . . . *you* won't get a damn thing!"

"Dad," Michael said quietly, "there's no need to say something like that."

Riley did not feel the need to respond, and Michael did not press him any further. My husband didn't fully understand the source of his father's words, but Riley and I knew that he had aptly hit his mark, which was to let me know the level to which, in his eyes, I had fallen.

Once back home and in our own bed, I could not sleep. Remembering the earlier time in our marriage when Michael had too quickly let Riley off the hook, my doubts resurfaced. Would he *ever* be able to stand up for me to his father? I wondered.

Michael and I had made serious efforts to conceive and had found out recently that they had proved successful. Now it was the dead of winter, and I was close to five months pregnant. We were thrilled that a close call I had with intense bleeding earlier on in the pregnancy had not ended in a dreaded miscarriage. I praised God for blessing us with another child and promised to give Him "all the glory." I prayed, too, for a healthy baby, whose birth I could take to mean that I had become more pleasing in God's sight. Seeking ways to please God had become my heart's strongest desire.

Everything that happened in our lives held a deeper meaning for us now. We believed that nothing occurred by happenstance or fate, and we were constantly curious to see what lay ahead for us in our "new life in the Lord." We talked about how the void we had felt in our lives had been filled with the love of Christ, and about how wonderful it was that our marriage was now "sealed in Christ." We prayed about every decision and trusted God for direction. We were extremely zealous in our "walk" and wanted "whatever God had for us." Both of us believed that we had found what we had always been searching for.

There continued to be dramatic changes in our lives, especially in our circle of friends. We disengaged ourselves from most of our old friends, since it was becoming important that we have only Christian friends who believed and lived as we did. We learned that the Scriptures taught that we were not to be "unequally yoked with nonbelievers." We also did not want to be frivolous with our time, now that it belonged to God. At first, to have Christianity take me away from our friends seemed like a great sacrifice, but in just a short while our desire to be "right with the Lord" came to take alarming precedence over everything and everyone else.

Even Paul and Susan, the close friends I had stayed with in Athens, had written an angry response to a letter we had written sharing our salvation experience with them and urging them to accept Christ as their personal Savior. We were determined that all of our friends would spend eternity in heaven. Instead, our evangelism offended them. We spent less and less time with our families, with the exception of Camille and Richard, who had "found the Lord" a year before we had. Once we were all four saved, we united in our aspirations to live out our Christianity, as well as to share Christ with our "lost" families. More often than not, however, the salvation message we imposed on family and friends was unsolicited, and not always gratefully accepted.

While we were casting off the old friends, we made some new ones. Four special young women came into our lives all at once, and I loved them immediately. Suzanne, Evelyn, Sherry, and Janet were four equally energized, distinctly individual roommates who had moved into the apartment just across the pool from us. All four were Christians, and they gladly let me assume the role of big sister, a part I had always wished to play. In various combinations, they would come to see me and tell me how their day went. As the nights grew warmer, we sat on the front steps long after Michael and little Michael had gone to bed, laughing and talking about anything and everything. It was great to have girlfriends again—especially ones that let me feel like my real age, twenty-one.

We spent a lot of time talking about God and the Bible. The four girls had all been brought up in Christian homes, an experience that I envied and asked many questions about. I had come to the conclusion that because my Episcopalian parents did not often speak about God, much less Jesus, in our home, they had therefore not provided their children with what the Bible meant by a Christian home. I now believed that being christened at birth provided you with neither a relationship with God nor entrance into heaven when you died. I wanted my children to grow up personally knowing Jesus as their Savior. I wanted their father to teach them the Scriptures, and I wanted to pray with them each night before I turned off their light. From these young women who had been blessed to grow up with experiences like those, I hoped to gain insight into ways of creating a "good Christian home."

The four girls loved to talk about their boyfriends and dreams of marriage—except for Janet, who would instead be sitting across from us, shaking her head in mock disgust. Ironically, though Janet never carried on about boys as the other three lustily did, she was the only one who had a serious boyfriend. She definitely was not amused whenever one of the other girls mentioned Harry or, God forbid, dared to tease her about how he had repeatedly begged her to marry him. I found myself thinking, She's so tough and self-sufficient, and it's obvious she wants it that way. The truth is, I really *can't* imagine her as a wife.

I began to notice how protective Janet was of the other girls, and especially of Suzanne. So perhaps it should not have been a surprise when Suzanne came alone to the apartment one day to talk.

First she told me about the days when she and Janet had been in college together, and of the unusually close group of girlfriends they had been with constantly. Seeing that I was not catching on, Suzanne suddenly blurted out, "Sally, I can't stand it anymore. I've got to tell you something awful! Janet and I were *more* than just friends."

"I'm not quite sure what you mean, Suzanne."

Her eyes teared up with humiliation, but she was desperate to talk. "At school, we were lovers," she said bluntly. "Janet had been telling me that she loved me for a long time, and I guess I fell in love with her for a while too." She looked at me; tears were streaming down her face. "I knew it was wrong! I knew it was sin. But Janet, and the other girls, said that the love we felt for one another *couldn't* be wrong! They said that God had made us that way!" She hung her head. "Still, I knew it was wrong."

There was a moment of silence before she added, "But, Sally, no one has ever loved me like Janet does."

Suzanne went on to tell me that her previous experiences with boys had not been pleasant; they had not been gentle or kind. But Janet had been both. I was reeling. What gross secret was this girl *telling* me? I blushed, remembering a time in seventh grade when I had spent the night at a girlfriend's house after a basketball game at school. We had both sneaked out of the game to go behind the stadium and make out with our boyfriends. That night in her double bed we had listened to the radio while taking turns tickling each other's backs as we always did until we would fall asleep. I clearly remember the song "Cherish," by the Associations, playing while we whispered to each other, wondering how it would *feel* to be "felt off" by a boy, and slowly touched each other's breasts.

I remembered how when my friend's finger had rounded my nipple, I had felt a particular surge between my legs—a feeling that something told me meant *sex*. Though I did not tell her *that* secret, I suspected she had felt it too, because we both had laughed too hard afterward, saying it was nothing and that boys were so stupid. Still, for a long time it had bothered me to feel like that because of a girl's touch.

Suzanne told me that since leaving college and moving into the apartment across from us, she and Janet had tried hard not to be lovers, only friends. "Most of the time it's okay. But sometimes," she confessed, "I'm just not strong enough to reject Janet's advances. I don't think the other girls suspect anything." Then, looking directly at me, she asked, "Can you help me?"

I had to fight with all that I had not to let Suzanne see how repulsed and close to hysteria I really was. "I promise I'll figure out some way to help. I'm glad you told me."

Suzanne sighed. "I'm relieved that I did. Just knowing you know will help me be able to say no to Janet."

"Don't worry," I assured her, "God has an answer for this. We've just got to find out what it is, and we will." I hugged her convincingly and she left full of hope.

I watched her walk down the grass to her apartment and thought I could almost understand how Janet could be a lot like a guy to a girl, and how a girl who felt as insecure with boys as Suzanne did might be persuaded to let Janet love her in that way. Then my mind wandered to what they might *do* as lovers, putting a fast halt to any more tender thoughts. Besides being repulsive—it was sin! Of that I was positive. I had to find a way of helping them out of such wicked, ungodly ways. In my prayers to God for the girls that night, I promised I would not let Him, or them, down.

I knew I would have to talk to Janet, and for some reason it made me nervous to think about it. I sensed that this "lesbian thing" was more seriously a part of her than it was with Suzanne. I would have to pray and ask God to do a work in my heart. I would ask Him to change my fleshly anger to a righteous one, and I would wait until I knew my heart was right before I confronted Janet. I would also have to tell Michael. He would find the whole thing disgusting, I imagined.

———

One Sunday Camille and Richard invited us to attend what they called a "charismatic service" at Mount Paran Church of God, the same church where the tapes on marriage given to us by our counselor had been recorded. The four of us found a seat as close to the front of the crowded sanctuary as we could. Folding chairs had been set up in the aisles for the anticipated overflow of people from all denominations who would come hoping to experience the full manifestation of God's "spiritual gifts." The year was 1975, and we were in the midst of what was called the Charismatic Movement.

Michael and I listened and watched with complete fascination. All around us people were deep in a form of worship that was like nothing we had ever seen. Professional-looking women and men in perfect business attire amicably shared pews with blue-collar workers and homemakers dressed in their best Sunday-go-to-meeting garb. Folks who had more than enough money worshiped in one accord with those who did not, and single persons gladly joined hands in prayer with small children in large families. A message of both love and anticipation emanated throughout the sanctuary. The music was electrifying and, after a while, intoxicating. Hands were lifted high above heads as people's faces shone with sheer ecstasy. Sometimes the congregation waved their hands slowly back and forth, back and forth, reminding me of a tree's high branches on a slightly windy day, and their bodies swayed just a little from side to side. Many kept their eyes closed in deep, peaceful concentration, broken only for an occasional outburst of "Praise the Lord" or "Hallelujah! Thank you, Jesus!" Still others fell down on their knees and wept.

The magnificent choir came onto the stage, and immediately the throng of praise and worship accelerated to a point of high excitation. Moments later, an exuberant Dr. Paul Walker, also a very handsome man, appeared in a nicely trimmed suit, with his sandy hair brushed and sprayed back away from his full face, showing off a smile that lit up the room. His husky baritone caught the voices of the whole choir and congregation, carrying them into more songs of praise and worship, and finally leading the whole room into an emotional and spiritual climax that was absolutely amazing to witness. It was impossible not to want to join in, to clap your hands and move to the beat of the music. I understood now why the church was called charismatic.

Suddenly Michael and I heard a woman's voice, speaking loudly and in the same strange language that we had heard on the marriage tapes. I quickly looked around to see who was speaking. Except for the fact that she had a very scrubbed look and that her hair was piled in a beehive on top of her head in true Church of God fashion, the woman speaking did not look unusual—or at all deranged. Though the service stopped while she spoke, and remained so while a man spoke afterward in English, it then promptly restarted as though nothing odd had happened. No one else around us seemed to be the least bit disturbed by the bizarre occurrence. Camille and Richard seemed perfectly fine, and no one was rushing to escort the woman out. Apparently it was some kind of spiritual experience, and Michael and I wanted to know exactly *what*.

After a few weeks of attending Mount Paran on Sunday nights, and a lot of discussions with Camille and Richard, we finally began to understand what the funny-sounding language was all about. First Camille and Richard explained that these people were full of the Holy Spirit, *not* deranged. They had been "baptized with the Holy Spirit," which, they explained, was a different baptism from the water baptism we had experienced at the Baptist church. A person usually received the Baptism in the Holy Spirit by the laying on of hands, and by his or her asking God for Baptism in the Holy Spirit through prayer. The Baptism in the Holy Spirit had been promised to the apostles by Christ when He had presented Himself to them after His resurrection, and it was first realized by the disciples on the day of Pentecost when they "spoke in tongues." From then on, whenever this experience happened to a Christian believer, he or she was given a personal "prayer language" as evidence of having received the Holy Spirit.

We thought we understood: the woman we had heard on the marriage tapes was speaking in her prayer language. Camille and Richard said no, that though it sounded the same, she was actually demonstrating what the Scriptures referred to as the corporate body's use of the "*gift* of tongues." They patiently and carefully explained that this gift of tongues is a message from God, given out loud, by an individual, and in an unknown language, during a gathering of believers. The message is followed by an interpretation (offered by a different person) in English, so that "the body of Christ" (the congregation) can understand what God is saying to His people. We thought this was complicated and very confusing.

The prayer language a person receives at his or her Baptism in the Holy Spirit is for use during personal prayer times. Therefore it has no need for an interpretation. Though both kinds of tongues sound the same, we finally concluded, the prayer language's purpose is to take one's intellect out of the way and thereby allow the Holy Spirit to "pray for you." The Scriptures speak about the Holy Spirit interceding for us "with groanings too deep for words" (Romans 8:26), which could describe what a prayer language sounds like and could also explain the belief that it originates from the spirit of God. Some describe it as a direct line to God. Others claim that it gives substance and power to their faith. The gift of tongues, with interpretation, expressed in church services is given by the Holy Spirit for the purpose of edification and encouragement for the whole body of Christ. We thought we were finally beginning to understand. One thing was very clear: Camille and Richard obviously went to a much more exciting church than we did!

Each week we went faithfully to the Baptist church in the morning, sang in the choir, and attended our Sunday school class. But on Sunday nights we worshiped with the charismatics at Mount Paran. We had begun to join in the worship, occasionally lifting our hands awkwardly, allowing ourselves more and more freedom in worship. Still, we felt we were missing what the charismatics were so full of, and, wanting everything God had to offer His followers, I grew impatient with waiting to ask God to baptize me in His Holy Spirit.

Finally the week came when both Michael and I were ready to experience for ourselves what we saw happening all around us on Sunday nights at Mount Paran. Along with several others, we left our seats and followed a group into the side chapel, where ministers were waiting to assist us in asking God to receive the Baptism in the Holy Spirit. We knelt down together, and I watched a man lay his hands firmly upon Michael's shoulders as they prayed together for a few minutes. I heard Michael ask God to baptize him in His Holy Spirit. And then I heard Michael crying and bubbling over with words I could not understand. Michael had received his prayer language. I was amazed! It really worked. Michael's face glowed with joy, and I was ready to take my turn.

Both the man and a jubilant Michael, who was grinning ear to ear, eagerly turned their attention to me. They laid their hands on me while I prayed as earnestly as I knew how, asking God to please baptize me, also, in His Holy Spirit. We waited. Nothing happened. Michael prayed for me. Still nothing. After a few minutes I began to feel a tremendous heat surge up my neck and flood over my face. I wished it to be the power of the Holy Spirit but knew it was only the deep embarrassment I was feeling at God's decision not to bless me as He had Michael.

That night, unable to sleep, I quietly slipped downstairs, where I knelt down and begged God to baptize me in the Holy Spirit and to let me have a prayer language as evidence. Still nothing happened. I was convinced that God was angry with me. I confessed all the sins I could think of and spent extra time tearfully beseeching God for forgiveness for what I decided had angered Him the most—my having left Michael, along with my unthinkable fantasies about being with a man other than my husband. Michael was so good, I thought painfully. He had always been such a good and faithful husband while I had been willing to violate one of God's most sacred covenants—marriage. I began to worry that maybe what I had done was *unforgivable* to God. I certainly had not forgiven myself and had decided that, until God had, I never would.

One night just a few weeks later, Michael and I went to a meeting where a "prophet" was to speak. We had been told that a prophet was a man who brought a fresh word for the day directly from God to His people, just like Jonah and Elijah in the Old Testament. Michael and I looked forward to hearing what this modern-day prophet had to say to today's church.

"Brothers and sisters! God's people are witnessing great signs and wonders all across this land—salvation, healings, prophecies, and miracles of every kind! By the power of the Holy Spirit and God's Word, these things—and more—will abound in the last days! Glory to God!"

A short, rotund man about forty years old, Norville Hayes sounded terribly loud and aggressive; however, before long we became used to this common style of preaching.

At the end of his message he gave an altar call to receive the Baptism in the Holy Spirit. When I realized he was saying that anyone who had asked to be baptized in His Holy Spirit, but had not yet received his or her prayer language, needed to come forward for prayer, I quickly joined the cluster kneeling at the altar. I listened hopefully as he emphatically stated that we weren't to doubt God's gift of His Spirit. If we had asked Him to baptize us in the Holy Spirit—we *were* baptized in the Holy Spirit. We needed only to accept it by faith.

Along with several others, I asked God to give me my prayer language and thanked Him for it in advance. After a few moments, I was aware of a sound inside of me that I was sure didn't originate in my brain. Feeling giddy, I began to speak. "Shananana . . . "

In tears of relief and gratitude, I obediently "claimed" these syllables as my prayer language. Added to my joy was the thought that maybe this was also evidence of God's forgiveness for my sins. I left rejoicing with all of the others who had received their prayer languages that night. It was great. I was no longer on the outside looking in.

One day shortly thereafter, I finally sat down with my sister and told her about Janet and Suzanne. I had told Michael a few days earlier, and, rather than being disgusted, he had been genuinely concerned for Janet and had encouraged me to try to find a way to help her. Camille, however, was as shocked and as greatly distressed as I had known she would be. I was relieved when she said she knew someone who would know what needed to be done, in accordance with God's Word. When she called me later that day, she said the girls probably needed "deliverance."

"Are you serious? Surely you're not talking about something like the heinous deliverance scenes in *The Exorcist,* which—I might remind you—gave me months of nightmares."

"Actually, yes. It could be sort of like that. Only . . . this deliverance is for real," Camille seriously reminded me, "not make-believe."

I was scared now, but I called Janet and asked her up to the apartment to talk.

"Janet, listen to me," I began. "Deliverance is the only thing that will set you and Suzanne free from all of this. You know homosexuality's sin, and you know you can't remain in sin and be a Christian. Besides, Janet, Suzanne *wants* to stop; you've got to think about her." I could see that she was angry.

"I don't know what I think anymore. I love Suzanne," she said emphatically, "and it's not so easy to see why loving her is such a sin." We sat in silence for a few minutes. Then, seeing the persistent frown on my face, she finally conceded. "Okay, okay. I know the Bible says it's a sin. I'll go through the deliverance, Sally—if for no other reason than for Suzanne."

The truth was, looking at Janet sitting across from me, moving her hands through her hair in angry frustration, I was puzzled myself. She seems so masculine, I thought. Whenever I was around her, I felt the way I did around Michael's youngest brother. Janet felt like a *brother* to me, I thought, with a surprising rush of love and compassion. Just then, I caught a brief flash of fear behind the anger in her dark brown eyes, so that for a moment I weakened in my decision, feeling guilty at having to push her toward something I knew would be painfully humiliating.

"Look, I know it's hard, Janet. But I'm sure that God will give you and Suzanne the strength to endure it. Satan's really had a hold on y'all, but I am sure he won't after next week! And, in the meantime, please don't make things any more difficult for Suzanne, okay?"

"I won't make any sexual advances toward her, if that's what you mean," she answered, a slight smile forming on her face.

"Good," I said, blushing, "and thanks."

"Look, Sally," she said, having become serious again, "as much as I hate to admit it, I know that being with me was probably a one-time thing for Suzanne. I just treated her a lot better than any guy ever had—or probably ever will."

With that, she smiled again. "Sorry—I shouldn't have said that. But, really, I'm sure she'll be okay, Sally."

I could see that Janet truly cared for Suzanne, which still mystified me. And I was terrified of the ordeal ahead. With both girls, however, I acted as though I knew exactly what I was doing, chanting to them over and over, "Greater is He who is in us than he who is in the world."

"Be careful," Michael said, kissing me good-bye. Whereas Michael had reacted calmly when I told him about Janet and Suzanne, his eyes had definitely widened with interest when I told him about the deliverance. On my way now to pick the girls up for our appointment, he looked concerned. "I wish we knew this guy y'all are going to see," he said. "But I'm sure it'll all be fine. I'll be praying for y'all."

As the deliverance minister opened the door of his suburban home, I saw that he was an ordinary-looking middle-aged man with dark hair and glasses. After we had introduced ourselves, he invited us into a small study. Pointing to two straight-back chairs placed in the middle of the room, the man asked Janet and Suzanne to be seated. Smiling, he showed me to a leather sofa, where I could observe everything but be out of the way.

Standing and facing the girls, he carefully explained, "There are basically two kinds of demonic activity. One is oppression—the lesser of two evils, so to speak—and the other is possession. The only way to accurately discern between the two is through prayer and God's Word. So I will need to pray with each of you separately in order to distinguish the spirits that we are dealing with, and then proceed. All right?" Both girls nodded their heads in agreement, and with that, he placed his hands firmly on Suzanne's head.

With a much stronger voice than somehow I would have expected, he closed his eyes and prayed: "Lord Jesus, I hold this young woman up to you and ask that you would expose the enemy right now! Thank you, Lord.

"Suzanne, I believe the Lord is saying that Satan's demons are oppressing you." Clasping her hands between his own, he raised them heavenward. "We call upon the name of Jesus and we claim His power to set you free! Glory to God!" With even greater authority in his voice, he said, "Satan, you are a liar. You have no power over Suzanne. She belongs to Jesus. I bind you and your demons from her. In Jesus' name—let it be so!"

After a minute he was satisfied and lowered Suzanne's hands. "Lord, we thank you for setting your daughter free! Suzanne, you are free! Lord, I ask you to place a hedge of protection around her that will protect her from any further oppression. I ask it in Jesus' name. Amen." There was a long pause. Then Suzanne looked up slowly. She was in tears, but relief clearly shone on her face.

He turned then to give me specific orders: "You must pray diligently for Suzanne, and she must stay accountable to you on a daily basis." My heart swelled with the pride of Christian duty, and I eagerly committed myself to her safekeeping.

It was Janet's turn now, and I thought to myself that she looked like a cornered and pitifully frightened animal. I hated to see her looking so weak and vulnerable. Silently I began to pray—and pray hard.

The minister began to pray over Janet with great fervor and intensity, while at all times keeping a firm grip—not on her head, but on her shoulders. "Lord, I now lift your child, Janet, up to you. I ask that you reveal the enemy and show us how to come against him in Jesus' name. Thank you, Lord."

He waited and, after a moment, calmly said, "Janet, the enemy has a very tight hold on you." Then there was a long pause.

"Satan!" he suddenly shouted. Startled, Janet gasped. "By the blood of our Lord and Savior Jesus Christ, and in His name, I *command* you to depart from this child of God. You have no more power over her. *Satan,* do you hear me?! In Jesus' name, I command you to *release* her and depart from her forever!" He tightened his grip on Janet, whose face was set in deep anger. I thought to myself that she looked as though any second she might bolt and run. She pulled away a few times, just before the sickening noises began.

I sat wide-eyed and frozen in place, watching and listening, while Janet began to wrestle with her unseen enemy.

Despite Janet's strength, the minister held on firmly. "Satan, I command you—*come out* of her this minute in the name of Jesus!" With that, Janet let loose a groan, grotesquely low and guttural at first, but then accelerating to a revoltingly high volume. She coughed and made painful-sounding retching noises until I was certain she was going to throw up. I had done some reading about deliverance in preparation for this, and the book had said that sometimes as the demon or demons came out, so did an awful green bile. It looked as if *something* was on its way out of Janet. The minister immediately threw back his hands as though he had been shocked.

She continued on like that, thrashing in her chair, fighting invisible tormentors, until abruptly she grew completely quiet. She sat very still, in perfect peace. The minister stood back and beamed triumphantly. "Praise God! Praise God in this place! Satan and his demons have departed, Janet, and you are completely set free—in Jesus' name! Hallelujah!" She tried to smile.

Janet was commissioned to my care as well, a job I gladly accepted. At last it was time to go. The minister sent Janet off with a chilling admonition: "You especially must stay very close to the Lord and avoid all temptation to return to your past sin. The demons that were commanded to depart from your body will seek a new habitat. According to Scripture, if—because of sin—the demons are able to return to you, they will come back *ten times worse!* And, believe me," he added, "they *will* try."

I drove us home, all the while imagining furious demons scurrying all around, biting at the air, seeking just one small crack through which to crawl back in. Finally I made myself focus on Suzanne, who sat in the backseat and whose countenance was decidedly lighter now. Janet sat beside me looking quiet and pensive. I told myself she was tired—which, in fact, I'm sure was true.

After a few months, I felt that I could ease up on my constant supervision of the girls. They seemed to be doing very well. Suzanne was finishing her education and was unquestionably happier. She always hugged me and had taken a real interest in little Michael. I often told her what a wonderful mother she would be one day. As for Janet, she had surprised us all with the sudden announcement that she and Harry were getting married. I believed she seemed much softer now, and often told her so, which I knew embarrassed her but seemed to please her as well.

The winter wedding was lovely, and Janet was a handsome bride. It seemed like the perfect happy ending.

That same winter, Michael made a difficult decision to join his family business. We needed more income, and he was tiring from the long days and nights of working and going to college classes. His father would help him get started in the managers' training program, and eventually we would be transferred out of Atlanta. It would be tough, as no favoritism was shown to family members. As hard as it was for him to temporarily stop studying for his college degree, it did seem to be the right decision.

Spring came, and I was feeling and looking *huge* with child. However, my pregnancy due date came and went. After two weeks had passed and there was still no baby, my doctor insisted that I be x-rayed to check things out. When he called me with the results, he stated frankly that the baby was too large for me to deliver vaginally.

So, on May 13, at 5:30 P.M., with no help from my sleeping body, Daniel (which means "God is my judge") Robert was lifted by cesarean section from his cramped, warm haven out into the bright lights of the delivery room, weighing in at a plentiful eight pounds, fifteen ounces.

Michael and I were thrilled with our second beautiful baby boy. Not having been forced to take the same bony route into the world that his big brother had been made to suffer, Daniel had been allowed to report to life in unusually perfect shape.

On one of our first nights back home, Michael and I stood beside each other, watching little Michael as he very gently held his baby brother in his big-boy bed. We had experienced a few moments of jealousy in little Michael, who missed his long-standing role as only child. Still, he was no less adoring and proud of his baby brother. Standing there, I felt swallowed up with joy. Leaning over to Michael, I whispered, "If God saw fit to give us only *these* two sons, no matter how much we want more children, I would be completely fulfilled as a mother."

Michael bent down and kissed the tops of both boys' heads. Standing back up, he pulled me close to him, kissed me as well, and said, "I couldn't be more content myself."

One Sunday Pastor Miller called Michael and me into his office for a private session at the Atlanta Baptist Tabernacle. With a deep frown, he asked us to take our seats. He wasted no time in asking us point-blank, "Do the two of you believe in the Baptism in the Holy Spirit?"

Michael and I smiled. "Yes, we do!"

"Am I then to assume that you also believe in speaking in tongues?"

"Not only believe in it," Michael said. "We speak in tongues ourselves!" We probably would have demonstrated it for him had he asked. But that was not where he was going. In fact, as it turned out, it was we who would be going.

Having heard all of the evidence he wanted, or needed, to hear, he abruptly rose from his chair and pointed an accusing finger at us. "You must both leave. Obviously you are a part of the group causing divisiveness in the church. It is clear that you cannot submit to Baptist doctrine; therefore, you need to find another place to worship."

We were officially "dis-fellowshiped" from the Baptist church, and he was not in the least bit sorry to say so.

Michael and I left his office, and the church, numbly shaking our heads in disbelief at the idea that anyone could throw someone out of a church for interpreting the Bible differently. Even though the resulting confusion was extremely hard on our tender, idealistic shoots of faith, we managed to leave our Baptist "friends" and join the growing numbers of charismatics at Mount Paran Church of God.

After only three months of marriage, Janet divorced Harry. She told me that she could have, and should have, left him after the first week. Bluntly, and without asking whether I wanted to hear it or not, she exploded with a blistering account of sex with poor Harry. "It was awful—in fact, it was disgusting! But, you know something?" she went on to say, with a determined look on her face. "I never had a problem having *great* sex with girls! I never should have married Harry, Sally. I wish to God I hadn't."

I did not know what to say except for a weak "I'm sorry." I had been taught, by then, that God was against divorce, which I told her—though I knew that her mind was adamantly made up. I secretly wondered if it wouldn't be the best thing. Janet made me feel so confused about what I thought that sometimes I wished I'd never gotten involved. I felt a rush of sadness for tall, skinny Harry, who at their wedding had looked at Janet with such adoration—and desire! I had thought to myself then, with silent envy of the bride, that Harry looked ready to famishedly devour her as soon as he could get his hands on her. And now here she was, telling me that sex with him was worse than lousy! I shook my head, not even caring if Janet saw me.

At first Janet and I didn't talk about what she would do now about relationships. I think I feared her response and she feared mine. I did not want to believe that the demons were back—God forbid—ten times worse! Instead, I asked Janet a safer question: "How are you doing in the Lord?" To this she replied flippantly, "Well, you know what the Baptists believe: once saved, always saved. So I guess I'm fine!"

I let it all go that day, with only a mild generic caution: "Stay close to Him, okay?"

Her reply was an unenthusiastic "Yeah, I will."

On our next visit together, Janet was more up-front with me, boldly declaring that she was a lesbian and that that was pretty much all there was to that. "I know you don't agree with it, but I can't pretend anymore to be something I'm not—straight! I also think God's fine about it, but I know you won't agree with that either."

She was correct. "I think that God very much disapproves of your choice, Janet."

"Well, Sally," she said, "that's the problem. It doesn't feel much like a choice to me—more like the way God made me."

For the next few years, Janet and I would exchange letters, each of us trying to persuade the other to come around to what we each saw as the "right" ways of living and loving. Mine, of course, always called for Janet to change her lifestyle and to stop listening to Satan, who, I said, was deceiving her with the lie that she was a lesbian.

In response to my lectures, Janet only grew stronger in what I saw as her "imagined" lesbianism and became bolder and bolder in telling me whatever she wanted to about it. I became harder and harder on her, finally resorting to saying that I believed the demons really had come back and possessed her ten times worse. Eventually, we stopped talking and writing, and after a while we abandoned all contact with one another.

The visiting preacher at Evangel Temple was a thin, wiry-looking woman of about fifty. Michael and I had been visiting the church ever since October, when we had moved to Montgomery, Alabama, for Michael to serve as assistant manager of the store there. Having read in the Bible that women were to instruct only other women and children—never men—we were both disturbed by the fact that the preacher who would be holding the weeklong "Holy Ghost" revival meeting was a female. Though we certainly took Scripture literally, Michael had decided that I should go anyway and check out the revival.

At the end of her daily morning's preaching, the woman urged anyone who needed *anything* from God to come down front to the altar rail for prayer. After a line of people had formed, she worked her way from one end to the other, pausing to lay her hands on each person and pray over him or her. Never having witnessed anyone being "slain in the spirit" before, I watched for a while before I, too, joined the line. It was a domino effect. One by one, as she passed, bodies slowly fell to the floor. A man stood behind each person, ready to catch each of "the slain" and gently guide him or her down to the floor to rest until he or she "came to." Another man stood ready to cover the ladies' exposed knees (or whatever) with a small blanket. As I stood waiting for my turn, I watched the female preacher and wondered if she was somehow pushing the people over. When she came to me, she simply said, "In the name of Jesus," and as I felt her fingertips brush across my brow, yes, there was ever so slight a push, and over I went. It was not enough of a push to actually force someone over, unless he or she *wanted* to go. It was more like an encouraging nudge. I fell as if in slow motion, trusting the stranger who caught me to set me down delicately on the red carpet. I was only vaguely aware of someone else rushing over to cover my possible indecency. Though as I lay there for several minutes I enjoyed the sensation of being engulfed in warmth, with my spirit and my mind in a state of rest such as I had never known, still, when at last I rose to my feet, shaky and feeling kind of heady, I was unsure of what I had just experienced.

I returned the following day for the morning service. Then at noon I grabbed Daniel from the church nursery and rushed to pick little Michael up from kindergarten, hoping to get back to church in time to catch the end of the Holy Ghost meeting. We were, however, too late. As we entered the rear of the church, little Michael stopped and stood perfectly still, staring at the bodies that dotted the church floor, their lower portions covered with blankets. To me it gave the appearance of an adult kindergarten class during nap time. Looking up at me, little Michael very calmly asked, "Are they all dead, Mama?" I took a second look at the room strewn with bodies and realized that it really did look like a mass murder had taken place. It was not easy trying to explain being "slain in the spirit" to a four-and-a-half-year-old, though somehow I tried. I knew then that I didn't want to be "slain in the spirit," attend Evangel Temple, or be preached to by a female preacher again.

In our first few months in Montgomery, life was good. We had been thrilled to find that we would be living in the same town as Mary and Ricky. As we settled into our cozy rental house on Audubon Road, Michael became engrossed in learning the responsibilities of his new job while I concentrated on learning my way around Montgomery.

Being away from Atlanta for the first time had already brought us closer as a family.

The emphasis in our Christian walk was consistently on our home. In my view, homemaking was the job given to me by God, and I began to treat it as such by studying Christian books and attending workshops at local churches that Mary would usually take me to. I was learning that a Christian woman's priorities were: God and her relationship with Him; her husband and his needs; children (which I was taught were an *excuse* for a messy home but never a reason); and outreach for church and others.

In my Bible-study notebook I jotted down these notes:

1. Get up and dressed attractively first thing in the morning, because the way you look in the morning is the way he will remember you all day. Remember: he *is* out in the world!

2. Pick up for him thankfully. Ask him what he wants cleaned around the house and see that it is done each day.

3. Give him much praise, and remember: no husband likes the "Honey-Do Club." [This referred to the proverbial list that many wives had of things that their husbands needed to do for them.]

4. Look your best when he returns home each day so that he will always *want* to return home! In doing these things you will please not only your husband, but your Heavenly Father.

Mary faithfully instructed me with a list of scriptures I was to read and learn to apply to my life, such as Colossians 3:18, "Wives, be subject to your husbands, as is fitting to the Lord"; 1 Timothy 2:11, "Let a woman quietly receive instruction with entire submission"; and Psalms 131:1, "O Lord, my heart is not proud, nor my eyes haughty; Nor do I involve myself in great matters, or in things too difficult for me."

Though I wrote such verses on index cards and taped them to kitchen cabinets, I still feared that my not so quiet and not always gentle spirit would never be changed enough to please God. I prayed often about this. I yielded more and more to Michael's opinions, asking his counsel before I decided just about anything on my own. I began to leave "great matters" to my husband, and, as Mary had told me I should, I tried to allow God to speak to his heart rather than giving him advice myself. Michael seemed to like the changes I was trying to make, and as a result, I felt more and more secure in my Christian life and in my home.

Being a mother gave me much gratification. During that time, I especially relished the sweet closeness and restfulness I felt while breast-feeding Daniel. A problem arose, however, in the form of Daniel's first, sharp little teeth. One minute we might be peacefully lounging together on the sofa—Daniel's bright green eyes peering trustingly up at me, his tiny hand absently playing at my shirt collar—when, suddenly, he would stop suckling and clamp those teeth down right on the very *tip* of my nipple. After going through this nine or ten agonizing times, I looked up the phone number of the local chapter of the La Leche League (a breast-feeding support group) and called them for advice. Their counsel was: "The next time he bites you—scream. He won't bite you again."

The next Sunday afternoon was pleasant, and Michael took his little family out for a drive. When it was past feeding time, I reached over the backseat, removed a fussy Daniel from his child seat, lifted up my blouse, and settled back down in my seat to nurse him. With Daniel now content, we continued on our drive. Suddenly, with the usual lack of warning, Daniel bit me. Remembering the La Leche League's advice, I screamed. Michael slammed on the car brakes just as I looked down to see a most pitiful sight: Daniel had let loose of my nipple, all right, and his beautiful face was now in shock. The corners of his mouth were on their way down, and his little lips were quivering as though he were freezing. He began to cry. No—he began to *wail,* and there appeared to be absolutely no comforting him. I tried everything I could, putting him back to the breast, putting him up high on my shoulder. Nothing worked, so I cried too. Little Michael began to cry as well, and big Michael, now frustrated and not understanding at all what had just upset our pleasant ride, chastised me, saying, "Sally—I can't believe you screamed at him like that."

"But the La Leche League *said* to . . ." I wept on. Daniel finally calmed down, as did little Michael and I, and we drove home. However, the sad result was that Daniel would have nothing to do with breast-feeding again. I suspected then that, though he might be *big,* Daniel would be a tenderhearted little boy who would grow up to be a tenderhearted man—which he was and has.

After gathering a small pile of fall leaves from the abundance still on the ground in March, Michael struck a match and lit the leaves. Then he took each record album and—along with each one's precious memory—tossed it onto the flames. Michael had become "convicted by God" about something he had been taught at a weeklong Christian conference the previous summer while still in Atlanta. There he had learned that inanimate objects could possibly be demonic because of oppressive evil spirits having "attached themselves" to the objects. Bill Gothard, the leader of the conference, told a story about a man who had bought a guitar and stored it in a closet for years, forgetting about it until his teenage children suddenly became very "rebellious." While the father was in prayer, God revealed to him that their rebelliousness was directly related to the guitar, which, God further "showed him," had been previously used to play wicked secular rock music. The man promptly burned the instrument, and his children immediately returned to their usual obedient state.

Because of this story Michael was suddenly uncomfortable selling, or even giving, our record collection to anyone else. We decided that the only thing to do was to have a bonfire and burn the whole lot. Besides our own secret regret, I know we also both saw dollar signs go up in smoke as into the fire went the Beatles, the Carpenters, Johnny Mathis, Creedence Clearwater Revival, Jimmy Hendrix, Chicago, Peter, Paul and Mary, Blood Sweat and Tears, and countless more of what today would be vintage classics. Holding hands, we said a solemn prayer over the burning pile of smelly, misunderstood vinyl: "God, please forgive us for having such sin in our home and around our children. Please bless our obedience now. In the name of Jesus. Amen."

After all the records had been burned, Michael took a shoe box from my hands, which contained all of our high school love letters to each other, and shoved it onto the center of the smoldering pile. The flames leaped back into life, and soon the cardboard box disintegrated before our eyes. As it did, my heart sank. Looking at Michael, I knew that he was remembering too and shared my mixed feelings. Still, I believed that we were doing the right thing.

Since the first of the year, Michael had determined that it was too difficult for him to work for his father, and I had become terribly homesick. As a result, we began to seek God's will about what we were to do. Before long Michael devised a plan for us to move back to Georgia and open a Christian coffeehouse, a place where Christians could informally gather to talk about the Bible, play Christian music, and be served a light fare of food and soft drinks or coffee. It sounded like a great idea to me—besides which, all I knew was that I wanted to go home.

We ran these thoughts of leaving Michael's family business and moving back home by my parents first, who, surprisingly, did not tell us we were complete fools to leave such a lucrative business. Michael's parents, however, became just as upset as we had anticipated they would. They had tremendous problems understanding why on earth we would choose to put our family in financial straits when Michael had "the opportunity of a lifetime" right in front of him. If we weren't happy in Montgomery, Riley unhappily but generously suggested, maybe we could be sent elsewhere. Michael thanked him but said no.

The first thing Michael and I needed in order to move back to Atlanta was money, which was why we decided to have a yard sale. For several days we boxed up what we would take to Atlanta, and hauled the rest to the carport to be sold. It was then that we made those two foolish mistakes—burning our record albums and burning our love letters.

Spring came, and with it the glorious pink-and-white blossoms of the dogwood trees and azaleas that stun Atlanta every year. By the beginning of April, we had been able to move from Montgomery to a small apartment in an affordable suburb of Atlanta. Michael tried hard to establish a Christian coffeehouse; however, he met with one financial obstacle after another. Eventually we had to face the fact that we would not be able to realize our dream. Discouraged, we began to earnestly ask God about what Michael was to do instead.

Daniel had his first birthday, and we spent what was probably our last dime on his toy riding horse and his party. About the time we were wondering if we had made a mistake by returning to Georgia, Michael went to talk to Clayton Ryder, owner of Ryder Sporting Goods, where he had worked during his first years of college. Clayton was happy to hear from him and, without hesitation, offered him a position in one of his stores.

Now the hot, humid days of summer were upon us and, though it meant I would have to take Michael quite a distance to work so that I could have the car for the rest of the day, I decided to help with the weeklong vacation Bible school at Mount Paran Church of God. We had happily resumed our worship there and were trying to become as involved as possible. During the week of Bible school, I met Charlene, a woman who was to become the link to our next fifteen years of spiritual journeying.

After a few months, and with some creative financing, Michael and I were pleased to be able to purchase our first "starter home"—in Marietta, another Atlanta suburb. One day not too long after we had moved in, there was a knock on my door, and much to my surprise, there stood Charlene and a friend with a homemade coffee cake to welcome me and my family to Marietta. I was touched by their gesture and delighted to see Charlene again. I was even happier to learn that we now lived close to one another. While the three of us ate and talked, Charlene invited Michael and me to visit a couples Bible-study group that met every Friday night. Knowing that we were eager for Christian friends and "fellowship," I enthusiastically assured her that we would be there.

"Good," Charlene said. "I think you'll like James Smith a lot."

chapter 4

The Dark Ages Begin

"Jesus never asked his disciples for their opinions. If you are a true Christian, you are a disciple of Christ and free to make only one choice—to obey the Lord. Following Christ's example of obedience to the Father, a disciple gives up his rights as well, and submits to the authority of his teacher." Although James Smith was an attractive forty-year-old man who stood about five feet, seven inches tall, with wispy blond hair and delicate features, his appearance was not his most arresting aspect. To me, it was his voice. While I cannot always remember my mother's voice perfectly in my mind, I can always recall the voice of James Smith, with its subtle, compelling authority.

"How exactly does a disciple learn how to live their life in obedience to Christ?" someone asked James. I listened carefully, hoping to hear specific examples that could be applied to my own life.

"Jesus tells his disciples in Matthew 16:24: 'If anyone wishes to come after me, let him deny himself, take up his cross, and follow me.' Deny your own will and instead yield to whatever *his* will is for your life. A Christian cannot seek to please both God and man. The best test of true discipleship is to observe how popular he or she is with 'the world.'"

Michael and I talked all the way home about how excited we were that God had shown us this group of "serious Christians."

The next Friday night, we returned to discover that there was a guest speaker talking about the group he was a part of, which lived "in community" in the heart of a nearby town called Roswell. They were attempting to live their lives according to chapter 2 of Acts, in which the disciples are described as "having all things in common." Self-sufficiency being a huge priority, they grew their own produce and raised their own rabbits, chickens, and cows for food. Believing in the concept of community ourselves (and remembering the time earlier in our marriage when we wanted to move to the Koinonia commune), Michael and I heard this man's words ring with a simple truth. We were terribly excited at having found James Smith's fellowship just as it was considering moving into community life.

After the meeting, we spoke to James about joining the group; he smiled and gently laid a hand on each of our shoulders. "There's no membership. We simply meet together weekly in one another's homes. But you are both more than welcome to be a part of what God is doing in this small part of the large body of Christ."

As we told James how excited we were about the prospect of communal living, he immediately called a couple over to meet us. "Michael and Sally, this is Stu and Becky Shores. I believe God would have the four of you get to know one another. It's my feeling that you share the same vision for your families. It could even be that God might want to use you together in some sort of ministry."

In talking with Stu and Becky, Michael and I understood that the four of us were somewhat more ready for "community" than the rest of the group. We found our discovery to be a little disappointing, but we were still glad to hear that at least the Shores and a few others were ready. We agreed that we should get together soon and pray for an understanding of what God had brought us together for. Nothing was happenstance. Everything was a distinct part of God's plan—as long as we heard and obeyed Him. Michael and I had found our niche in James Smith's group. For the next eight years we would be completely committed to all that he would instruct us to do with our lives.

My brother-in-law Richard and my sister Camille had decided it was God's will that they move to Wilmore, Kentucky, where Richard would attend Asbury Theological Seminary. They moved in with us for a few months in order to save a little money before the move, and, in spite of our not having much room, things went well. During those months of living together, we took turns, one couple having the master bedroom, one using the pull-out sofa bed, a week at a time, so that both couples would have their privacy. One night, when it was our turn on the sofa bed, Michael and I had a disagreement. I cannot remember what it was about; I can only recall that we made up once we pulled the covers around us and that, too late, Michael remembered that the condoms we were depending on in those days to prevent an untimely pregnancy were in the bedside table in our room, where Camille and Richard were sleeping. A month later I discovered that I was pregnant again. To us, it seemed clear that, by allowing me to become pregnant, God had shown us that birth control was probably not His will for our lives. If, after all, we believed God to be in total control of everything, that control surely included the "opening and closing" of a woman's womb to allow for conception.

James Smith's group, and many others like it, allowed only males to be in leadership positions and operated under what was called an "umbrella of protection." God "covered" us all with His protection and was the ultimate head. The pastor/elder was directly "under" God and "answered" to Him. The husband, as "head of the household," was next in line, with the wife submissively "under" his authority. A single woman had no option but to submit directly to her pastor or elder. Beneath the wives were the children, who answered obediently to their parents. Under this "umbrella," there would be little to no excuse for poverty in our midst (though no one would ever be comfortable with being well-off, either), no reason for divorce, no excuse for hunger, and less need for God to have to get our attention by "allowing" us or our children to become ill—or worse. (God was not blamed for sickness; rather, He *allowed* it for our good.)

I was all too ready and willing to attach myself to James Smith's fellowship. I came seeking the family continuity I had previously lacked and was eager to find others like me who yearned for an extended family with strong Christian values in which to securely bring up their children. In the fellowship I saw how my husband could learn to be a "strong man of God"—the strong authority and head of household I craved. Someone I could depend on. Someone who was bound to protect and love me forever. It seemed certain now that all of my prayers were being answered. As for Michael, he felt his own need to control something, or someone, in his life, which easily translated to his dominance over me. To me, submission to his control was a small price to pay for a guaranteed, indestructible life.

One Saturday morning, Michael came home from a men's prayer breakfast, during which James and the other men had prayed for my friend Charlene's estranged husband, Darin, and recounted a portion of the meeting to me: "While we were praying for Darin to return to Charlene and their children, James said that, in God's eyes, Darin had forsaken his paternal rights the day he left Charlene. I've never heard it put like *that* before."

"Me either," I said.

"Anyway, there's more. James said that the last time he spoke with Darin, he told him he'd better repent quickly, and return to his wife and children, before God had to break one of his legs—or worse—to get his attention!" Michael's eyes were opened wide while repeating James's shocking admonishment. Frowning deeply, he added, "And he was completely serious, Sally."

I sat there stupefied, unable to shake the thought that one day I might actually hear that Darin's leg was in traction. Still, as extreme as that sounded, I finally said, " Well, I guess that's what happens when a family gets out from under God's umbrella of protection. All we have to do is submit to His will and everything will be the way it's supposed to be. How hard can that be?"

Though Michael and I had different reasons for being susceptible to this type of fundamentalist Christian group and for allowing such fierce restrictions to be imposed on our lives and those of our children, both of us were nevertheless seeking to fill chasms that had been left empty within us since childhood. Also, we needed to find answers to questions that so far had seemed unanswerable. We were entering into a world of legalistic extremes. A rational person might easily have looked at that world and wondered why we did not see through it immediately and flee. But, for complicated reasons, Michael and I didn't—and couldn't.

The extremes that were espoused in the fellowship never bothered or frightened me in the least. At this turning point in my life it was not difficult to believe that I was a very undisciplined soul. It came as no surprise to me to discover that what I needed was the strong hand of God (the Father) to straighten me out. And though the extremes did bother and frighten Michael, he tried desperately to live under their promised protection. For the first time in his life, he had what he considered to be positive role models—men who he sincerely hoped would help him attain the sort of Christian life he so desired for himself and his family. In a sense, Michael figured that if he could get into the corral with these strong Christian men, they, in turn, would help him stay fenced in. Therefore, the more boundaries and restrictions we were given (even when we found them difficult to "walk in"), the safer we both felt—and the closer to God we felt. James Smith's own teachings, and any others he encouraged us to embrace, more often than not made perfect sense to me. And they quickly and easily became Michael's only hope.

Together we willingly joined our forces with those of the fellowship, and during the next eight years we tried hard not to return to our sinful past—tried hard, as the fundamentalists say, to "never go back to Egypt."

Though at first those times seemed as clear and bright as a sunny day, in reality our dark ages had begun.

Every Friday night we went to the fellowship meeting. Another man, Jeff, shared in leadership with James, which afforded the group two pastor/elders. Even though these men were not ordained in the traditional sense (but were "anointed" by God), a pastor or an elder was the highest-ranked spiritual overseer of a group such as ours. Whenever the group recognized God's anointing of someone, they would respond submissively (yielding up all rights) to the leader "as unto the Lord." Jeff was the less outspoken of the two leaders and the one Michael would come to respect the most and feel closer to.

The women of the group got together weekly to pray, to "fellowship," and to attempt homemade crafts. We planted gardens together, we canned green beans, we quilted, we sewed curtains. We baby-sat and cleaned each other's houses when one of us was sick. We talked about raising children and how to be the best "helpmate" to our husbands. Within our circle of women, there was a great deal of love and genuine friendship. However, there was also a good bit of pressure imposed on all of us women to be a part of each activity. Our emphasis always remained on the common good—*not* on the individual's. Secret interests—perhaps to work outside the home or go to college—usually *stayed* a secret. When a woman did dare to pursue something on her own (or simply decline to can green beans with the group), she knew she would likely incur a rebuke either from a leader's wife or, worse, from the leader himself.

James said that we were living out a type of community life that greatly excited him. He strongly believed that God was creating community in our hearts before providing the land on which we would build our actual community. Slowly but surely, the families in the fellowship moved closer together, until before long most of the families lived within two or three miles of one another. Michael and I had never experienced such love and support in our lives. If ever any of us had a true need, God would provide for it somehow through our tight little world.

Spring passed quickly into summer. Before I knew it, I was in my last month of pregnancy. On July 26, 1977, around six-thirty in the morning, James Smith and the other men from the fellowship joined

Michael in the hospital chapel to pray. At 7 A.M., Matthew was born. (We had chosen the name Matthew because it meant "God's gift." Had the child been a girl, her name would have been Sarah, a derivative of my name that meant "God's princess.") He weighed seven pounds, thirteen ounces, which seemed so small after Daniel.

In the hospital I recovered quickly, just as I had with Daniel. "With the way you heal," my obstetrician said upon examining me, "you can have as many babies as you want. You can be like Ethel Kennedy. I should just put a zipper in you!"

Later that evening, I lay on the hospital bed thinking about a conversation Michael and I had had a few weeks before Matthew was born. We had been talking about what size family we wanted and agreed that we wanted to have as many children as God would allow us. I remembered a Proverb we had discussed that said that when a man is blessed by God with many children, it could be likened to a man being blessed with a quiver full of arrows for his hunting bow. Since arrows were not easily come by in those days, a man who had a full quiver was considered fortunate indeed. God willing, Michael had told me then, he wanted his "quiver" to be full of children. We knew that, in Hebrew, a "quiver" was said to mean seven. Seven children! I could not imagine that God would see fit to bless us with that many children. Still, I was extremely happy that Michael and I shared the same vision for a large Christian family. Considering how favored boys were in the Old Testament, three sons seemed like quite an accomplishment, too. Whenever God is ready for the next one, I smiled to myself, I'll be ready too.

Envisioning a house full of happy, well-behaved children pleased me to no end. I would be the godly mother. Michael would be the godly father. Feeling even more content than I had after Daniel's birth, I rested well with these thoughts.

The only foreseeable problem with our hopes and plans for a large family was the fact that we were barely making ends meet as it was. It was tough for four people to get along on the salary Michael was making at Ryder Sporting Goods; it would take a miracle for it to support five.

James Smith strongly and consistently discouraged his flock from entering into any debt other than, at the most, a house payment. We should owe as little as possible to the world. More and more it seemed that the favored lifestyle our parents had raised us to pursue conflicted with the life we had now come into—a life in which God shows no partiality (especially to the wealthy) and about which Christ promised:

"The last shall be first and the first shall be last." Our prayer was to live a life that reflected Jesus, who we knew had owned not even a bed in which to lay his head at night.

Because we "trusted the Lord to meet our needs," we never had a savings account in those days. Already we had sold much of Michael's stock in the family business to move into our house, plus all of our sterling-silver flatware to purchase outright an old green station wagon. Believing it was not right to ask God to meet a need that we had the wherewithal to meet ourselves, we had been "convicted" (a Christian idiom indicating that God had suddenly made a person aware of something He saw was in strong need of attention) to sell the stock and the silver. It was hard to watch the happy buyer leave my house with eight place settings of King Richard silver tucked under his arm, but I forced myself to look at it as our casting one more encumbrance aside from the old world—a world from which we were aspiring to remove ourselves in every way possible.

Thanks to a Mennonite cookbook and the examples of other women in the fellowship, I became fairly adept at low-budget living. I prided myself on the fact that I could stretch a pound of ground beef to feed five people and could make one whole chicken last two meals. Needless to say, we never ate out.

My clothes were looking old and dowdy. Except for the clothes that he purchased through his Ryder discount, Michael's were just as bad. The boys wore each other's hand-me-downs as well as clothes that were passed around the fellowship. When we weren't pregnant at the same time, my sister and I shared maternity clothes and baby clothes as well. Every time we visited her in Kentucky, a box or two full of clothes went with us in one direction or the other. Matthew's T-shirts and bibs were permanently stained from the strained baby food dribbled down the front by previous users, and the ends of the bibs were curled up and crinkly on the back side from too many washings. I machine-washed his diapers and hung them outside on the clothesline to dry—all in a continual effort to be frugal and, I admit, to impress God and man with my diligence.

During one Friday-night meeting, someone asked James, "Can we know for certain that we are saved?"

"Yes," he answered. "But to be assured of salvation you must strictly adhere to the terms of true discipleship. What it boils down to is the fact that we *still* have a voice and a will." Each week James would show us his disappointment and dismay about this fact. We would shamefully nod our heads in agreement, knowing that, in order to truly love Jesus and be His disciples, we were allowed to have neither voice nor will.

"The cry of your heart has got to be: '*I* no longer count!' When we deny ourselves and lose our identities, then only Jesus is there for men to be drawn to. We must become so transparent that only Christ is seen in us—and nothing of ourselves.

"Count the cost *before* you enter the race," he would admonish us. "There is no point in entering if you are not going to finish."

"What *is* the cost, James?"

"The cost is forsaking everything." Frowning with the weight of his own words, he would repeat, "Everything."

James also taught us: "We must love one another enough to risk the relationship in order to tell a brother or sister about a weakness in their life." That last sentence alone did more to breed disunity than it ever bred love. Time and time again one of us would go to another with the pretext of "speaking the truth in love." In reality these "truths" were harsh personal judgment calls offered with little or no love.

More than once Michael was called to James's office, where James "risked the relationship" in order to tell him about an area in which he felt one of us was weak. One time he called Michael in to say we were not disciplining our boys correctly. "Too often I hear you end a command to your boys with a question. I hear you say, 'Do so-and-so—*okay?*'" he chastised. "Obedience is not a choice, Michael."

James had observed correctly: little Michael was a strong-willed six-year-old, and it was true that we did sometimes ask—not tell—him to do something. James reminded Michael that it was up to us to teach our children about obedience to authority: "Whenever we reject God's delegated authority, Michael, we are rejecting God."

The "true discipleship" teachings were instilled in us from 1977 to 1979. James diligently urged us to "deny the flesh" to be more like Christ. It wasn't long before everyone in the group was trying hard to accomplish what James insisted God desired of us. Before long, different ones among us were being "convicted" during their "times with the Lord" about things that they felt God would have them deny. As this happened (for example, Stu stopped eating meat once, because he claimed it had been revealed to him that it clogged his brain and made it hard for him to "hear God"), the person would stand up during a meeting and "share" with the group his or her latest "revelation from God." In our group, there was seldom an edict issued as to what we were to do; however, it was difficult to ignore someone's God-given revelation. The revelations were—for all intents and purposes—contagious. Once one of us would share, the majority of those listening would, almost without fail, follow suit. The thinking was simple: if what God is saying is good for one, it is surely good for all.

We called this "being like-minded," and it influenced us in all areas of our lives. If God revealed to someone that sex was for procreation and that to give attention to the pleasure associated with sex could be a way of "feeding the flesh," it was certain that many would begin to frown upon sexual pleasure. To be sure, this did much to inhibit women from seeking any pleasure at all in lovemaking. (The lucky men, of course, received their pleasure regardless.) If a respected member or teacher said that God had told him or her that He forbade anyone (even a married couple) to engage in a *particular* sex act (other than the acceptable "missionary position" intercourse), those listening had a decision to make. If they had been indulging in the forbidden act, either they immediately quit, or they continued secretly and somehow lived with the guilt. Homosexuality was completely off the sin chart. There was no need for much discussion or decision there. It was not only ungodly but unnatural. We were told that God had good, healthy reasons, all for our benefit, for keeping us bound to such legalism and under what we knew to be "the Law." The Bible said so, and that settled it. But again, most of us wanted to please God more than anything else in the world. We had come to measure our worth to God by how closely we were able to walk in the way we believed things *ought* to be, not in managing the reality of the way they were.

A frequently confessed sin in our group was that of watching R-rated movies. I can count on one hand the movies we felt it was okay to view during those years. When we did go out to see a movie, it was usually to one that James had determined bore some sort of Christian message. *Chariots of Fire* was acceptable because its hero stuck by his conviction to honor the Sabbath. *Raiders of the Lost Ark* was encouraged by James because it gave such a piercing, unforgettable example of the wrath of God.

Alcohol of any kind at all was frowned upon. However, there were occasional inconsistencies among us—which I discovered once when I was cleaning up after a meeting at the house of Jeff and his wife, Bonnie. While putting something away in their refrigerator, I was shocked to discover several bottles of beer. Leaning close to Bonnie, who was washing dishes at the sink, I whispered, "Does the beer in the refrigerator belong to Jeff?!" Bonnie was always just a bit on the radical side, which would later prove an asset to us both, and she only blushed slightly when she answered me: "Actually, it belongs to us both!" She laughed at my big eyes, patted me on the arm, and said simply that they liked to have an occasional beer, leaving me to deal with my confusion over the fact that one of the group's leaders drank, while the other definitely did not.

The fundamentalist teachers of that time, both James and others, encouraged us to read and listen only to Christian material—not material from "the world." From 1978 until around 1986, I did not read any secular books or listen to any music other than what was purchased at Christian book and music stores. We canceled our newspaper subscription and closely monitored our television viewing. Many families threw their TVs in the trash, but we counted too much on *Sesame Street* and *Mr. Rogers* to provide a few minutes of peace and quiet each day.

I couldn't have told you who was running for political office on a local level or, except for president, on a national level either. I voted only once in eight years—for Jimmy Carter, and then only because he professed to be a Christian. Michael was always more aware of what was going on outside of the cloistered world we shared, and I asked him to explain to me what was happening in the world whenever the need arose, which was not often.

We were extremely strict when it came to any conceivable influences on our children and their activities. Instead of *shopping* at the shopping malls, some of the group's children would stand passively near an entranceway for hours, dutifully handing out salvation tracts (palm-sized booklets that explained how to "get saved").

For years, on Halloween, a holiday unquestionably "of the devil" and strictly forbidden, we locked our doors and turned off the outside and inside lights in an attempt to discourage unwanted trick-or-treaters. Inevitably several determined kids would ring our doorbell anyway. Our boys would peer around from behind us while Michael gave the trick-or-treaters either a tract that explained the evil origins of the holiday or a verbal explanation of the same; then they would run to the picture window to watch the witches and ghosts, dressed up and happily carrying bulging bags of candy, make a hasty retreat down our driveway. At the bottom, the children would turn to point and laugh at the strange kids who weren't allowed to trick or to treat. Every year, one of our boys would cry, "Why can't we celebrate Halloween? What's so *bad* about it? It's just for fun!" Though it bothered us to see the hurt looks on our children's faces and to have to explain *again* every year why they could not observe Halloween, for the most part we stoically accepted this annual event as the necessary beginning of their learning to "deny the flesh."

"Remember," James reminded the adults on Friday nights, "we live in the middle of Satan's kingdom. Therefore, we constantly do spiritual warfare with the enemy. The remnant of overcomers from this battle will be raised up with Christ only when we obtain the perfect unity which comes from denying oneself."

Citing Luke 13:23–30, James had decided that heaven would be sparsely populated, whereas hell, on the other hand, would be overcrowded with surprised sinners who had foolishly believed themselves to be saved. The fear of losing my salvation took deep root in my soul. James's chilling weekly cautions bound the fellowship together with "ties that could never be broken": we were tightly lashed together by the fear of the Lord.

During that same period, we lived near a couple named Lyn and Joey. Lyn was outspoken, funny, and intelligent and always had something to say. I liked her as soon as I met her and was pleased when she and Joey agreed to come to a Friday-night meeting at our house.

After the meeting, most of us stood around our dining-room table helping ourselves to dessert and discussing that night's teaching. Joey, a soft-spoken, shy man, sat on the sofa with little to say. Lyn, however, was her usual talkative self. On my way back into the room from the kitchen, I heard her blithely telling James, "Of course we have a choice!" I stiffened as I placed more coffee cups on the table. Laughing out loud (it must have seemed ridiculous to her to even consider otherwise), she then said, "Really, James, everyone *always* has a choice, don't they?!" She stood smiling broadly at our dauntless leader while waiting for his reply.

Without hesitation, James returned her smile and softly answered her, "They don't if they are true disciples of Christ, Lyn. A disciple's only choice is to do His will."

"But who determines what His will is? Surely you don't mean to tell me that there is only one way to think—to interpret the Bible—and to know Jesus' will?" she asked incredulously. James nodded yes. Lyn looked around at all of our faces before she spoke again. Still managing a smile—though her cheerful laugh had become more nervous than fun—she tried once more to find some place of compromise with James. "Well . . . at least someone can disagree with *you*, can't they, James? This *is* a democracy, isn't it?" she asked, waving her arm around to include us all.

There was silence for a moment. Without raising his head from the plate he was serving, James answered her: "The truth is—no, Lyn. This is *not* a democracy." He looked at her then, and his face was completely serious. Lyn's smile slowly faded as she began to comprehend. It was the first time I had heard James be that pointed about who was in charge. And everyone present, including Lyn, knew exactly who that was.

Of course, Lyn and Joey never came back to the group. In fact, two months later Lyn left Joey, took their son with her, and moved to Florida.

At the next Friday-night meeting, James exhorted us all: "Mercy comes by way of judgment. Remember . . . Satan must ask God's permission to touch any one of us. And when permission is granted, it is for the sake of discipline, which *is* God's mercy." Sadly, I thought to myself: then I guess Satan must have obtained permission to touch Lyn. For the longest time, I prayed for God to discipline Lyn and was convinced that someday she would repent and return to her husband. But she never did, and I never saw her again.

"Beware of natural talents," James warned. "God rarely uses a person's natural talent in ministry, but rather He uses that which we are ungifted in, so that He might be glorified. Be careful that you are not operating in the flesh, which can lead to pride." The "flesh" referred to your own heart and instinct, neither of which was ever to be trusted.

A young single woman came to the fellowship who was brilliantly gifted in playing the guitar and intuitively sensitive to the direction of the Holy Spirit when leading worship songs. For several months the group enjoyed some of its best times of worship; then the dark day came when James informed the young woman that pride had entered into her heart. "Your identity has become too wrapped up in your natural talent," he told her. "God would have you lay your guitar down for a season, until He has humbled you and said you are ready to resume playing. For now, Stu will lead worship."

No one seemed to notice how much pride and pleasure Stu derived from being held up as a godly example. Nor did anyone seem concerned while the young woman was made to tearfully suffer through meeting after meeting, watching as Stu ineptly attempted to pull off what came to her so naturally. To admit that this scenario was disturbing would have been a clear indication of resisting authority—something anyone rarely found the courage to do. Eventually it was decided that God had "dealt" with the young woman's pride, and she was allowed to lead us in worship again—but only under the watchful eyes of our leaders.

Our house church had no name. James believed that in order to "lose our identities to Christ" we must resist being called anything but simply Christians. He also hoped that if we remained untethered to a name it would alleviate the temptation to become exclusive or divisive, which he saw as the downfall of traditional, denominational churches. Our claim was that we never wanted to become "ingrown." The disconcerting part was that which we all knew to be true: we already had a name—James Smith's Group—and we were indeed exclusive.

The larger and more self-supporting the fellowship became, however, the more it also became necessary to establish a bank account for the depositing of tithes. Consequently there had to be a legal name on the account. Unhappily, James finally gave in to what had to be. The men of the fellowship went away to ask God to show them what the fellowship should be called. They returned claiming that God had revealed the scripture Hebrews 6:1: "Therefore leaving the elementary teaching about Christ, let us press on to maturity, not laying again a foundation of repentance from dead works and of faith towards God." So our name became the Hebrews Six Fellowship.

From that point on, our unofficial creed became the sincere tenet that we had been called by God to press on to maturity, to a much higher level of spirituality than most could "walk in"—all of which pleased our leader immensely.

"We have been given eyes to see and ears to hear what others have not. It is time for us to stop needing to be fed milk as our spiritual food, and instead be fed meat," James told Hebrews Six.

It would be a steady diet of tough, raw meat that we would be fed in Hebrews Six—hard to chew, and even harder to digest. James believed that God had chosen him specifically to speak His most provocative and demanding messages to "whosoever would hear them and obey." Less meant more; in other words, the fewer people who were able to live out the difficult messages, the more convinced James—and, in turn, we—became of their validity. At last, our maxim became: the harder the "word," the more likely it is to have come from God.

"Check whatever I tell you against what you think God is saying to you Himself, and against what the Bible says. Never believe it just because *I* said it," James would tell us after a difficult message. Twenty years later, Jeff's wife, Bonnie, would sarcastically call this challenge James's Jedi mind trick, because in this way he smoothly absolved himself of blame and in addition put the burden of proof back on us. Most of us readily took his every word as inspired truth. Who would dare to be so un–spiritually minded as to question his authenticity? At that point, none.

James also taught us: "Never tell a person who comes to you with a need, 'Go and be warmed. I will pray for you.' If we have the means to supply that person's need, there's no need to ask God what to do—just meet the need."

Considering the fact that we took what he said completely to heart both as a group and as individuals, it came as no surprise when our elders decided that God would have the fellowship take full financial responsibility for a single mother, Sher, and her two children. This included finding a home for them, furnishing it, and providing Sher with a check each month to cover her expenses. This way she would never need to use the "ways of the world" (i.e., welfare or child care), a plan that suited the broke—but not stupid—Sher just fine. Anyone who was around Sher for ten minutes knew she had an attitude (no doubt perpetuated by the fellowship's big heart) that stemmed from her wanton belief that *somebody* on this earth owed her. And it might as well be Hebrews Six that anted up.

Sher came to my home a few days before she was to move into her newly provided apartment. As she shuffled through our living room and into the nursery, supposedly to see our newborn son, Matthew, she abruptly stopped, turned to me, and boorishly said, "I see that you have *two* rocking chairs in your house."

"Yes . . . I do," I answered cautiously, fearing that I knew where this conversation was going. Secretly I thought that Sher was quite deranged, and I was actually somewhat frightened of her. But she had a way of presenting her needs and her opinions in such a "spiritual" light (quoting Scripture and "hearing from God") that it was difficult even for our elders to dispute her—much less deny her.

Now as Sher stood scowling at me for a moment in my living room, she said nothing, only flung her hands on her hips like a petulant child. She was wearing a dingy T-shirt, jeans at least one size too big, and ragged tennis shoes without laces, and her unbrushed hair fell in greasy clumps around her severely acne-pocked face. She looked her disadvantaged part well. I suddenly found myself completely void of the godly compassion I was supposed to have. In fact, all I could think about was how much I loved both of our rocking chairs. I stood there recalling to myself how calming it was to nurse Matthew at 2 A.M. in the rocker in his nursery, and in the daytime how relaxing it was to rock him next to the big picture window, enabling me to watch the two bigger boys playing in the front yard.

Just then—as though creepily able to read my mind—Sher abruptly broke through my tranquil thoughts: "God would not want you to have two rocking chairs when I don't have one. He wants you to give one of yours to me. I can come and pick it up when I move." I felt myself obediently nodding in agreement. However, in my heart (where I was aware sin most often originated), I was furiously thinking that I despised this woman and did not want to give her anything. Noting, I'm sure, her easy victory over me, Sher smiled menacingly and lumbered out the front door, followed by her two blank-faced, miserable-looking children, their mouths hopelessly hanging open.

As I stood watching them drive away in the car the fellowship had paid for, my face burned with anger. At the same time my lips automatically began to form necessary words of repentance for my very ungodly thoughts about Sher and the rocker. I knew I had allowed sin into my heart. "My flesh and my heart, they fail me. But God is the strength of my heart. You are my portion both now and evermore. There's none that I desire but Thee!" The words of this worship song came to me, and I concentrated on them as I walked back into the house. Chastening myself with the conviction that Michael and I and our children had so much compared with Sher and her kids, I decided I had better be grateful that it was only the rocker God had said to give her.

When Michael came home I said matter-of-factly, "God wants us to give Sher one of our rocking chairs because we have two and she has none."

"How do you know that?" he rightly asked.

"Because . . . Sher said so," I answered, half hoping he would say, "Forget it then."

By the look on his face I could see that he was doubtful about God having actually said that. But, reluctantly, he concurred. "Just as long as you don't let her have the one that was mine when I was little—the one that has my initials carved on it" was all he added.

Michael was at work when, on the following Saturday, I stood by the front door and watched the man delegated to help Sher move carry the rocker to the moving truck. When it was loaded, Sher brushed past me without so much as a thank you. I blushed and lowered my reddened face, hiding it in the hope that she wouldn't see me. I was shamefully aware of how it would displease God for me to expect thanks for having simply been obedient to His will. Would I ever learn? I wondered, angry again at my unruly flesh and heart.

Sher was one of a number of folks (some of them authentic down-and-outers and some out-and-out con artists) who seemed to hear of the fellowship's reputation for generosity. Some took only what they truly needed and were grateful. Others were greedy and, while a part of us, took full advantage of our altruism.

And then there were some who took advantage in even worse ways. There were those who came into the group who benefited from our imperious belief that wives should be in complete submission to their husbands and that God stringently opposed divorce. For instance, though a husband might have abused his wife until she finally fled, he could be sure that she would be encouraged by the fellowship (after a cooling-off time) to forgive him and return to him time and time again. James expected us to respond to sin from a higher spiritual place of forgiveness. It was the same forgiveness that Christ did indeed preach about in the Gospels—but with a James Smith spin on it.

1 Corinthians 7:16 was interpreted to give yet another warning to remain married. It reads: "For how do you know, O wife, whether you will save your husband? Or how do you know, O husband, whether you will save your wife?" We never knew, then, if we might be our spouse's only means to salvation, making divorce even less of an option. The complexity of these and other scriptures were not taken into consideration. They were taken only one way—literally.

By late winter, our personal finances had become unmanageable. Something had to be done, but neither Michael nor I could see where we could cut back any further. Eventually Michael decided to seek counsel from James and Jeff about what to do. Michael knew he probably needed to find a job that paid more, but he was reluctant to say so because James usually urged us to be content with less, not more. He was happily surprised, then, when both men agreed that he should immediately look for a better job. When he returned home and told me their counsel, I could see the nervous relief on his face. Both of us were wondering what would be next.

I had to assume that our financial situation was critical if James and Jeff were encouraging Michael to increase his income. I had very little knowledge about our finances because Michael handled all of the money. I never balanced a checkbook or paid a single bill; Michael took care of it all.

Each week, not in a stingy or unpleasant way, Michael told me just how much money I could spend on household expenses. If a need arose unexpectedly—such as a haircut or shoes—I needed to ask him before I wrote a check. I usually had no idea even of how much money we had in the bank. Nor did I know what we owed on our house or even what utilities cost us each month.

As wives, we were taught to stay out of God's way in order for Him to place the burden of responsibility properly on our husbands rather than on ourselves. Inasmuch as the husbands were the providers and heads of household, our place was to pray for them to have the godly wisdom to manage our lives, and our children's lives, along with their own. If absolutely necessary, we were permitted to "wisely appeal" to our husbands about a specific issue with a carefully worded sugges-tion. Once the appeal was made, it was to be left for them to consider. The final decision always remained with the husband, and we were to trust God with the outcome.

Even though the sense of being taken care of appealed to my need for security, I sometimes had trouble being soft-spoken in my appeals to Michael. And I found it impossible to be silent. My tendency to be strong-willed was, I knew, my worst enemy. I also knew that having a resistant spirit could mean all kinds of trouble for me and my family with God. I hated that I sometimes rebelled against yielding my rights, and over and over I prayed for God to give me that "quiet and gentle spirit" described in 1 Peter.

Since the husbands in the group were accountable to the elders, they were subject to a sound rebuke, or worse, if found to be inadequate providers. If a man's "rebelliousness" persisted, the elders would often "take over the finances." This meant that the head of household was now under their constant supervision regarding all spending. When he had learned to budget, not to overspend, not to use credit, and to tithe at least 10 percent and the elders felt his finances were "in order," he could resume his responsibility. Fortunately, Michael never suffered this particular humiliation, though many men did.

While Michael was trying to decide what he should do next con-cerning a job, his father offered him a suggestion: Why not consider becoming a manufacturer's representative? Riley said he would be glad to contact several good manufacturers he knew and inquire about positions. He admitted that it would mean working on commission and some travel for Michael, which might be hard on us. However, it would also mean considerably more money. After prayerfully considering this new suggestion, Michael gave his dad the okay to make the contacts. In only a matter of weeks, Michael began interviewing with those companies that had expressed an interest in him—thanks largely to his father's high recommendations.

In the early spring of 1978, Michael was offered a job with a solid company that sold quite a bit of merchandise to his family's stores all over the Southeast. Living strictly on commission was a little frightening to us. Plus, he was told, he would have a territory that would demand him to travel as often as two nights a week.

A whole new way of living was about to begin for us. I knew that my husband would now be "out in the world" in ways that he had never experienced before. I would have to commit myself to praying for him more fervently. While I wondered what, besides financial freedom, his new job would mean to us, my main concern was how I would manage our three young sons in his absence. Neither of us knew then that Michael's new job would afford him somewhat of a temporary freedom from the strong emotional ties he had at home. Traveling would also provide him with the anonymity necessary to begin to cautiously explore another life—one he had so far forbidden himself to even consider.

After a few short weeks of training, Michael kissed the four of us good-bye and left for his first merchandise market, six hours away in North Carolina. He would be gone for two full weeks. I didn't know how I was going to stand being without him for so long.

Michael left on Saturday. On Sunday morning, James and his wife, Laura, came over to help me get the boys ready to attend another church's Sunday meeting. James was speaking to the congregation and had requested that the members of the fellowship attend the service. At church, I felt so lost without Michael beside me that I cried most of the way through the service. Embarrassed at my own weakness, I tried to hold back my tears. We had often been told that an excessive display of emotion was an indication of not trusting enough in God's sovereignty. We were to be strong in the Lord. When I finally dared to look down the row at James and Laura, I was relieved to see them smiling compassionately at me. I thought to myself how kind and considerate they were being. I relaxed and gave myself a little more permission to be sad and miss Michael.

Though James believed that he kept his family under strict control, he and Laura were obviously devoted to one another and to their children. That morning I felt very grateful for my closeness to their model family. I lowered my head and promised God that I would pattern my relationship with Michael after theirs and my mothering techniques after Laura's. After my resolution, I felt peaceful and prayed then for my husband—that God would protect him in his absence and bring him home as safely and quickly as possible.

After what seemed like forever, the two weeks were over and Michael returned home. Little Michael and Daniel were wild with excitement to see their daddy drive up. I could hardly contain myself either. It was not hard to tell from his tight hugs and very happy face that he had missed us as well. A consolation for being away so long was that Michael could work from home for a week or so. Spring had come in Michael's absence. We all looked forward to the warmer days and nights—with plenty of time to enjoy them together.

Soon things were settling down nicely around our house. It was at about that time that my parents announced that—with Daddy having completely retired—they were going to sell their house in Atlanta and move to St. Simons Island. Having bought two lots across from the lush marshes of Glenn, on the East Beach section of the island, Mother and Daddy had by July built a lovely home on one.

That summer Camille and Richard with their two boys and we with our three spent our vacation together on the island. Late one afternoon, after a swim in the pool, we lazily returned to the villa we were staying in. We were all standing in one of the bedrooms when Matthew, clad only in a tiny swimsuit and holding on to the bed, took his first wobbly steps across the carpeted floor. Smiling at the round of applause he had received from his surprised audience, he promptly dug his little toes into the rug's deep pile for balance and happily performed a few more steps. I suddenly realized that my baby was growing up fast.

I looked over at Michael—clapping his hands and grinning and saying incessantly, "Yea, Matthew!"—and thought: he really does love being a daddy. Watching Matthew now as he toddled from person to person—clapping his hands with sheer and utter joy in himself—I thought how very much I loved being a mother. I hoped that, God and Michael willing, we might have number four on the way by fall.

Later that evening, Michael and I decided to drive down to the pier with our children. With islanders and fellow vacationers, we took our evening stroll on the pier just as the warm sun began to touch the water's edge. While pushing Matthew along in his stroller, we cautioned little Michael and Daniel to stay away from the pier rails. With the boys, we lingered to watch the fishermen slowly haul in their daily catch.

The last time Michael and I had been on St. Simons Island was in 1973 when we had been on the verge of divorce. So much had changed between us since. Now to me it seemed that the island was reaching out its blessing to us. With the sea breeze feeling so good on my face, I thought about how perfect it was to return to my special childhood refuge. Standing there with my husband and our three young children, I was engrossed in the thought that as Mother and Daddy were making their home there, the island would become mine again. Michael and I and our family could visit it whenever we wanted. The dreams he and I had spoken of there six years before were coming to pass.

On top of the pier, the atmosphere is always relaxed and easy. Below, however, the ocean waters are treacherous. Warning signs, nailed onto huge pieces of driftwood and stuck into the sand, grimly prohibit swimming at all times. And walking down the long pier can be a little scary, especially when you get to the end, where there are no guard rails—save, you hope, a loved one's protective arms.

Life can be that way too. Nice and easy on the surface—raging seas below. And one always hopes that someone's protective arms will be there to catch you if you start to fall.

chapter 5

The Sin That Sickens God the Most

St. Luke's Episcopal Church in downtown Atlanta was my parish until Michael and I were married and began attending the Roman Catholic Cathedral in Buckhead called Christ the King Church. For as far back as I can remember, I sought to know God and thought about Him a lot. Sometimes I made atrocious attempts to get His attention. Once when I was eight, and had left my spelling book at school, I sat in the bathtub and said, "God, if you're real and you hear me, make my spelling book, the one I left at school, be on my bed when I get out of this tub." Needless to say, it didn't work. I wasn't discouraged, however, but instead continued to find ways to figure Him out.

When I heard that the father of Taylor, my sixth-grade boyfriend, had died when Taylor was small, I had a few questions. I had never known anyone with a dead parent before. One day while I was at St. Luke's working on a project, I asked one of our ministers, "Can a person see you after he is dead?" I was concerned that Taylor's dead father would be able to see me making out with his son. And if he did so, would he tattle on me to God? I told Reverend Andrew that Taylor and I had made out, that I knew it was very wrong, and that I felt miserable.

The young priest looked at me carefully. "Quite honestly, I don't know whether or not a person can see what happens on earth after death. But I wonder, Sally, could you perhaps be confusing dead people with guardian angels? Because if you are, even an angel's job description would not include being God's tattletale. I'd like to suggest that it might be your own *conscience* that is watching you."

He explained this further. "According to the Episcopal prayer book and tradition, our conscience is given to us by God as a tool for us to use to determine right from wrong. Maybe you might want to check out what your conscience is saying to you about this matter."

I took a deep breath. "Okay, I'll try."

"Let me assure you," Reverend Andrew gently added, "that what you and Taylor did was *not* bad. God cares deeply about you, Sally, and He is not angry. Out of consideration and respect for *yourself—not* from fear of being caught by anyone either dead or alive—you might choose to not make out again until you are older."

Of course, Taylor and I broke up shortly thereafter and before long I was kissing somebody new. I quickly discovered that my guilt didn't nag me half as much with my new beau as it had when I feared the possibility of a vigilant ghost.

What a loving, merciful view of God and sin was presented to me by Reverend Andrew that day in 1964 compared with what fundamentalist Christianity had taught me was true about God. By the fall of 1978 I had begun to fear all kinds of "ghosts." Not the least of these was the ghost of my separation from Michael, which still hovered over me and filled me with guilt and fear. How, I worried, might that shameful act affect our future? I grew convinced that nothing in me—not my thoughts, not my heart, and surely not my fleshly instincts—was to be trusted. I was deeply aware of my subjection to God's wrath and punishment.

Throughout the week James visited in the fellowship homes, where he charged the head of the house with the responsibility of the spiritual growth of his wife and children. His only charge to the wife was: "Obey your husband as unto the Lord." It was about this time that I first began to sense that maybe I was more willing to follow James's commandments than Michael was. I found myself wishing that my husband would be more consistent in Bible study and prayer so that he could accurately teach me and the boys. Sometimes I asked Michael if he would pray with me more regularly, to which he would always respond with a promise that he would; but in fact he rarely did. I knew I had to submit to Michael, so for a while I tried hard not to question his spiritual authority.

Being "in leadership" was becoming very important to the men in James Smith's group. Everyone knew that James and Jeff were considering certain men to be the fellowship's first appointed deacons and servants to the church, and one man to act as an aide to the overseer or pastor/elder. According to 1 Timothy 3, both elders and deacons had to be men "above reproach," who had, as James put it, "a character that cannot be defamed." I knew that most people in the fellowship thought that Stu Shores and Michael would more than likely be "raised up" by God to serve as deacons, and it seemed that Michael wanted very much to be recognized by God in this way. I secretly feared, however, that God would not choose Michael because of my having left our marriage five years ago. And I worried because I had not yet fully acquired the submissive attitude that I so often wished God would just go ahead and slap into me.

One man in the fellowship had already suffered disqualification as a deacon. It came to our elders' attention that the wife had been divorced before her present husband even knew her. 1 Timothy 3:12 said, "Let deacons be the husbands of only one wife," and our elders took this passage literally, holding that no church office should be bestowed upon a man who had previously been married, or whose wife had previously been married. It also said, in verses 10–11, that "women must likewise be dignified, not malicious gossips, but temperate, faithful in all things." In the marginal notes *women* is defined as "deacon's wives or deaconesses." Concerned that I had not been faithful in all things, I decided there was only one thing for me to do: I had to counsel with James. After asking one of the fellowship women to baby-sit the boys, I nervously set up a time to see James at his office. On the way there, I felt like I was going to my well-deserved doom. I thought back to the only other time I had counseled alone with James. "James," I had asked, "how can I experience joy in the Lord more fully? It seems like other people have such an abundance of joy in their Christian lives. What am I doing wrong?" To me, it seemed like a reasonable question.

"Sometimes I feel as though a dark rain cloud is hovering over me," I continued, describing what I know now to be a classic symptom of depression. "I think I lack something others have in their walk with the Lord. The truth is, I want more from God, James. Do you have any suggestions?"

James looked at me hard for a moment, then harshly reproved me: "You should be grateful for what God has already done in your life! Jesus warns that only a foolish and perverse generation seek after signs and wonders. Is that what you want, to be a part of that foolish generation?"

"No," I said, instantly full of regret for disturbing Jesus or James, "I do not."

"Sally, you ask too many questions," he impatiently said.

"What do you mean?" I responded. Then, realizing I had asked another question, I immediately turned bright red.

James was irritated now. "Your incessant questions annoy God."

I was shocked. How had he determined this? I didn't think I had spoken out too much in meetings. Had his wife, Laura, "shared" with James some of the confidential things we had talked about when we got together for ladies' meetings? I suddenly remembered a time when the extremely quiet and submissive Laura had suddenly rebuked me for "not letting Michael finish a sentence." When she saw the horrified look on my face, she had further clarified her comment with: "You simply *have* to learn to be quiet and let Michael be the head."

James went on: "You should learn to be quiet and content with what God has given you—three boys and a husband from which to learn whatever God has need of you to learn."

I wanted to protest, "But I *am* grateful for all of that. Can't I be grateful and still desire a richer, more joyful spiritual life too?" But I kept silent.

"Sally, you are the kind of person who is persistent with questions like this: 'Can God create a rock that is too big for Him to break?' Then, when the answer is yes, you demand to know: 'Then, can He break it?' I repeat: learn to be content with what you have from God, Sally. Stop badgering Him for anything more. Until you learn this, you won't be in God's will."

I had left James's office that day under a much darker rain cloud than the one that had followed me in. I chastised myself all the way home. Whatever it took, somehow I would learn to be a content and quiet woman. I would beg God every day, if necessary, to change my rebellious heart into one of perfect submission.

Now here I was, back again, and he did not look too happy to see me. I was convinced, however, that this time would be different. Surely James would be pleased that my concerns were for my husband, not for myself.

"James," I began nervously, "before I came to the Lord, I did something awful that I want to tell you about. I left Michael, and I intended to divorce him. I also had a desire to be with another man. I am so worried my past sins might hold Michael back spiritually and might even be the cause of some rebelliousness in him." By *rebelliousness*, I was referring to the fact that Michael had disagreed with James more than once about certain matters and had been reprimanded each time for questioning James's authority.

"What should I do, James? I have confessed my sins to God over and over, but maybe it's not enough. I fear that Michael is suffering in his relationship with God because of my past disobedience." I sincerely believed that this was true, and the mere thought began to upset me. When I paused to regain my composure, James spoke.

"First of all, I want you to *absolutely* tell me no more. I do not want to know the details of your sin." I was mortified. I had no intention of telling him *any* details of *any* sin. He continued a little more softly, "Sally, if you have confessed all of this to God, then leave it there. And do not tell Michael the details, either, because it would only cause him unnecessary distress. Just recommit yourself to God and make it your business to be submissive and loving to Michael. I trust you will not ever entertain thoughts of leaving your marriage again."

His last words made me feel sick to my stomach. How could I convince him I was completely positive that I would never repeat the foolish behavior that had almost lost me everything? I knew I couldn't do it with words. My behavior would have to be the proof of my changed heart. Why, I asked myself, had I done this? Why had I come to James again?

I knew that I had accomplished nothing by confessing to James—except to display more of my spiritual inadequacy. I had probably also done Michael more harm than good. God must be *really* pleased with me this time, I thought ruefully. As I drove away from James's office, I promised myself two things. Number one: God willing, I would lay to rest, once and for all, my guilt over leaving Michael five years ago. Number two: I would never counsel with James Smith alone again.

I was able to keep one of these promises. I never counseled with James again.

As the fall of 1978 approached, the days grew blessedly cooler. One day while little Michael was at school and the other two boys were spending the day at a neighbor's, Michael and I planned to meet for a rare lunch together at a restaurant. Our finances had greatly improved—at least enough that a lunch out was possible.

Michael knew that I had gone by the doctor's office that morning for the results of a pregnancy test taken a few days before. We hoped this would be a celebration lunch. Once seated, I happily told him that, just as we had hoped, the results of my test were positive. It had taken only two months for us to conceive our forth child. Reaching across the table to grab his arm, I laughed and told him what the doctor—who was a specialist in infertility, as well as in problem pregnancies—had said after giving me the results: "I wish I could bottle whatever it is that makes you so damn fertile! I'd be a millionaire!" ("Yeah," I had come back with, "and I wish someone would bottle whatever it takes to *stay* pregnant." I was taking weekly hormone shots to prevent a miscarriage.)

After we ordered, I smiled and said, "Well, I'm sure it's another boy."

Shaking his head, Michael beamed and said, "There's no way God would ever bless us *that* much!"

This remark took me aback. I knew that Michael didn't want a girl. He always expressed the concern that if we had a girl she would be "bratty," like certain other people's girls. I always replied, "No. Ours would be different." Still, his lack of desire for a girl hurt me a little. However, I was happy to hear that another son would thrill him, because I felt fairly certain that God was giving us another boy. I had honestly reached the point where I enjoyed having only sons—each one having unmistakably emerged as patent individuals.

During my pregnancy with Matthew, Michael and I had decided that if we ever had a girl, her name would be Sarah. So at lunch that day, we spoke only about what we might name another boy. Believing names were very important and inspired by God, we carefully decided on the name Timothy, which means "honoring God."

When spring came that year, it was time for our fellowship retreat. For a couple of years we had rented a ramshackle dorm-style bunkhouse in Toccoa, Georgia, that had formerly been a chicken coop. The men and young boys slept on one side of the large dorm room, in a row of bunk beds, and the women and girls and babies slept on the other. Sheets hung on clotheslines to separate male from female. Not much sleep was ever achieved, what with snoring men (and women), crying babies, and countless outbursts of "I need to go potty, Mommy!" throughout the night. Still, we laughed about it in the mornings and, for the most part, took the inconveniences in stride. As heavy a group as we were, we did have our lighter times, and the bond of love fused between us was as real and strong as was the bond of fear.

There was a large meeting and dining room, and a small kitchen where the women prepared meals for the whole group. We talked together as we cooked and set the food out on the long tables. Some of the women worked on sewing projects; others read or studied their Bibles. The men read their Bibles as well, and talked with one another. They played ball games with the older children. For the most part the children played well together on the vast acres of fields and woods. Often, in the afternoons, groups of parents and children hiked to the nearby waterfalls. And at night, the children fell into their bunks completely exhausted, making it easy for the adults as they then gathered together for James's teachings. We always expected God to "move on us by His Spirit" in especially mighty ways while on retreat. James was even more intense than usual—as, in fact, we all were.

One beautiful Sunday morning James announced at breakfast that we would meet outside for worship on top of a huge grassy hill. We happily trudged up to the top and settled down on heaps of blankets and quilts. Once everyone was quieted, James began to speak. In our fellowship, a serious part of managing one's household was keeping the children under complete control during meetings. As a group we vacillated between the belief that children should be kept in the meetings to hear God's word and to teach them discipline and the belief that they should be kept with a sitter, away from the meetings, so that the adults could concentrate. On this particular Sunday, we were together as families. Matthew was about fifteen months old, still in diapers. Our family sat together on two quilts. Michael held Daniel cuddled up in his lap. Little Michael sat next to me with Matthew lying in his lap, sleepily sucking his thumb and softly rubbing his "shazzy" (the name he had affectionately given his blanket). He stayed that way until about halfway through James's message, at which point he moved over to my lap, then quietly stood up. He stood there with his feet on the ground between my legs and his thumb still in his mouth.

Without missing a beat of his teaching, James glanced over at me and motioned for Matthew to sit down. Embarrassed, I pulled him down hard and fast. His bottom hit the grassy ground, his thumb popped out of his mouth, and out burst a loud, disapproving grunt. I quickly grabbed his "shazzy" and handed it to him. For a few minutes everything was peaceful. Matthew sat quietly sucking his thumb, his eyes blinking from the bright sun. Then I heard determined little *uh, uh* sounds coming from around his thumb. Once again he stood up, and again James motioned him back down. We continued this jack-in-the-box routine for the duration of the meeting. At one point, Michael leaned up and asked, "Can't you keep him still? Do I need to hold him?" I shook my head no.

I wanted to cry, and yet I wanted to laugh at the same time, because I was the only one who knew why it was impossible for Matthew to be still. Finally the meeting was over! I picked up my messy child and headed straight for James.

"Here," I cried. "Just hold him for a second and you'll see why I couldn't make him stay sitting down!" James and Laura had always had a special affinity for Matthew, and, though looking puzzled, James smiled warmly and took Matthew from my arms into his.

"Why hello, Matthew! Why *were* you so unruly this morning?"

It took only a second before James's nose turned up. His face reddened and he laughed. "I am so sorry, Matthew!" he said to my oblivious baby. "I *really* didn't know!" Feeling pleasantly vindicated, I started down the hill with Matthew to change his diaper.

As I think about that story now, it seems so clear that Matthew's odor—which was especially pungent on that nice warm day—was solid proof that what sometimes appears to be disobedience might, in truth, only be someone in desperate need of a change.

June 1979 was here at last, and with it my due date. I was hot, miserable, and ready to have this baby. Looking down at my stomach, I could think only of a fat missile. As before, I shopped for groceries and thoroughly cleaned and organized the house so that it might run as smoothly as possible during the five days I expected to be away.

Finally, on the morning of June 12, Timothy was born. Since I had opted to have an epidural anesthetic, Michael was allowed in the delivery room for the first time ever. He was terribly excited to finally be a part of the birth experience. We audiotaped the delivery. On tape, the ecstasy in Michael's and my voices is obvious as the obstetrician pulls our eight-pound, five-ounce baby boy from my womb.

"It's another boy!" the doctor shouts first.

"All right!" Michael says, his voice cracking with emotion.

Then, as Timothy lets out his first gusty wail, I exclaim, "I knew it!" through tears of joy. I had been sure all along that he would be a boy.

As we drove up to the house from the hospital, I saw, hanging lopsided across the front door, the huge Welcome Home Mama and Timothy sign that the boys had made. Timothy's brothers thought he was totally fascinating and fought over the right to hold him. As Timothy was passed from lap to lap by unsteady hands, I was glad that he was a big, sturdy baby. I didn't worry as much that he might break as I had with Matthew.

James Smith was often asked to teach at other fellowships that were similar to ours. One that he frequented was located in the small town of Cullowhee, North Carolina, where Western Carolina University is located. The home church there, whose members were mostly single students, was pastored by a young married man who looked to James for spiritual guidance. The young pastor did so especially in matters he believed he did not know how to handle alone.

One week James shared with our group a story about a member of the Cullowhee fellowship, a young woman named Jodi. It seemed that James and her pastor had recently come to the conclusion that it was imperative for Jodi to leave Cullowhee—that she had to do so in order to overcome an enormous area of sin in her life. James said only that Jodi was struggling with a very evil temptation and needed us to help her change. Though we had no idea what James was referring to, we were more than willing to open our doors to Jodi and do for her whatever God would have us do. Jeff added that while she was with us, Jodi would be staying at his and Bonnie's house. "It will be good for her to be a part of a family and to be under Bonnie's influence," he said.

A few weeks prior to Jodi's arrival, Michael was made a deacon in the fellowship during an especially somber Friday-night meeting. The group prayed together for a long time before and after James and Jeff laid hands on Michael, anointing him for leadership. The experience was very moving for Michael, who cried as the elders spoke several specific words from God to him. In addition to saying that he was "set aside by God for ministry" as a deacon, James and Jeff also prophesied that Michael would be used by God as an evangelist whenever he was out in the world.

When it came time for Michael to pray, he said, "Thank you, Lord" several times. "Please, Lord, protect my family from the enemy and, Lord, use me in any way that you desire. I give myself to you and ask you to cut away the hardened scar tissue from around my heart. Scar tissue is thicker and tougher than normal skin, Lord, so I ask you to please remove it from my heart, that I might be free to better serve you in the ways you have called me to tonight. Amen."

That was a strange prayer, I thought to myself. For the first time I sensed an aching wound buried deep within my husband, and I quietly began to pray for God to heal him. Though I wanted to know what the scars were, something told me to not probe too deeply. Just be glad he's praying about it, I thought. Maybe on some level I was afraid to know what the scars were from. But whatever possible reasons for his pain I mulled over thereafter, I never came even close to discerning the truth.

As I learned years later, Michael's prayer that night was as sincere as any he had prayed before or since. What he was referring to was a terrifying six-month period of time when, at age thirteen, he had been violently raped by two high school seniors and threatened with worse should he ever tell anyone. He never had. Instead, he had carried inside him, from that day to this, the sickening memories of those violations.

And he carried inside him something else, too: the mortification of knowing that, even as he had been terrified by those boys, he had experienced a physical attraction to one of them. Now his fervent hope was that the memory that had caused him so much shame, pain, and resentment could be removed by God. Even though Michael knew he had been attracted to boys even before the assault, he still told himself that the rapes themselves were what had caused the confusion he now suffered concerning his sexuality. If God could heal the emotional scars left from the rapes, then, Michael hoped, he could be delivered from his attraction to other men once and for all.

There were two prophecies for me as well that night. As the elders laid their hands upon my head, I could think only of how much I cared for Michael and how much I wanted to be the sort of wife God wanted me to be for him. I ended my prayer by asking that I might be "just what he needs, Lord." Then James spoke to me "from the Lord." He began, "God would say to you, 'Have I left you barren, my daughter? No, nor shall I leave you barren of heart. I'd have you know, my daughter, that as you've borne four healthy boys, you shall bear up in faithfulness to your helpmate, you shall bear up in faithfulness to me. . . . It shall not be by your own strength that you shall know faithfulness or servanthood. I'd have you know, my daughter, as I've taken the boys by cesarean section, I also take from you my pleasure. I'd have you know, my daughter, that you shall serve and I shall know joy. But as it has been with pain that you have borne sons, it shall be with pain that you shall serve. And your joy shall be that you know me.'"

Then Jeff spoke: "Sally, I think the Lord would have you know that your strength will be in your weakness, your wisdom will be in your submission. And your joy will be that strength and wisdom that He gives you. As you recognize your weaknesses, you will learn to submit."

"Amen," I said. "Thank you, Lord." I was humiliated to realize that God had been forced to use particularly painful childbirths as His method for teaching me submission. Why was I such a difficult case? I believed that every word of the prophecies was true, since it was clearly God who had made it necessary for me to deliver by cesarean section. And God knew how much I wished I could have natural childbirth, and how jealous I was every time another woman in the fellowship delivered a baby at home or at a birthing center. Still, more than anything else I wanted to please God, and if this was His only way to teach me submission, then so be it. I hoped that being a deacon would encourage Michael to be more consistent in his responsibility as spiritual head over me and the boys, which would make submitting to his authority a more rewarding task for me.

Jodi arrived from Cullowhee and was quiet and subdued at the first fellowship meeting she attended. While I knew she was a few years younger than I was, she seemed a whole lot tougher. I thought to myself that something seemed familiar about Jodi. She had on coaching shorts and a short-sleeved golf shirt—left over from her days as a P.E. major, I mused. Her brown hair, which she ran her fingers through nervously, was cropped short. It wasn't until halfway through the meeting that it hit me. Jodi reminded me of Janet; the way she looked, walked, and talked was masculine. My heart sank, and I hoped I was wrong.

One night, Michael returned home from a meeting of the fellowship leaders saying he needed to tell me something. "First, you have to promise not to talk about this with anyone else in the fellowship, except for Bonnie, Laura, and Becky," he said. After I assured him I would tell no one, he told me the real reason Jodi had been sent to our group. "Jodi was involved in homosexual behavior in Cullowhee and could not seem to stop while she was still there. Apparently, after the last escapade in which Jodi admitted to having initiated sex with another woman in the Cullowhee group, her pastor called James in a panic. James agreed that she had to be sent away and said she could come here."

So, I thought, Jodi is here to be reformed. My heart went out to her, thinking how much I'd hate to have to answer directly to James in regard to a sin like that.

"Had you already guessed?" Michael asked.

It was true, I was not as shocked as Michael had expected me to be when he told me. "Yeah, I guess I really had," I admitted guiltily.

"Oh" was all Michael said. He was quiet for several moments. "Well, the point is, we need to do all that we can to help Jodi get out of this. She needs to spend as much time as possible with you, Sally. She wants to break away from the sin in her life, but it is really hard."

Michael gave me no clue then or at any time in our involvement with Jodi of how strongly he identified with the young woman in the agony she was going through. For the next few years, as Michael watched the saga of Jodi unfold, he vacillated between feeling a viable hope that Jodi could be changed (which meant, of course, that there was hope that he might change) and feeling that the whole effort was absurd. He hoped with her and cried for her while at the same time crying inwardly for himself.

Michael didn't have to convince me to spend time with Jodi. I liked her, and even though the thought of "that" particular sin put me off, I enjoyed having the chance to get to know her. God, I felt, was giving me another chance to help someone break away from the lies and bondage that I knew came from Satan. At least, I thought, I could show her how wonderful it was to marry and have children. I wanted badly to see Jodi "healed" and God glorified as she one day walked in His plan for her life as a woman: to become more feminine, marry the man He had for her, and have as many children as God would allow. Wow, I thought, what an awesome victory for the Lord that would be!

It seemed that Jodi was improving in her efforts to reform. Some days she followed Bonnie around almost to the point of annoying her, though Bonnie truly loved Jodi and never made a serious complaint. Thanks to Bonnie's hairstylist, her hair was now longer and permed. Thanks to my influence, she wore more skirts than pants. At first it made me want to giggle to see her curly-haired and "dressed up." But instead, knowing what a serious task we were trying to accomplish with her, I quickly told Jodi how pretty she looked, making her blush terribly.

Jodi had begun to confide in me, and, as with Janet, I found that I both did and didn't want to hear about her sexual exploits. It sometimes seemed that she enjoyed telling me. She knew I disapproved of her past and that my "job" was to cheerlead her on to becoming the heterosexual woman God had created her to be. One day she told me more about the woman she had "had relations with" at Cullowhee, the affair that had caused her to come to us. She took pleasure in describing the college student as a gorgeous, sexually inexperienced blonde. I noticed, however, that she described the delicate loss of the other woman's virginity with tremendous sensitivity and respect. Shaking my head, I thought, I really *do not* understand this and am not sure that I want to. Afraid that I was encouraging Jodi more toward her sinful past than away from it by even engaging in this conversation, I asked her to stop telling me about it. Though she at once grew sad, Jodi said she understood how I felt, and from then on she mostly refrained from giving me the details of her "sin."

Jodi spent a lot of time at our house, which Michael seemed to enjoy. The boys did too, even though Jodi, having been a P.E. major, was very strong and muscular, which sometimes proved a bit intimidating for my little guys. Like the time, for instance, when Michael was out of town and Jodi came for dinner. She had taken a special liking to Daniel and often amused herself and him by playing "boogeyman" and chasing him around the house. It was fun until once, when Jodi carried it a little too far. She chased Daniel to the bathroom but didn't stop. With one fast sweep of her arm, she was dangling a terrified Daniel headfirst over the toilet, while he loudly begged for mercy.

"I'm gonna drop you in!" she laughed and shouted way above his cries for help.

"*Nooo! Pleeease!* Put me down!" Daniel screamed.

Quickly I came running. As soon as I saw the scene above the toilet, I yelled, "Put him down, Jodi. *Now.*"

She looked at me and realized for the first time that Daniel was not having a good time. She immediately placed the whimpering boy on the floor, and he ran to me as fast as his stubby little legs would carry him. Only then did Jodi realize how frightened Daniel really was. Her face completely sobered as she sheepishly came over to the two of us, apologizing all the way. I had never heard her speak so tenderly as she did to him then: "Daniel, I'm so sorry. Gosh, I am stupid. I swear, I wasn't really going to drop you! I wouldn't ever hurt you. I'm sorry." Daniel continued to keep his head buried safely in my shoulder, and the closer she got to him, the louder he bellowed. Backing off, Jodi, I saw, was crying. As angry as I was at the stupidity of her doing that to a child, I knew she adored Daniel. Seeing her now, I felt almost as bad for her as I did for him. Daniel let go of me and ran to find little Michael, no doubt to share his tale of woe.

"Sally, I am so sorry," she cried to me then. "I promise I wasn't going to drop him. I swear—I don't ever want to have children. I'm afraid I'd be the worst mother!"

"No, you wouldn't. It's okay, Jodi. It really is." I meant it. I hugged her then, and she held on to me miserably, as though now she were the child in need of comfort.

It was weeks before Daniel would go anywhere near Jodi. She apologized to him from time to time until he was about ten years old and stopped only after he told her he didn't even remember the event. She breathed a sigh of relief then, while I thought to myself what a neat kid Daniel was to forgive and forget.

Through another pastor, James heard about exciting things taking place at a Christian community in Charlotte, North Carolina, called Lambs' Chapel. Our group was invited to attend their next biannual retreat, and Michael and I were invited to stay in the home of a couple named Chuck and Lou Ellen, whom we would become close friends with over the next eight years. We were eager to experience a viable Christian community in action. The people at Lambs' Chapel lived together in well-made, attractive houses on a huge piece of land. They farmed and had cottage industries, and for a time they had their own school. When a family was ready to move onto the farm, the community built a house for them. While the majority of the fellowship lived at "the Chapel," still others came only for the Sunday meetings held in a huge enclosed pavilion. Besides those of us from our fellowship, people came from fellowships all over the United States and England and were also assigned homes to stay in—some at the Chapel, some in Charlotte.

The first retreat that Michael and I and the boys attended at Lambs' Chapel was another life-changing experience for us. Once all of us were settled with our host families and had enjoyed a wonderful supper, the adults gathered back at the pavilion for a meeting. (The children were not just baby-sat during the meetings, but were given fun and interesting programs designed expressly for them.) Once the adults were assembled, a rotund man about fifty years old, with fluffy curls like a halo, stood before us. His smile, along with his distinctly Charlotte accent, warmed the room as he graciously welcomed everyone. The man was Harold, pastor of Lambs' Chapel. He and his wife, Mary, lived in "the big house" and oversaw the Chapel's varied ministries as well as the farm itself. Pastor Harold and Mary were deeply loved and respected by the fellowship and had quickly become mom and dad to many of the families present. Michael and I both felt drawn to his gentle spirit. And though in many ways our two fellowships were similar both in beliefs and in operation, it wasn't long before we saw the obvious differences between Pastor Harold and James Smith.

The weekend would be full of the most glorious worship we would ever experience. The atmosphere was one of abandoned jubilation. It was as if we were captives being suddenly set free. Songs were sung that exalted Christ and praised Him for setting people free from sin, then filling them with His forgiveness and love. During those lengthy meetings, God set people free from all manner of sin—lust, anger, unforgivingness, and much more. And, though I had not actually witnessed it, I knew that God had even set some souls free from homosexuality, the sin that, because it was so grossly unnatural, was often said to sicken God the most. With each account that testified to any sort of miraculously changed life, my hope for Jodi grew. The good news was that God could set a person free from anything if he or she was a willing vessel.

Worship was enhanced by a band with drums, piano, guitars, tambourines, and trumpets. There were lively singers who led the worship with infectious enthusiasm and clear, melodious voices. The accent was on spontaneity. Someone might feel led to sing a beautifully moving solo, or a quartet might suddenly explode in magnificent harmony. The worship leaders were passionately inspired as they led us in twenty or so songs of praise and worship per meeting, each one more exhilarating than the one before it, and each repeated until the Spirit moved the singers to begin another.

The women from Lambs' Chapel were easy to pick out. For one thing, they all appeared *happy.* They wore bandannas folded into triangles that neatly held back their hair, which in most cases was long. Later I learned from Lou Ellen that the belief was that if a woman's head was covered with a "symbol of authority," she was protected from the angels (fallen ones, of course, not heavenly ones) and could then freely speak forth a word from God in a meeting. I knew that head coverings were spoken about in 1 Corinthians 11, and had James Smith suggested that the women in our fellowship wear head coverings, which he never did, I would gladly have complied. Not only did I want to obey everything written in God's Word, I also wanted all of the spiritual protection I could find. Finally, most of the Chapel women wore loose, flowing skirts, peasant style. After a few visits to the Chapel, I began to emulate the women there as best I could. Michael seemed to like this look a lot, which made me all the more eager to attain it.

I soon came to understand one reason why the women wore such skirts. When the music for worship began, women and men alike jumped not only to their feet, but out into the extra-wide aisles, where they could *dance* more freely. Skirts swished and feet moved to the upbeat music. Some danced alone, with their hands raised in praise, while others grabbed hands and danced in circles. Men with men, women with women, and couples too. Michael and I were awestruck. Every part of me wanted to join them—so much so that, as we neared the end of our first retreat, I could no longer refrain from dancing in front of my chair. When we returned for our second retreat, Michael and I both ended up in the aisles, enjoying our newfound freedom in worship. I loved watching Michael so exuberant, so absolutely delighted—the way I wished he always looked. As I grew less inhibited during worship, more able to lose myself in "the Spirit," my mind would ease into a place where my full focus was on God. For me, these were the purest and most affecting experiences of worship I had ever known. It was at the Chapel that I felt the closest to God and to the joy of the Lord I had been seeking.

Shortly after we began visiting the Chapel, Michael asked me to wear only skirts and blouses and dresses. No pants, not even jeans. I was happy to comply, because I was always pleased when Michael asserted himself as head of the household. It made me feel secure and confident to know that Michael was listening to God, then telling me what I should do. That was the way it was supposed to work, and I thanked God whenever it did. Not wearing pants was a statement to the world that I did not "wear the pants in the family." It was also a statement against the fast-growing feminist movement. I wore my hair waist length (Michael's preference) and wore little makeup and little jewelry except for a simple wedding band and tiny earrings. My "uniform" was a denim jumper, plain blouse, and knee socks, with simple functional shoes that usually laced.

Thinking back, I see that I had made myself as far from sensually attractive, even subtly so, as was possible. All done in a pious attempt to be certain I would never be a "stumbling block" to any man in the area of lust. From 1971 to 1985, I was always either pregnant or nursing a newborn or ready to get pregnant again, and I always seemed to be twenty or thirty pounds overweight. I wonder now if I didn't hide beneath those skirts and extra pounds partly because I was frightened of my own sexuality and fantasies. Sometimes I dreamed about men I didn't even know (and sometimes about men that I *did*). Whenever this happened, I prayed for God to deliver me.

My being "chunky" never seemed to bother Michael. I could never see that our sex life was suffering. There were many times when I didn't *feel* very sexy, but it wasn't likely that I would think about that very often. An interesting thing to me, and something I considered very touching, was that Michael seemed to love my body most when I was pregnant. During the long months of each pregnancy, it seemed we grew more sexually and emotionally intimate. Yet even sexual intimacy was problematic, since many teachers of fundamental Christianity had made it clear that our emphasis should remain focused on things of the Spirit, not things of the flesh.

Once while we were planning another retreat to Lambs' Chapel, Michael suggested that the children and I might ride back to Marietta with Stu Shores, Becky's husband, once the retreat was over. Michael needed to go directly from Lambs' Chapel to the High Point merchandise market. Stu would be attending the retreat alone that year and therefore would have plenty of room for me and the children on the return trip. I felt uncomfortable with Michael's suggestion of riding home alone with Stu and told him so.

"Why?" he asked. "You won't be alone anyway, you'll have the kids. Why would it be any big deal to ride with Stu?"

"Kids or not, I just don't feel right about riding for six hours with another man." It bothered me as much to have to explain why the plan unnerved me as it did to think of riding with Stu. I couldn't see it as a very godly or wise idea, and I resented Michael for coming up with it. I wasn't worried about anything specifically with Stu; it just felt wrong.

In fact, I had never had the opportunity to develop friendships with men outside of the one I shared with Michael. There were few such friendships in our fellowship—if any. I knew, though, that what really upset me was Michael's nonchalant attitude. I thought to myself angrily that Michael did not seem to have a protective, much less jealous, bone in his body. Maybe I just wasn't attractive enough to worry about. That was an unpleasant thought, but one I began to ponder.

My days (and nights) were consumed with the needs of my family, the fellowship, and my "relationship with the Lord." I always felt I was falling the most short in the latter respect. My journals during those days were labeled *prayer notebooks,* so that even as I wrote my most private thoughts, they would be "of the Lord," not "of the flesh." I censored each entry by writing only what I thought would be acceptable to God.

March 1980: Dearest Lord, Forgive me dear Father for falling again and again and again. Why you and Michael don't just give up on me, I don't know. Lord I am so sorry for the way I behaved on Sunday to Michael. When am I going to grow up, to mature? When are my desires going to become my walk? The guilt feelings and feeling so sick of myself are more than I think I can stand and yet I continue to allow days like that to happen ... What am I doing wrong? ... I am desperate to go on and "forget about myself and concentrate on You and worship You" [these were the words to a worship song] and to come into a true oneness with Michael. Lord please do a work in me soon. Whatever it takes. I do love You Lord and my desire is You. And

I do love Michael and my second desire is him. Thank You for your forgiveness. In Jesus' Name. Let it be so!

That Sunday I had questioned my husband's authority by asking him, as I had before, why it was that we didn't pray together, and then not being content with his answer—that he was just too tired at night. I had further provoked him by asking why he didn't seem more interested in "things of the Lord" than he did. An argument had erupted after which I felt horribly guilty and apologized for the way I had behaved. Michael had accepted my apology and again promised to make our praying together a priority. The expectations we put on ourselves to "grow spiritually" and to be "mature in the Lord" were enormous. So were my constant feelings of inadequacy. No matter how much I aspired to change, I just couldn't seem to measure up to what I felt was required of me, either in my marriage or with God. I wanted to know, really know, both my husband and God. Yet both seemed out of reach, and I was convinced it had to somehow be my fault. Unfortunately, I had no knowledge then of how much Michael was suffering in his own efforts to hold on to the impossible standards of excellence we had embraced. I had no idea of what his own cries to God were and what a failure he, too, often felt like. I now wonder if, while focusing so much on my own imperfections, I didn't miss some of the clearer signs of distress Michael might have exposed. At least my shortsightedness helped Michael retain his "cover"—for a while longer.

What Michael was in fact going through then was one of the most agonizing times of his other life. Many years later, Michael told me about a man with whom he became intimately involved while traveling in Buford, South Carolina. He met Don at a gas station. A conversation had sprung up easily between the two men, which they continued as they walked and talked together for several more hours. Don was single and in his late twenties, a successful real-estate agent, closely involved with his family and community—much like Michael. Later, they had drinks, then dinner, and finally ended up in a motel room in each other's arms.

At 2 A.M. the next morning Michael woke up with a sudden jolt. Quickly going back through the events of the night, he realized, with a sinking feeling, that things had gone way past what he had intended. So far, Michael's gay life had consisted of browsing gay bookstores or having a few drinks in a gay bar, which on occasion would lead to a one-night stand. As soon as the sex was over, he would abruptly leave. So far he had managed to handle that other life and, with the exception of an enormous amount of guilt, had taken no other feelings home with him.

While talking the night before, Michael and Don had found that they had a lot in common. Michael had not been indifferent with Don, as he had been with the others, and by giving him his real name and phone number, something else he had never done before, Michael had also not been discreet. Now he wondered what had possessed him to do something so foolish. Of course, he knew the answer. He had *felt* something with Don that he had never before felt, or at least had never allowed himself to feel. Looking at Don now, a suffocating panic besieged him. He had to get out of there fast.

While Michael threw his clothes on, Don woke up and tenderly asked, "What's wrong?"

"I can't do this," Michael cried out. "Not to you, and not to me. I've got to go!"

Emotionally distraught, Michael ran from the room and jumped into his car. Speeding down the highway, he passed several bridges that crossed over the deep Atlantic Ocean onto peaceful, sleeping islands. An all too familiar pain now burned in his gut. "Good God, what have I done?" he said out loud. "And what the hell am I *going* to do?" Then he looked out the window again. "That next bridge," he said, "that one coming up . . . I could—"

Suddenly headlights glared from behind. Was it a cop? Michael wondered, then realized that it was Don. That's the last person I need to see right now, he thought, and sped up to lose him, flying right past the last bridge—and very possibly past his own death.

Two days later, Don took a risk and called Michael, who, in return, let him know he was glad to hear his voice. Don told Michael he had been really worried about him and hadn't known what to do. "I followed you that night until I lost you . . . or . . . you lost me," Don said.

"I know. I'm sorry," Michael answered. "Thank you." As they talked, Michael explained why he had left the motel room so hastily and how terribly torn he was feeling about his life. Don understood and was extremely compassionate. Finally he told Michael that he cared very much for him and would like to see him again. Michael said he definitely felt the same way.

"But," Don added, "I will not be what takes you away from your family. That would be a wrong I can't live with." Michael assured him that he completely understood and promised that that would not be the case.

Don and Michael met sporadically for the next four or five years, then lost touch for about a year. When Michael finally called Don, he learned that Don had become happily involved in a long-term relationship. Michael was sincerely glad for him and wished only that he could have the possibility of that for himself. From then on, they remained close friends.

Though I honestly don't understand how Michael persevered during those years of living two lives, I am very glad he drove past that bridge that night. He didn't know it then, but hope and new life were ahead for us both.

I usually felt the best about myself when I thought about my mothering abilities. Since an early age, I had wanted lots of children. Sometimes I wished for a break, but mostly I considered my children to be God's one sure act of pleasure in me. Being "allowed" to have them said to me that not *everything* I did made God angry.

Since I took a fair amount of pride in mothering, I had to guard myself against that sin as well. I felt that a good way of handling that was to always give God the glory of any compliments I received for being a good mother. That opportunity was often presented to me in unusual and even backhanded ways. One day I strolled Timothy and walked with the other three boys to a nearby grocery store. After I had paid for my purchases, the cashier carelessly said to me, "Oh my God. Are all four of those boys yours?" When I said yes, she foolishly went on, "They must make you absolutely crazy! I only have one and he makes me nuts!"

I looked at my three oldest sons staring up at me, waiting to hear their mother's reply. I knew they had seen me act pretty "crazy" sometimes, and I did not want them to ever think, as I had so often done with my mother, that they were to blame. Balancing my bag of groceries on my hip, I chose my words carefully: "Yes, they are all mine. And no, they do not drive me crazy. I have *very* sweet boys. Each one is precious to me and a blessing from God."

The cashier was taken aback by the seriousness of my answer. "Oh. Well, that's good. You have a nice day!" She turned and got back to her register.

The boys and I walked out with big smiles on our faces. Once we were outside, I knelt beside them on the sidewalk. "I'm sorry, boys. I am so sorry that some people feel that way about their children. And I *really* feel sorry for her little boy." They nodded their heads in agreement. We "group-hugged" and began our walk home. Watching them play along the way, picking up discarded "treasures" and then running to show me, or picking dandelions as gifts for me until my hands were full of the weepy weeds, I only hoped they knew how loved and wanted they really were.

Michael and I had become friends with a new couple, Russell and Scarlett, who, along with their three sons, had recently joined the fellowship. Our friendship had developed naturally, rather than as the result of a "word of God" ordering it into existence. Simply put, we enjoyed one another's company.

One Friday night Russell brought a friend of his to the fellowship meeting. Larry was an attractive, soft-spoken single man, and it quickly became obvious to everyone that he had an eye for Jodi. She, however, did *not* have an eye for him—a fact she made perfectly clear to me at lunch one day.

"What am I going to do?" she cried, dramatically burying her face in her elbow on my kitchen table. "Larry drives me crazy. He talks to me all the time even though I'm mean to him. I can't stand him. I think he is the biggest nerd in the world." Her eyes widened in panic. "What if God makes me marry him? I'll die."

It was understood that God sometimes "put couples together" at His singular and often inexplicable discretion. I had also been told that at some point during the process He miraculously created "a heart for one another" in the couples He matched.

Thinking about that now, I assured her, "God won't do that unless He first gives you a heart for Larry, Jodi. But I have to say, Larry's really not all that bad. I know he won't stop talking when he starts and he's sort of boring . . . "

"Sort of?!" she groaned.

"Oh, Jodi. It's so sad. Larry is obviously so in love with you. But I do understand why you don't like him. I know it would take a big—okay, *really* big—miracle for God to change your heart."

"Please promise me you won't pray that He does, okay?" she begged me. "I know James and Laura and Jeff and Bonnie probably already are."

"I promise," I laughed. And as I never did ask God to give Jodi a love for Larry, I was in for a big shock when, only a few months later, Jodi came over for lunch again sporting a silly grin on her face. "What's going on with you?" I demanded to know.

"You won't believe it, but I think I *like* him. I actually think I like Larry. He doesn't gross me out anymore. I think he's *sweet*. I still can't think about him touching me, or—oh gross—kissing me, but, Sally, God is doing *something!*" she exclaimed excitedly.

Well, apparently it was so, because in only a matter of months Jodi and Larry announced that they were getting married. The whole fellowship rejoiced in what God had done in Jodi's life. To me, it all seemed very strange and yet very wonderful at the same time. Jodi told Larry all about her past experiences with women. He remained unshaken in both his love and his desire to marry her. When Jodi told Larry that she wasn't sure when she would be able to feel responsive to him sexually, he calmed her fears by saying God had given him a patient heart and promising her he would wait until she was completely healed before they attempted to make love. I told her she was blessed indeed, that Larry seemed too good to be true. Jodi seemed to have at least gained a tremendous amount of respect for Larry, if not true love.

The day finally arrived when Jodi and Larry were wed. As Jodi took her marriage vows with Larry, she later told me, she made a private vow to God as well. She promised God that from that day forward she would never touch another woman sexually. During the ten or so years that I remained friends with Jodi, she would confess to me that there were times when she thought she might self-destruct from the intense temptation to be with a particular woman. When that happened she would tell Larry, and they would pray together, asking God first to forgive Jodi, then to give her added strength to abstain the next time temptation came her way. I could sometimes detect a weariness in Jodi's voice, but if she ever broke her promise, I didn't know about it.

Jodi would tell me from time to time that she hoped her life with Larry would be like mine with Michael. I knew she patterned her marriage after ours, and while I was flattered, at the same time I was sometimes uncomfortable to hear the trust in her voice. I only hoped that Michael and I would be able to live up to her expectations.

Jodi and Larry started their family right away and did not stop until they had four children, one girl and three boys. Jodi asked me to be an attendant, along with Bonnie and Larry, at the birth of her first child and their only daughter. I was honored to be asked. When the actual time of birth came, I wept tears of thanksgiving and joy while watching a precious, wet baby girl pour out of a woman who only a few years before had told me she never wanted to be a mother.

Larry was an exceptional man, I thought to myself, watching as he lovingly bent down to kiss his wife. Their newborn daughter was snug in the crook of his arm. I knew from Jodi that there were still those awful times when she said Larry made her sick, times when she could not bear to let him near her. But, I thought, Jodi was determined to repress any "unnatural" feelings and to find a way to enjoy loving Larry. I admired her commitment. Sometimes the pull toward her old life was so strong, she told me, that she felt like she was going to climb out of her skin. I would hear those exact words from Michael one day, and they would frighten me then as they had when I first heard them from Jodi. I could not for the life of me understand why God allowed this kind of conflict in a person. But who was I to question God? I didn't know what else to say except to urge Jodi to continue to be strong and quickly flee from the temptation to sin. Watching Jodi with her husband and tiny baby, I found myself hoping that in the delivery of her daughter, God had miraculously delivered Jodi once and for all. Maybe all temptations would cease. I sincerely hoped so.

In the spring of 1980, the fellowship was introduced to something new called Atlanta Christian Cursillo. A derivative of the original Catholic Cursillo, Christian Cursillo was an ecumenical movement intended to further unify Christian churches. A couple in our group had attended Atlanta Christian Cursillo, and I could see the disturbed look on James's face as they now told us how it had improved their relationship with God. I knew James struggled with anything "being of God" that originated in a denominational church—especially Catholic. As it turned out, James neither condemned nor condoned Cursillo, partly because Jeff and Bonnie were the next ones to attend a weekend.

Cursillo tradition was that the husband "made his weekend" first, and then, a few weeks later, the wife "made her weekend." (Since then I have found out that in some Cursillo groups, couples "make" their weekends together.) No one who had been on a Cursillo would tell anyone who had not been on one much about it. "Candidates," as newcomers were called, were encouraged to have no expectations about the weekend. Someone let it slip that candidates were asked to remove their watches during the weekend in order to be completely free from worrying about time. It sounded interesting to me. I was pleased when Michael said that Jeff had asked to sponsor him on a weekend and that he had decided to attend. Bonnie would then sponsor me on mine. Stu and Becky would also be going.

While Michael was away for his Cursillo weekend, I prayed for him daily as Bonnie and Jeff had asked me to. I had seen a change in Jeff and Bonnie since their Cursillos. There was a softness about them now and a greater sense of peace and well-being. I hoped for the same for Michael and me.

When Michael came home late that Sunday night, he would tell me little about his weekend. He "glowed" his first night and day back home. People I had never heard of called him and sent him letters telling him to have a "great fourth day"—whatever that meant. I was curious, and eager to experience Cursillo for myself. Over and over Michael would say, "Have absolutely no expectations, Sally. Just go and let God do it all. I promise you will not be disappointed."

Later he said something unusual. I was complaining, as I often did, about how undisciplined I was in one area or another and how I was just sure God wanted to bounce me on my head. After listening to me for a while, Michael smiled and sarcastically said, "That's right, Sally. God probably doesn't even love you, does He?"

I wanted to answer yes, of course I knew He did, but the words stuck in my throat. I suddenly realized that I wasn't too sure whether God *loved* me or just tolerated me. I couldn't blame Him at all if it was the latter. Though I hadn't said a word, Michael reached over to hug me. I couldn't understand yet what was going on inside of him, but I knew it was something different. Whatever it was, it seemed good, and I was ready to find out about it for myself.

I had to wean Timothy from breast-feeding a few months earlier than I had planned in order to be gone from Thursday until Sunday on Cursillo. Doing so made me a little blue, as did the fact that I rarely left Michael to go anywhere overnight by myself. He was the one who left me to travel each week. It felt odd, and yet somewhat exciting too. After kissing Michael good-bye, I climbed aboard the bus of women, some happily chattering and some, like me, looking apprehensive. Becky and I had gently been separated from one another, which was good. It would have been too easy to cling to one another.

I leaned back in my seat and tried to relax. Fidgeting with my watch, I wondered when someone would come around to take it from me. Sunday seemed a million years away, and I thought I might cry. Just then a woman I didn't know sat down beside me and began to talk. She was extremely friendly and understanding, especially when I told her about having to wean Timothy to come on the weekend. While we talked, a peaceful feeling began to replace my angst.

After a time of introductions followed by a chapel service that re-minded me more of my Episcopal upbringing than anything had in years, we were escorted to our beds. A little gift was on the pillow with a note from someone I did not know, who said she was praying for me. Before lights out, someone pleasantly suggested that we put our watches away only so that we might not be concerned about time, or anything else for that matter, during the weekend. I shoved mine to the very bottom of my suitcase. All that was asked of us was that we explicitly follow any instructions given by the rector (who, to my surprise, was female). It was promised that we would be glad if we did. I could hear some of the women grumbling that they thought even those instructions were too demanding. My strict years of discipleship with James Smith made this simple obedience child's play for me.

The next morning in chapel I was moved at the gentleness of worshiping with only women. At breakfast I was amazed at how happily the workers flowed together and how eagerly and graciously they served each one of us.

After breakfast, the talks began. I was surprised when the first woman to speak was the same woman who had been so kind to me on the bus. Now she stood at the front of the room, a lovely corsage pinned to her Sunday dress, beaming confidently as she spoke to us about God's love for us. The serenity in her voice told me of a peaceful rest in Christ that I had not yet entered. Thinking about her gesture of love toward me the evening before, I began to cry quietly.

I was surprised once more when Bonnie gave a talk. Seeing her so poised and self-assured as she spoke candidly about her life and how God had been gracious to her, I knew that the changes I had seen in her were genuine. I had never heard her speak so openly, and it made me want to get to know my friend better.

I had expected the talks on Cursillo to be similar to the ones I usually heard at our meetings. They weren't. In talk after talk, I heard testimonies about how God meets us at the point of our need, how priceless we are to Him, how He desires a relationship with us, how we can find our security in His unfailing love for us, and how compassionate He is toward us. By contrast, James taught us that our sinfulness could separate us from God, that only a "chosen few" would be with Him in heaven, and that God's compassion toward us was in direct proportion to our obedience to Him.

Slowly, over the course of the weekend, I became aware of how judgmental I had become. I had to face how wrong I had been to think that those who were still in religious denominations were less "serious Christians" than those of us in nondenominational groups such as Hebrews Six. It was a humbling experience and exposed conflict after conflict within me. In not one of the talks did I ever hear anyone insist that it was her way or none. On Cursillo, I was challenged to see each person as an individual, created and loved by God. I realized how pragmatic I had become in my disregard for individuality as a result of believing that God had only one way of dealing with us all.

I found myself thinking about my old friend Lyn, who had run away to Florida. Suddenly I saw how narrow I had made the way to Christ seem for her. No wonder she had chosen to flee! I should have been more patient, more tolerant of her aggressiveness. Why had I been afraid to love her the way she was? Having no idea how to reach her, I could only pray that God would heal the hurts I knew I and others had inflicted on her in the name of Jesus.

One morning after I had returned home, I wrote in my journal (no longer a "prayer notebook," but still a somewhat censored record of my own thoughts): "My experiences need to catch up with my so-called knowledge." Both Michael and I were slowly making a turn back in the direction of our original quest for truth. It would be a long row to hoe. The important thing for us at that time was that we each took home from Cursillo something that both of us had had little knowledge of when we came. The reason was that neither of us had experienced much of it in our lives before then.

That life-changing message can be summed up in four words: *the grace of God*. And one day we would come to know it well.

chapter 6

You Shall Go Out with Joy

A month after our Cursillo weekends, Michael surprised me by insisting that we take a trip away together. He had a beautiful place in mind, he said: Cashiers, North Carolina. I balked a little at first, asking him what we would do with all the kids. He said simply that we would work that out later.

Considering the fact that I was much more pleased that he wanted to go away with me than I was worried about how we would manage it all, I quickly said yes to Michael's enthusiastic offer. While Michael planned the weekend and together we arranged to farm the kids out to various people, I worked hard to lose a few pounds, then purchased some new clothes. I also went to the optometrist for new contact lenses. So by the time we were ready to go to Cashiers, I felt a lot better about how I looked. To my added pleasure, Michael seemed exceptionally excited about being away and alone with me. I still wasn't sure exactly what all was going on with Michael, but whatever it was, I liked it and hoped it would continue.

I could only think that ever since Cursillo, Michael had a much more upbeat attitude about life and about God. He continued to gently reprove me whenever he found me worrying about God's displeasure with me. Over and over again he tried to ease my endless worry and guilt by reminding me of God's love and grace. On one hand, I found his words encouraging. But on the other, I wondered if Michael had forgotten about the punitive side of God. While I had come to understand, in part, how much God loved me and had extended His unmerited grace to me, it was still a love that I did not know how to fully accept or implement in my life. It occurred to me that if God loved us so much, we ought to strive that much harder to please Him. Looking back, I'm sure this was my attempt to weave the teachings of Cursillo together with James Smith's. So, while I ached to know the God of grace that I had only barely glimpsed, I didn't dare allow myself to forget the God of vengeance that I knew so well.

Sometimes I worried that Michael was looking for an easier route to God. This frightened me. A life of total grace was far too loose, too charitable, for me to fully grasp yet. I still needed the boundaries of legalism, because they still spelled security to me. Eventually, Michael would return to them as well. At this point, however, he was trying with all his might to hold on to what he hoped might provide relief from his exhausting inner conflict.

We had a delightful drive together to Cashiers, talking and laughing as we drove through the magnificent mountains of North Carolina. I gasped when I saw the stately High Hampton Inn, where Michael had rented one of the charming cottages for the weekend. The air was breezy and just slightly warm. In fact, the nights were so cool that a blanket was already spread over the bed. We were alone for the first time in I couldn't remember when, and it was wonderful. Michael was being very attentive to me. He seemed to be enjoying each and every detail of the trip he had so carefully planned.

At night we had dinner in the huge old inn, which had a long row of comfortable rockers spread across its wide porch. As we went inside, Michael remarked how great it would be to one day have a front porch with rockers like that. Maybe we will, I said, if God ever allows us to move out onto land. We were tired of waiting for God to show us land for community, but we still held out the hope that He would, knowing that we could then enjoy a more peaceful life.

The Old South tradition of wearing a coat and tie at dinner was still alive at the High Hampton Inn. From across our dinner table, I said that Michael looked especially handsome in his. Earlier, before we left our cottage, Michael had told me I looked pretty. Michael's compliments were sparse and, I had noticed, were offered almost shyly. This whole scene was such an unusual one for us. I sat at our table in the immense dining room watching the people, the majority of whom were obviously wealthy longtime habitués of the inn. After dinner, we took a walk across the huge, sprawling lawn. Near our cottage, Michael surprised me with a bottle of wine and a blanket, which we spread under a tree. Because we had believed drinking was sinful, we hadn't had an alcoholic drink together in years. I was a little taken aback, but so happy with this romantic "new husband" of mine that I wasn't about to spoil the night with any hesitation.

Nor had I hesitated for long when, earlier that afternoon, Michael had said he hadn't thought it necessary to bring any protection to use during our lovemaking. Ever since Timothy's birth, we had struggled to discover God's will for us about birth control. We had recently come to the conclusion that it would be all right with God if we gave ourselves a little more time before we had another baby. That meant the use of condoms again, something we had not dealt with since before the birth of Matthew. That afternoon, however, we had agreed that it was a safe time, since my period had just ended the day before. Certainly there was no way I could get pregnant.

The weekend passed too quickly, and soon we were back home and into our old routine. The children had survived our absence so well that Michael and I agreed we needed to make such trips a regular habit, which we did. Still in the afterglow of our unusually passionate time together, I determined to lose more weight and to keep the fire burning between Michael and me.

At first I thought it nothing more than a little amusing when my period did not begin on time the next month. But when it hadn't come in a few more days, I grew more seriously concerned. For the first time ever, I was angry at the possibility of being pregnant.

I had recently begun getting up early in the morning, before Michael and the boys woke up, to pray with three or four women in the fellowship. One morning I took my problem to them. We prayed and I asked God to forgive me for having such an un-Christlike attitude toward the possibility of having another baby. While praying, I mused to myself that God must not have been in favor of us using birth control after all.

Finally I gave in and took a pregnancy test. When the doctor called me back with the news that number five was indeed on the way, I cried on the phone. Having finally grown used to the idea that we wanted an unusual number of children, he was shocked. When I then asked him, almost accusingly, how it could be possible for me to have become pregnant when we had been so *sure* that our weekend away was during the "safe" time in my reproductive cycle, he roared with laughter. Much to my chagrin, he explained to me how long those little sperm rascals actually live. He commented on how strong and healthy Michael's sperm must be—not exactly what I was interested in hearing—and said once more that if he could just bottle the good chemistry Michael and I made together, he'd be rich and famous.

At twenty-seven years old, I felt pretty foolish not to have known about the longevity of sperm. Before we hung up, my wonderful old German-Jewish doctor asked me seriously if Michael and I had not wanted another baby. When I gloomily answered that we did, just not yet, he shouted exuberantly into the phone, "Well, then—what's to worry? Be happy!" and hung up.

Soon enough, I *was* happy. Once I stopped being disappointed at the prospect of losing my newly slim figure, I became quite excited about the arrival of our next child. I began to have the strong feeling that this surprise pregnancy meant a very special child indeed. Michael had always been fine and happy about it—though at first he, too, was amazed at how fertile we were together. I did think it was getting to be almost embarrassing. Michael's mother was right—we were like rabbits.

My mother didn't think it amazing or impressive at all that we continued to have baby after baby. Once she had caustically asked me, "Can't you do *anything* besides have babies?" Her words stung and angered me. But mostly I resented her lack of support. Michael's father, for his part, thought it outrageous that we spent our money on nothing but children; he said we could have so much more if we would just stop reproducing. We grew weary of repeating our explanation: "Our children are a blessing from God. We choose to spend both our time and our money on things that are eternal, not temporal."

The fellowship had finally found a place better than the old chicken coops in which to have our retreats: a large retreat center, in Tiger, Georgia, called Covecrest. It was a truly beautiful setting, absolutely pastoral, with rolling hills, streams, and an outdoor chapel for Sunday services. Families stayed either in the Billy Brown Cottage (a neat little log cabin), in tidy trailers, or in single rooms adjacent to the meeting hall. We had grown in number and praised God for allowing us a new place to get away and hear His word.

This year's summer retreat proved to be a life-changing one for Michael and me and for Stu and Becky. During our Saturday-night meeting, someone said he "had a scripture from the Lord" for the group. It was from Ezekiel 12:2–6 and read in part: "You live in the midst of a rebellious house . . . go into exile from your place to another place. . . . Perhaps they will see, though they are a rebellious house." The text was hastily interpreted to mean God was telling the fellowship to "go into exile" away from "the world" (the rebellious house) to live lives that would encourage others to take notice. During the remainder of the weekend, God continued to send messages for the fellowship to prepare itself to live apart as a community. It was also prophesied that God already had the land set aside for us and would reveal its location shortly. That produced a great time of rejoicing, even though a few in the fellowship were still not "ready" for this "exile" God was calling us into.

The next day, Michael and I were loading up our car to return to Marietta when James stopped, looked at Michael, and said, "It's time to sell your house." We shouted, "Praise the Lord!" James gave the Shores the same instructions, and the For Sale signs went up immediately in both of our yards.

Our house sold quickly, and the Shores' shortly thereafter. Now we had to find a house to rent until the land was "revealed" to the group. Looking for a house that a landlord would rent to a family of six (soon to be seven) was a humbling experience, to say the least. It seemed no one wanted to bear the burden that seven people would place on a septic tank, or to deal with any other wear and tear caused by a big family. Finally we found a house that was large enough, still close by the old neighborhood, with a landlord willing to give us a six-month lease. We did not expect to be there for long. We were sure that we would be moving to "the land" very soon.

Once a possible parcel of land for community had been found in West Cobb County, the leaders and the other men of the fellowship went away for a weekend to fast and seek God's will. Apparently although many of us were sure this land was "it," others were not. James reminded us that "God is not the author of confusion, but of a clear head and a sound mind"; therefore, He would clarify His will for us. The other leaders' wives plus some of the other fellowship women came to our house to fast and pray for the men.

When the men returned on Sunday, it was not with the news I had hoped for. There had been considerable disagreement over what God had meant by His words to us during the retreat several months earlier. As a result, the elders were no longer certain that community was God's "direction" for the entire fellowship; therefore, plans for moving were put on hold. James, Michael, and Stu were the most disappointed. James said it was possible that in deciding to form a community we had "gone ahead of God." I did not like the sound of that at all. James's advice to us and the Shores was to continue to be faithful to whatever God spoke to our hearts about community for ourselves. It might still be possible that God wanted us to be forerunners for the rest of the group. But the four of us knew that our vision was shaken, maybe destroyed, and that God had allowed it to happen. Michael and I were more than a little disheartened. We had obediently sold our homes as James had instructed us, and now it seemed to have all been in vain.

I knew this did nothing to encourage Michael's allegiance to James. Interestingly, where Michael now had begun to doubt James's infallibility, Stu's loyalty had increased. He was more devoted than ever to our leader. It seemed we were no longer "of one mind" with the Shores.

By winter the fellowship had moved beyond the shock of not moving into community and had settled back into a routine of regular meetings. It was tacitly understood that Michael and I had abandoned our plans for community with the Shores. Try as we might, it just didn't seem to be what God wanted for us. It seemed as though we were stuck in some sort of holding pattern.

Michael now led a small group called a "cell group," which met in our home each week. James and Laura, during a trip to Korea, had attended cell meetings and had come back to Georgia believing that it was God's will for the fellowship to form such groups. The concept was based on biological cell division. You begin with one leader and a group of about ten. Those who are called to evangelize bring others in until the group becomes too large and must divide. From that point on, the addition and division continues until many cell groups form and eventually fill the earth with seriously dedicated Christians.

It was around that time that *accountability* became a consequential word in our fellowship. James taught that it was important to be accountable to someone (usually a leader or, in the case of a woman, a leader's wife), which meant giving that person permission to "speak into your life" about whatever he or she thought needed correction. How well a person could tolerate being held accountable became a test of his or her spiritual maturity. I saw that this whole concept made Michael uncomfortable, and when I mentioned it to him, we argued.

"Why don't you meet with one of the other leaders to discuss things in your life like the other men do, Michael?" I asked.

"Because I don't like the idea of being held accountable to someone—or the thought of holding someone accountable to me."

"Why not?" I argued. "Why are you sometimes so rebellious to what James tells us to do?"

"I don't think I'm rebellious, Sally. And how about if you just let me handle this, okay?!"

It was not a question, and I knew it was time for me to be quiet.

Still, I worried about the fact that Michael's proclivity toward privacy seemed to become more pronounced as the group itself inclined toward increasing openness. Before too long, other members of the fellowship began to notice and comment on this. And since I was much more of an open book, our differences seemed even more pronounced.

In the meetings of both the cell group and the larger group, it was also not at all uncommon—in fact, it was encouraged—for someone to specifically confess his or her temptations or actual sins out loud. Michael did *not* subscribe to this practice. In fact, he rarely asked for prayer about anything of a personal nature at all. At times I told myself that my husband was just stronger than most of the other men; but at other times I wondered if it was not merely his sinful pride that made Michael so reticent.

Once, while we were driving somewhere without the children, I asked him, "Michael, do you ever struggle with lust?"

"Why on earth are you asking me that?" he responded. I had never thought to ask such a thing until several women in the fellowship had shared with me how much they worried about their husbands' problems with lust. Already it embarrassed me that I had brought it up, but I continued because suddenly I really wanted to know the answer.

"Well, you know, so many of the men both in our fellowship and at the Chapel say they struggle with it. It seems like someone is always tearfully confessing his problem at the meetings. I just wanted to ask because I've never worried about that with you. Maybe I'm being foolish. Maybe I *should* worry!" I laughed nervously.

"No, you shouldn't worry," he said, attempting a smile. "I really do not struggle with lust at all."

"Why don't you? And why do they?" I asked. He looked a bit shocked now, but he answered me.

"Because," he began slowly, "I just do not think about other women, Sally. It's just never been a problem with me, I can assure you. I really don't know why some men have such a big problem with it. But the only woman I have ever thought about, and think about now, is you."

Most of what Michael told me that day was true. It just wasn't the *truth*. But I believed him. I was so proud and felt secure: What an incredible husband I have! Every woman on earth should envy me. He never thinks about other women—no one else but me! What I *didn't* know, and of course he couldn't tell me then, was that at that very moment I had inadvertently unleashed Michael's carefully confined, lustful thoughts of the last *man* he had been with, probably only days before.

From that moment until more than ten years later, I felt safe. And why shouldn't I have? I inhabited a cocoon in which I was incapable of suspecting Michael of heterosexual, much less homosexual, infidelity. Little did I know how different Michael felt in that world—a world in which he couldn't even consider coming out as homosexual, a world whose teachings about homosexuality, and everything else, he gave every indication of concurring with. How could he even think of telling me the truth—let alone telling it to himself?

Continually, the emphasis in the fellowship was on growing, striving, and maturing in the Lord. The constant challenge we heard from James was: "Can you see God working in you?" It was 1981, and Pat Robertson was calling for a "cleansing of the nation" beginning with the household of God. Sin was rampant in our land. In Hebrews Six we were constantly praying for God's healing for both the church and the world. "Serious Christians" everywhere were told to be on constant watch. We should "test the spirits" to be sure we were listening to the Spirit of God, not the devil. According to the "latter-day prophets" (who were cropping up everywhere), things were only going to get worse. I had only to look around at the condition of the world—drugs, promiscuity, divorce, and the like—to believe that it was true.

Before long, my fear of losing God had doubled. I began to have vivid dreams about the end times that always found me scrambling frantically to pull everyone (even Michael's mother, in one dream) into the house, or some other place of presumed safety, before it was too late. I dreamed about tornadoes and about being caught under huge, crushing waves in the ocean, in both cases panicking because I could not see Michael or the children. I seriously feared being separated from those I loved when the end came. The thought of anyone in our extended family being sent to hell when Christ returned and the world as we knew it ended haunted me in the daytime as well. In my nightmares, it seemed to be my responsibility and mission to save everyone from disaster, and each time I woke up feeling completely hopeless and inadequate.

Our lunatic fringe of Christianity became even loonier, for a while, with the temporary addition of a couple for whom James's teachings, as it turned out, were not demanding enough, and the rest of us were "spiritual weaklings." Peter was a superficially gentle man with a boiling rage hidden just beneath the surface; Nicole flat-out terrified me with her cold eyes and her sunken face that never smiled. Both were extremely intelligent. When we met them, however, they were out of work by choice. God, they said, had instructed them not to *seek* employment; it would come to them if it was supposed to, and in the meantime, God would supply their needs. If something—say food, for instance—was not "supplied," Peter and Nicole assumed it was not

God's will that they have it. This assumption definitely simplified their lives, though the fact that they had two daughters, aged eleven and nine, made their slow trek to starvation especially difficult for the rest of us to watch.

We all knew about the scripture that says: "A man who does not provide for his family is worse than an infidel." Peter and Nicole, however, had "heard God"—and such experiences overrode even Scripture. They declared that they would stand on "His specific word" to them no matter what. If no one believed them, then so be it. That part sounded familiar, so much so that we all watched to see how our leader would handle these two.

Before long it was clear that neither James nor anyone else knew what to do with them.

One day Peter calmly called Michael and me, asking us to inform the fellowship that a DEFACS (Department of Family and Child Services) social worker had placed Peter and Nicole's two daughters into foster care. A schoolteacher had noticed a large red mark on one of the girls' thighs, and the girl had admitted that it was from a hard spanking; she had also told the social worker that her parents had almost no food in the house. Both children, painfully thin, had immediately been taken into custody. After a short, pointless battle with DEFACS, during which Peter and Nicole refused to stop spanking their children, to find jobs, or to accept government aid, both girls were sent to live with relatives in another state.

The fellowship was seriously perplexed as to how to handle this latest turn of events. (Whenever anyone in the fellowship had questioned Peter and Nicole about the condition of either themselves or the girls, their answer had been to ask God; it was His will.) As a group we preached strict adherence to whatever God's word was to a person, no matter how foolish or absurd it might seem to the world or the church. James himself had certainly propelled us in a walk that was far from comfortable. Peter and Nicole were only living out in a bolder way what James had taught us about denying oneself.

One morning my phone rang. "Hello?" "Hello. This is Nicole. I'm calling to tell you that I love you."

I felt my heart soften a bit toward this odious woman. Maybe God was doing something after all. Still shocked by her unusual display of affection, I managed to stammer out only "Thank you, Nicole" before she interrupted me.

"Don't thank me," she said firmly, returning to her usual monotone. "God told me I had to call and tell you I loved you—even if I don't." With that, she said a brisk good-bye and hung up. For a moment I stood there holding the receiver, trying hard to make sense of what had just happened. Then I hung up. James may say Christians are to be a "peculiar people" all he wants, I decided, but Nicole and Peter are just too strange.

My phone call from Nicole was followed by an event witnessed by the whole group. It happened after a meeting at Jeff and Bonnie's house, when we were enjoying our usual dessert. The group was particularly hungry that night, and in no time at all the cake brought by one of the women was almost gone. Bonnie reached for the last piece at the same moment that the pale, skinny Nicole also reached for it. As soon as Nicole saw Bonnie's hand, she quickly retracted her own. Bonnie immediately did the same.

Nicole firmly and loudly said, "*No! You* take it! God does not want me to have it."

Those of us around the table were stone silent. Bonnie could find nothing to say, feeling that whatever she did say or do would make her seem terribly ungodly. Finally, a red-faced Bonnie left the piece of cake and walked away. So did Nicole. I'm sure no one present that night has ever taken the last piece of cake from a plate again without remembering Nicole's stinging words.

Soon James decided what to do about Peter and Nicole. He met with them and honestly told them that our fellowship was not equipped to give them what they needed. They wasted no time in leaving the group. Everyone, even James, felt a sense of both relief and defeat. Perhaps we had let them (and God as well?) down. No one spoke about it much after they were gone, but the air seemed lighter, easier to breathe.

From time to time Michael and I would see the Peter and Nicole. With each sighting we noted sadly that they looked more cadaverous.

On the morning of March 27, 1981, I set my alarm to go off early so that I could slip out of bed and have some "quiet time with the Lord" before everyone else was up. While I sat at the long kitchen table, quietly reading my Bible and praying, the words to a scripture song, one I did not often sing, kept going through my mind: "Blessed be the Lord God, the God of Israel . . . Who only doeth wondrous things . . . And blessed be His Holy name forever." With each verse, I became increasingly cheerful. Finally I went to wake up Michael. Making my way slowly down the hall to the bedroom, I suddenly realized that I had fluid running down my legs and it was very sticky. My water was breaking.

I woke Michael, then called the doctor. Before I knew it, Michael and I were in the delivery room. I realized that it had been about four hours since my water had broken and I had not had the first labor pain. I was amazed. At 2:47 that afternoon, Josiah was born. As always, choosing a name was very important to us. Virginia had suggested the name Josiah while we were visiting at their house several weeks before his birth. We liked it instantly, and liked it even more after looking it up and finding that it meant "God's chosen one." We felt that the name suited him well, since it seemed clear to us that God had had His hand on this child all along. Weighing only seven pounds, eleven ounces, he seemed small, like little Michael and Matthew, as compared with Daniel and Timothy. He was beautiful, with a dark complexion and a head full of dark hair. Immediately, I was in love with our unplanned bundle of love.

Spring came; then summer. The more we talked with the Shores, the more obvious it was that none of us knew what to think or do about our longtime vision for community. Finally, Michael and I decided that we had to stop renting and buy a house. We found a large one in a neighborhood where several other fellowship members lived. Russell and Scarlett lived close by, which pleased us, because we wanted to get to know them better. We bought the house, and eventually the Shores bought one down the street. Life in the fellowship continued, though not quite in the way we had planned.

James's spiritual focus, we discovered, had shifted again, this time to an even more passive faith, in the sense that we were admonished not to resist any trials or adversity that came into our lives. Instead, we were to accept all things as being God's divine will for our lives. He encouraged us all to read books by a woman named Madame Guyon. A Roman Catholic, Madame Guyon had been extremely self-abasing. Eventually she became so convicted that to have any sort of physical pleasure was contrary to following God that she told her husband she could no longer have a sexual relationship with him. He divorced her. Finally her messages from God were renounced by the Roman Catholic Church and she was put to death during the French inquisition.

It was then that many began to seriously question where James was going. Once the questions began, it was only a matter of time before the foundation of Hebrews Six Fellowship would begin to crumble.

For a year and a half longer the group tried either to figure out or to ignore the signs of trouble brewing. "What's happening to the fellowship?" was the usual topic of our conversations with Russell and Scarlett, with whom we had developed a deep friendship. Scarlett and Michael enjoyed discussing history and politics together. Russell had become my first male friend, and together we discussed everything from art and poetry to the interpretation of scriptures—even daring to question what James had taught us. The word *discontent* was frequently heard among the four of us, and among others in the group. Our tight little world was slowly strangling us all, yet no one was quite ready to see it yet—except perhaps Michael, who knew quite well what it was about it that was torturing him. He knew he couldn't remain where he was for much longer.

By the fifth grade, little Michael had developed some serious difficulties in school. I felt dreadfully out of touch with my own son's learning, which now, it seemed, had become quite troubled. I recalled one night the previous spring, when we had been invited to a friend's house to hear a couple speak about their positive experiences with home-schooling. Some of their radical words echoed back to me now: "*Any* school severely limits time with your children." Though we did not disagree with their decision to home-school their child, it still seemed drastic, especially to me. How could I teach little Michael while caring for four others as well? Besides, I was not trained to teach; I hadn't even gone to college.

Now, halfway through fifth grade, little Michael had become so distraught with his schoolwork and so irritated with himself that he had begun to call me in the middle of the day, sometimes begging me to come and get him. Every time, I tried to calm him down and urged him to finish out the day, and he did so. It was painful for both of us. At home he was tense and angry so much of the time that I wondered if home-schooling would be any easier on us.

Over the long Christmas break, Michael and I began to notice subtle changes in little Michael, in that he seemed happier and more agreeable. Bad weather forced the schools to remain closed for an additional two weeks, and it was then that we noticed unmistakable changes. Little Michael was decidedly calmer, sweeter, and more content. He helped me around the house; played exceptionally well with Daniel; and was gentle and affectionate with Matthew, Timothy, and Josiah. His daddy and I agreed he was a real joy to have around. When the weather improved, I actually dreaded his return to school, afraid that his "old self" would return.

Mother, never meaning to be a home-school advocate, sent me an article by Dr. Raymond Moore entitled "School Can Wait." The article really hit home. Dr. Moore spoke about how detrimental it was to "force immature little boys into a structured first-grade classroom" and emphasized the need to let kids be kids as long as possible. Too much academic learning too early, he said, was a sure way to burn them out fast. Michael and I had to admit to each other that little Michael was definitely burned out. It was then that we decided to give home-schooling some serious thought and prayer.

Since Daniel was now in first grade, and doing fine academically, if we decided to home-school, we would have to do it with him as well or else run the risk of little Michael feeling that he was way behind his little brother. Home-schooling both boys would always be a challenge. I would have to find a way to catch little Michael up without letting him feel he was back in first grade with Daniel. I began to feel the truth that home-schooling was indeed God's will tugging at my heart, but at the same time, the responsibility still seemed beyond my capabilities.

A few days later, Michael told me he had been praying about what to do about little Michael and how we could best help him. He looked at me calmly and said he seriously believed God would have us home-school both little Michael and Daniel. I was surprised that he had come to this conclusion so fast, but very appreciative that he had taken the time to seek God for the answer. As we then discussed home-schooling in further depth, we agreed that our sons ought to be firmly grounded in Christian character and morals before we sent them back to school, especially public school, which might corrupt or at the least challenge their beliefs. Seeing my obvious apprehension, Michael assured me that whenever he was home, he would help.

In just a matter of weeks, Michael had converted a room in the basement into a classroom. We researched material and decided upon a Christian curriculum called A BEKA. In March 1982, we removed little Michael from fifth grade and Daniel from first grade to begin teaching them at home. The boys did not resist the move, and were in fact excited, though at first they missed their friends and teachers.

I found out quickly that home-schooling was not easy and required a lot of scheduling, preparation, and discipline. Still, our attitudes were positive. One of the first things we learned was to be a lot more flexible and patient. I considered home-schooling to be an added dimension to the full-time job I already had with mothering five sons. I felt good about the sense of purpose and order that it lent to our days. Best of all was seeing the relaxed look on my firstborn's face as we began our day together.

Michael continued to travel professionally and was very successful in his sales. Consequently, our finances continued on an upward swing. One night he took me out to dinner at one of our favorite restaurants, the Old Vinings Inn. After we were seated, I said I thought it was extravagant to dine at the inn when it was not even a special occasion. The waitress came, and Michael ordered a bottle of wine and two racks of lamb—our favorite.

"Sally, you really need to relax about money," Michael gently admonished me. "God has blessed us financially and you can honestly stop worrying, okay?"

"Okay, I'll *try*," I smiled back with a look of mock hardship.

Michael's mood turned serious. "I want to talk to you about something important," he began. "I have been praying about something, and I think God has given me an answer," he went on carefully, watching my face. "I believe that God has told me to look for land for us."

"What exactly do you mean?" I asked, confused.

"I believe God has said it is time for us to move. I want our family to be out in the country, away from the hassles of the city. I want us to have some land, animals, creeks, and fresh air! So, what do you think?"

"It sounds great," I answered quickly and rushed ahead to other questions. "Where will we move?" "How soon?" "What about the Shores? Are you at least going to ask them if they want to go with us?" I was excited at the thought of moving out but still wanted to be sure we would not "miss God" in any way.

The enthusiasm in Michael's voice dropped a little when I suggested including the Shores in our plans. "Yeah, I'll ask Stu if he wants to look for land with me. But whether he decides to or not, Sally, I still feel that it is the right thing for us to do."

I agreed, and we spent the rest of the night planning our house, talking about the horses we could have, the vegetable garden he wanted to plant, and, best of all, the freedom from the strife of city life. It would be great to home-school the boys on a farm! Suddenly I was filled with such a warm happiness, mostly from knowing that Michael had spent time praying about our future. I relaxed into a safe assurance that we were finally on the right road, and that the joy and peace we both seemed to lack would finally be ours.

Michael had several reasons for his decision to move, some of which I knew and some of which I didn't. I did know that while he truly believed God might use us in a new way on the land, he was tired and frustrated by the legalism constantly rammed down his throat by James. I knew he was struggling to remain loyal, even though he no longer believed that James possessed the only "truth."

Unbeknownst to me, however, there was something else Michael wanted to escape: an increasing temptation to experience Atlanta's gay life, which, so far, he had managed to resist. He sincerely hoped that moving far enough away from Atlanta would serve as the control factor he prayed was all he needed. Furthermore, he felt that if he poured all of his energies into working the land, allowing it and his family to become a place of refuge for him, perhaps after a little while his longings would subside.

As he saw it, moving to the country could only be a good thing for us all. Ultimately, he would be right.

I was hopeful for my husband as well, but for different reasons. I had watched Michael's growing dissatisfaction and restlessness, which I mostly attributed to his hurt and disillusionment with James Smith, but which I also feared was due to his holding himself back from God. Though I shared Michael's mixed feelings about James, it still disturbed me to think of us being out from under his authority. What would we do on our own, without a fellowship? Would we try to remain attached to Hebrews Six Fellowship? Somehow I doubted that. Finally I decided I had to rest in Michael's decision. I set my hopes on the move he had initiated and prayed that it would be the outlet Michael needed to at last be free to be the man God had intended him to be. After all, I reminded myself, that's all I had ever wanted.

When Michael approached Stu about our looking for land together, Stu was apprehensive about leaving James and Hebrews Six. After some prayerful consideration, however, Stu said that he and Becky and their three children would join us in the move. Presently Michael found a suitable piece of land, thirty-four acres in Forsyth County, near a small rural town called Cumming, roughly sixty miles north of Atlanta. Michael's old family lake house had been in Forsyth County, so Michael knew the area fairly well. Michael and Stu decided that log houses were the best buy and that we would build two of them, about one hundred feet apart. We hoped to have them completed by the summer of 1983.

I had never seen Michael so excited. The only thing that seemed to trouble him occasionally was that the Shores were moving onto the land with us. Sometimes he seemed glad to be sharing plans and clearing land with Stu. At other times I was sure he would have been happier had it just been the seven of us moving to Forsyth County.

Michael and I had talked about Stu and Becky many times and had admitted—to each other, at least—that there was a strain in our relationship. We loved them and knew that they loved us, too, but much of the enthusiasm we had once shared with them was gone. We had very little in common besides children, church, and an aging "call from God" to be in some sort of ministry together. I began to wonder how we would all survive in such proximity, yet I was certainly not ready to move to "the sticks" alone. We could only hope that God would "do a work in our hearts" toward the Shores before the next summer.

It had been with heavy hearts that Michael and I told the rest of the fellowship about our plans to move. We and the Shores weren't the only ones with such plans: Jeff's career would soon take him and Bonnie to Raleigh. Everyone knew that the absence of the six of us—Michael and me, Stu and Becky, and Bonnie and Jeff—would drastically change the flavor of the group. The impending changes served only to heighten the general discontent. No one wanted to say what we all knew—that God was bringing to an end what had been the core of all of our lives for eight long years.

Meanwhile, James's words had grown even more gloomy. In fact, on our fellowship's last venture to Lambs' Chapel, when James had spoken, he had reprimanded the "house of God" sternly for our "rebelliousness" and had declared the way of the Lord to be so narrow that it seemed no amount of striving would assure anyone of salvation. At one point, Bonnie had leaned over to me and said, "I swear I can actually see the dark cloud that follows James everywhere he goes. The sun all but goes out whenever he speaks!" It was true: James had altered his teaching direction to the extent that most of us knew better than to follow. It was a very sad, but necessary, time of reckoning.

During our last year in James Smith's fellowship, James had asked Michael and me to help him lead what had become quite a large group of singles. Thinking it would be interesting, we had agreed. It proved to be a much more wonderful experience getting to know them and seeing life from their perspective than we had expected. They dealt with issues that we—or at least I, in my cloistered world—might not otherwise have encountered.

It was in 1982, at the singles meetings, that I first heard about the horrible disease called AIDS. "It is a curse sent by God," James explained.

"How do you know it's a curse?" I carefully asked.

"Because," he said, "it is a result of sexual promiscuity and originated from homosexual behavior.

"Why should we be surprised?" James asked the group. "It makes sense that God would, in these last days, send an unmistakable form of judgment in the hope of waking sinners up."

Thinking about the immoralities of the day and lumping homosexuality in with them, I had to agree. We bowed our heads and prayed in earnest and with power for those who had been deceived by Satan into believing they were homosexual. We prayed for them to be delivered and for God to continue to use AIDS to show them the vileness and horrible consequence of their sin.

Michael prayed too.

At the end of May we finished our first few months of home-schooling, feeling fairly successful. Little Michael's reading skills were improving dramatically. The boys had finally accepted me as a "real" teacher. Michael, for his part, had kept his word by teaching the boys' Bible classes and by relieving me of history or math whenever he was available. Michael also began to take little Michael or Daniel along on business trips, along with a book bag full of schoolwork. Eventually all of our sons, except the last, would go along on at least one business trip with Michael; for each of them, these became treasured memories.

Home-schooling, of course, wasn't popular with everyone. It was then in its infancy in Georgia and was widely regarded as dubious. Michael and I had joined a home-schooling organization, and he took part in the political struggle in Atlanta, the capital, where home-schoolers protested for the right of parents to educate their own children. As for Michael's and my parents, they were simply appalled at the thought of our teaching the boys at home. How could I teach the boys without a degree? I carefully explained to them that it is not difficult to teach a child elementary subjects, as long as you are willing to study them first yourself. Then came the socialization questions, which it was a little tougher to convince them we were handling. Our boys joined with other home-schoolers in the home-schooling organization for regularly scheduled field trips. The boys had plenty of friends. But how could I teach the older boys with the babies around? our parents asked.

That part, I had to admit, was hard. Matthew, Timothy, and even Josiah were constant distractions that required creative tactics. Still, the longer I taught, the more I realized that it took only a few minutes to comfort a crying baby or to show a two-year-old how to mold his Play-Doh into a ball. Besides, we had all day. A few minutes were not all that crucial. The older boys learned to be patient. The younger ones grew up thinking school with mama was a treat, and one they were eager to be big enough to be a part of. On a "good" day, school might be over at one o'clock. On a day with more interruptions, it could take until four o'clock to finish. The boys became less self-centered, a lesson that never once hurt them. They grew up knowing how to share not just their toys, but their time.

Finally I told both sets of parents that we firmly believed we were doing the best thing for our boys *at that time*. I could promise them only that whenever we felt that home-schooling was a disservice to any one of our boys, we would enroll him in conventional school. I invited their input on this but asked them to withhold their judgment at least for a while. The results were gratifying. Before the first full year of home-schooling was over, both Michael's and my parents had complimented us on the children. They congratulated us on the improvements they saw both academically and in the boys' behavior. For once our peculiar way of doing things seemed to have met with their approval.

By that summer, it was evident that the boys had developed a closeness with each other that was rare even for brothers. As for me, I could not imagine a more important job than teaching the boys, besides which I loved having the chance to spend so much time with them. While vacationing in St. Simons, however, I made a distressing discovery about myself. One day I stood on the beach, as I often did, watching the two older boys ride the waves with their daddy. All at once, out of the corner of my eye, I saw Timothy jump up from his drip castle and begin to run toward me. Then I saw myself, as if watching from a distance, raise my hands—not in greeting, but to break what I knew would be an enthusiastic hug. In a flash, as the painful memory hit me hard, I was the little girl again rushing up to greet my own mother only to find her arms tensely braced, just as mine were then to my son. I realized then that never once in my life had I experienced a satisfying hug with my mother. Without another thought, I vowed that it would not be that way ever again with my sons. As I knelt down to fully embrace Timothy, I sensed that a long chain of pain and loss had been broken at last. The promise I made that day was one that, by the grace of God, I have managed to keep.

For over a year, Michael had expressed interest in visiting Last Days Ministry in Tyler, Texas. Last Days was a ministry developed by the late Keith Green, a powerful Christian singer, and his wife, Melody. The focus of the ministry was on preparing Christians for the last days, with an emphasis on repentance and living fully for the Lord. Keith Green and two of their children (Melody was pregnant with a third child at the time) had been killed in a private-plane crash just that summer, and Christians all over the country had felt the loss. Christians were now being petitioned by Melody to come to the ranch to lend a hand and to experience a personal time of retreat.

In September 1982, Michael at last journeyed to visit Last Days Ministry. He decided that he could fit in a week there before a scheduled business trip to Dallas. By now I had determined in my mind that the reason Michael's "walk with the Lord" was inconsistent was because he held part of himself back from God. I hoped that at Last Days he would be encouraged to completely "sell out to God." Michael had told me many times himself how much he wanted that very thing for his life. We had begun to argue about what I saw as a conflict between what he said he wanted and how much of himself he had actually dedicated to God. Sometimes he admitted that it was true: he was not "sold out." At other times he denied it and we fought. At any rate, I knew Michael hoped as much as I did that a trip to Last Days would help resolve things. Unfortunately, that was not the case.

Over the phone, Michael told me that throughout his entire week on the ranch, which he spent doing mostly manual labor, he had encountered an abundance of arrogance, ungratefulness, and self-righteousness that were equal to, if not worse than, what he knew existed in Hebrews Six Fellowship. I knew that he left for Dallas spiritually disillusioned and in despair.

Years later he would tell me how deep his despair had actually gone. Having become almost totally disenchanted with the belief that James and the Hebrews Six Fellowship could help him, he had gone to Last Days Ministry with a hope in his heart that, once there, he might experience a group of Christians who were truly altruistic and less legalistic in their walk with God than what he knew at home. When that failed to happen, Michael, no doubt seeking solace and peace of mind, ended up in a gay bar in Dallas. As God would have it, there he met a former Roman Catholic priest who was completely "out" as a gay man. Extremely interested, Michael listened to his story. Then he shared his own, both about the Hebrews Six Fellowship and about his recent experience, still weighing heavily on his spirit, at Last Days Ministry. They talked at length about Catholicism and fundamental Christianity. From the priest's own experience both as a Catholic and as a Christian, he enlightened Michael with the "good news" that it was indeed possible to be both Christian and gay. And, for the first time, Michael felt normal in his desire for both God and man. The two men ended up spending the night together, then never saw each other again.

Michael returned from his trip to Texas much more content than I would have anticipated after our phone call. Little did I know then that Michael's edification stemmed not from his experience at Last Days Ministry, but from a brief affair with a former priest who, out of his own rejection by the Roman Catholic Church, had come to better know the true heart of Christ.

One night in October, while waiting for Michael's nightly call, I turned on the eleven o'clock news. Channel eleven, one of our local TV stations, had a weekly segment called "Wednesday's Child." This segment focused on special-needs children who, for reasons varying from chronic bed-wetting to mental retardation, were hard to place for adoption. Individual children were shown on the program in the hope that someone would give them a permanent home. On this particular night, I was watching absently until a beautiful, copper-haired baby girl suddenly caught my eye. "Sarah is fifteen months old," I heard the reporter say. "She is physically and mentally handicapped. Prospective parents should also know that Sarah is blind."

"Sarah?" I said, surprised. That was our chosen girl's name.

I was completely engrossed as I watched Sarah. Her eyes were sad and blank as she sat still—too still—on a caseworker's lap. Her mouth appeared fixed in a constant O shape. Throughout the show she just sat there; she never smiled, never made a sound, never wriggled to get down. Josiah's her age, I thought. He would never sit still like that.

Still, I found myself drawn to her lost face. And her name was *Sarah!* I could hardly wait for Michael's call so that I could tell him about her. We had discussed adopting a special-needs daughter, thinking perhaps that that might have been one of God's purposes in giving us only sons. Still, I didn't know how Michael would react to one with so many needs.

I was thinking how much this little girl needed a family when the phone rang. I immediately told Michael all about the red-haired little girl. When I finally paused to let him speak, I held my breath, hoping I had not scared him too badly. On the contrary, Michael did not even hesitate: "Call DEFACS about her in the morning and we'll take it from there."

I was shocked. "Are you serious? Do you really want me to call?"

"Yeah, I'm serious and I do want you to call. You can tell me more about it when I get home tomorrow." Michael's positive reaction was all the confirmation I needed to begin to believe that if God wanted Sarah in our home, it would happen.

Bright and early the next day, I made the call to DEFACS. When Michael came home that night, I surprised him with the news that we had an initial interview the next week. "Really? That's great," he said.

Good, I thought to myself, he's still interested.

During the interview we learned more about Sarah's medical problems: she had been born premature and hydrocephalic. At five months pregnant her mother, a suspected drug addict, had hemorrhaged and almost lost Sarah. The doctors said that this had probably caused Sarah to suffer a stroke in utero. Sarah's hydrocephalic condition had not been detected until she was six months old, at which time she was permanently "shunted" to relieve the buildup of fluid that pressed on her brain. But the pressure had caused an undetermined amount of brain damage and blindness.

DEFACS presented us with mountains of paperwork to fill out and return as soon as possible. Michael and I each had to accumulate numerous references, take physicals, and show that we were financially and emotionally stable. The process took the remainder of the year to complete. Then came the long wait for the state to decide. We completed each step desiring only that Sarah would come to have a good home. I prayed daily for God's will to be done concerning her future.

I began asking God to prepare my heart in case we didn't get Sarah. I could not imagine God giving us such a fabulous gift. The next few months went by so slowly. I taught school and began to wish I was pregnant (another way of coping with the fear of not getting Sarah) or that the caseworker would call with good news.

Nothing happened until May 27. Scarlett and I had just returned from taking our boys to the park for an outing to mark the end of the school year. She and her boys had headed home, and now Michael and I were outside on the patio, discussing how long our waiting to hear about Sarah had dragged on. The phone rang several times, interrupting us so often that Michael almost took it off the hook. It rang once more and Michael, exasperated, went inside to answer it. The next thing I knew, he was tapping on the window, motioning me to come in with the biggest grin on his face. I knew it could only be about Sarah. "Here," he said into the phone, "you have to repeat this to Sally. Otherwise she'll never believe it."

He handed the phone to me. It was Sarah's caseworker, Mary Ann. "The results from the home study are in, Sally," she said, "and y'all were selected to be Sarah's parents!"

I had to sit down on the kitchen floor. My legs simply would not hold me up. I tried to absorb the fact that God had said yes. He didn't have to say yes, I thought. He could have easily said no and I would have understood.

Though I still felt in a way disbelieving, I looked up at Michael and said, "We are really going to have our little girl, our Sarah." He could not have looked more pleased.

I thanked God so many times for Sarah that I was sure He was growing tired of hearing me. "Enough already, Sally," I could imagine God wanting to say to me. So I switched my prayers, telling God that I was rededicating myself to Him as a mother and asking Him to use Sarah in my life to teach me, as He had with the boys and Michael. I thanked God that through Him, I would be made strong in my weaknesses.

I had no idea then what a mirror Sarah would be for me. Through Sarah, I would come face to face with my worst frailties as a mother. Nor did Michael or I know how much heartbreak would come into our lives as a result of having "won" Sarah—but not before she would bring a tremendous awareness to each of us, and to many others around her, of exactly what being mentally and physically challenged really meant and how we, as her family, could best meet her needs.

On June 2, Michael and I drove to Ringold, Georgia, where Sarah lived with her foster parents. There we were met with a surprise—an unpleasant one. We quickly observed that Sarah, now a week shy of two years old, was spoiled rotten. Her foster family's idea of loving Sarah was to indulge her in everything she wanted. Sarah, while she held on to the furniture for support (she did not yet walk), systematically went from person to person, pushing each from his or her seat. With each rude shove, a foster-family member roared with laughter, whereupon Sarah would go on to the next occupied seat. We immediately saw that Sarah was not so mentally challenged that she did not know how to play to a crowd!

It was all that either Michael or I could do to restrain ourselves long enough to listen politely to their reminiscing about Sarah, then endure their tearful good-byes so that we could get her out of there. They had given Sarah love, that was for sure; and for that we were grateful. But, I told Michael, Sarah's behavior had reminded me of the bratty Helen Keller in *The Miracle Worker*. It was certain that we had our work cut out for us when it came to discipline.

Together, we agreed on the first thing about Sarah that would have to go: the bottle that hung continuously from either her hand or her mouth. The second was her expectation of being carried everywhere she needed or wanted to go. At that point, besides being able to walk while holding on to furniture, Sarah also crawled upright, on her knees—a strange sight! We were determined that Sarah use her legs to gain strength so that she might walk as soon as possible. Michael and I promised each other not to coddle her. We would be firm and treat her as much like the boys as was possible. Staring at the red-haired beauty asleep in her car seat behind me, I thought how dreamlike it all still seemed.

The boys adored Sarah, plain and simple. They would be the ones we would have to teach not to coddle her—although, at two years old, Josiah was sometimes the exception. He was sweet with Sarah at first, sharing his toys, tiny bites of food—even a runny nose. He was obsessed with her long hair and stroked it for as long as she would sit still. After two weeks, however—when, I suppose, Josiah realized that Sarah was here to stay—his attitude changed abruptly. After he had clobbered her a few times, and she had shed more than a few tears, I knew I had to figure out a better way to make this work.

I decided that, with the addition of Sarah to our domestic unit, God was redefining my job description. From now on it would be full time plus overtime. I could fight the added load and have two cranky two-year-olds on my hands or give in to it and simply enjoy them. I began to play *with them*, actually sitting down on the floor with their miniature Fisher Price people, cars, and trucks. Whenever I joined them in their play, Josiah would share nicely with Sarah. After a while, the extra attention seemed to soothe the savage beast in Josiah, returning him to his former sweet self. I was confident once more that Sarah would survive life in our home.

One night, while Michael was away on business, he called to relate something to me that he felt God had shown him. Michael said that while he was praying, God had reminded him that it was His will for humans to live in the same peaceful, harmonious order as the rest of nature. Michael said he felt that when we moved to the land, God was going to somehow use us in a "ministry of reconciliation." Immediately I had visions of God perhaps using our home as a small retreat, where burned-out Christians could come for renewal. Thinking, then, about how worn-out and disillusioned Michael and I were from the rigid authority of the fellowship with its strict rules, I told him that I hoped God's reconciliation would begin with us. He agreed.

After that phone call, I had the words of a praise song on my mind for days. Finally I shared them with Michael, as confirmation of the word he had received from God about our future: "You shall go out with joy and be led forth in peace. The mountains and the hills shall break forth before you. There shall be shouts of joy, and all the trees of the fields will clap, will clap, their hands."

I couldn't wait for our move to Forsyth County. I was so certain that new life awaited us there.

chapter 7

A Happy Medium

In October 1983, Michael and I and our six children moved to Forsyth County and began life in the country. The log house, much of which Michael had built himself, was at best roughly finished.

Though it would be weeks before the house was actually complete, we were all happy to be there. Along with constructing tree houses, fishing on the lake, and building secret forts easily hidden in the twenty acres of woods, the boys worked on the house as a part of their after-school activities. It was spacious and had its own sort of rustic charm, set back on a knoll and nestled in dozens of wild dogwood trees that bloomed with exquisite white flowers every Easter.

Little Michael, Daniel, Matthew, Timothy, and Josiah were all immensely happy living in the woods; it was a virtual paradise for little boys. Sarah, who by now we were certain was *not* blind, was managing well in her new surroundings. Michael and I especially loved our bedroom, which was downstairs, far from the madding crowd. In a year or two we added behind our bedroom a room we called "the little room"; this room was off limits to kids, unless specifically invited, and became, for me, a place of solace. Over the next nine years I spent as much time as I could manage in that room, reading and writing and, sometimes, sorting out some of the most painful issues of my life.

I was hopeful for Michael. I saw his tension being replaced by a real enthusiasm for country living. He loved working the land. He even enjoyed the old-timers at Leon's Store, who kept him engaged in conversation for hours. It seemed to me that God had already provided us with much of the peace we had sought for so long.

The Shores planned to move up to the land the following month. If the house they were building next to ours was not yet ready to move into (which seemed likely at this point), they would have to move in with us. This was not a benign prospect, for a serious problem had been developing in our relationship with them. One factor was that Michael was ready to break away from James's authority entirely, while Stu argued that he and Michael ought to be more devoted to James than ever. Becky and I had our own problems, the chief one being my discovery that I was pregnant yet again. Whereas Michael and I had no trouble conceiving, it had taken four years for Becky to get pregnant after the birth of her second daughter. Every time I got pregnant she got upset. This pregnancy, my sixth, seemed to be the last straw for her.

For both Michael and me, sad to say, our friendship with the Shores had become little more than a necessary drudgery. I had suspected all along that Michael didn't exactly relish the idea of the Shores joining us in Forsyth; now I realized that I dreaded it as well. So uncomfortable did all four of us feel together, in fact, that we eventually admitted it to one another and, at Michael's and my suggestion, decided to have a talk.

It lasted four hours. Michael and I spoke honestly about our desire to separate from James and the fellowship, and all four of us discussed the problems that had developed between us over the last few years. By getting our feelings out in the open, then reaffirming our belief that God had directed us to Forsyth together, all four of us felt we had achieved a new understanding. Yet later I wondered if Michael and I had made peace not out of a true sense of shared calling with the Shores, but out of a fear that God would be angered if we reneged on our decision to share the land with them. Were Michael and I clinging fearfully to an imagined "commitment in the Lord" when in fact God wanted to do something entirely different with us? This question would resurface often during the years we lived cheek by jowl with the Shores. But for the time being, we tried to make the best of it.

Toward the end of November, the Shores moved in with us. For three months, the thirteen of us lived communally, as we had always dreamed of doing. Becky and I home-schooled five children between us. At the same time she oversaw the building of their house. It was difficult, sometimes to the point of breaking mentally and physically, but it was also fun. The kids, of course, thought living together was fantastic. To them it was one long sleepover. Since we heated our log house with only a huge wood stove, the nights were especially cozy. Everyone gathered in the great room, and the adults took turns reading to the children.

While the boys thrived in our new home, Sarah became much more difficult. Before moving from Marietta, Michael and I had taken Sarah to a developmental center for psychological and physiological evaluations. These had proved somewhat helpful—and very expensive. The right side of Sarah's brain was damaged, which explained why the left side of her body showed spasticity. The physical therapist from the center had given us a daily routine of exercises that, it was hoped, would stretch and strengthen her left arm and leg. Michael and I took turns helping Sarah do the painful exercises, which she screamed her way through. Occasionally when Michael would come downstairs after his turn with Sarah, I would accuse him of being too rough. Then, when it was my turn and Sarah screamed just as loudly, I would apologize to him. Michael and I ended up despising the exercises and were greatly relieved when Sarah's new physical therapist in Cumming prescribed a much gentler routine. Everything with Sarah was a learning process, much of it hit-or-miss. But all of it took its toll. Fortunately, Michael and I learned to share honestly with each other about our ups and downs with her, and consequently, our guilt and frustration, instead of tearing us apart, brought us together.

I was upset with myself, however, for exhibiting what I felt was a lack of consistent maternal love for my little girl. One minute I would be irritated by her constant demands on my attention; the next minute I would be flooded with compassion. I despised these inconsistencies on my part and asked God to change my heart. Some days I felt like a lost cause. Why wasn't I able to at least overlook the small things about Sarah that irritated me? I didn't want to admit to myself that the absence of a biological bond made a difference to me. Nor did I want to acknowledge that, although Sarah hugged and kissed me and could even parrot "I love you," her mental limitations meant that her attachment to me would always be superficial.

On some days, Sarah felt like such a burden that I would bitterly complain to Michael: "All I needed right now was this pregnancy! I can't even manage all of the responsibility I already have."

"Things will be all right," he would reply.

Actually, things were about to get much worse.

The timing of this pregnancy was a little chaotic, but Michael and I both felt it would be good for Sarah to have a baby brother or sister so that she might be ahead of someone developmentally. Little Michael, now twelve, rolled his eyes irritably when he heard that there would be yet another child for him to baby-sit. The other four simply took the announcement in stride. Josiah, two and a half, was the exception. He rubbed my tummy every day, saying, "Dis is *my* baby." The new baby was not due until June, which seemed very far away. I had experienced some bleeding during the first few months of pregnancy, but that had stopped. At my last doctor's appointment, the baby's heartbeat had been strong. Halfway through January 1984, however, I wasn't sure whether or not I had felt the baby move, and that worried me.

By February, my concerns had risen to the point where Michael was worried too. On Friday, February 3, Michael went with me to my scheduled checkup and sat by my side while the doctor, then two nurses, all attempted to hear the baby's heartbeat. When they were unable to do so, my doctor ordered a sonogram. And two hours later, he sadly told us that the baby had died, then explained the rough procedure I would have to undergo to deliver the baby.

Unfortunately, I was already familiar with it. Just before Michael and I had moved to Forsyth County, my friend Jean had lost a baby during her sixth month of pregnancy. I remembered vividly her description of the painful effects of the drug given to her to induce labor. It had been, she said, like the worst possible case of stomach flu combined with horrendously intense labor pains. "The only good thing," she had said, "is that it's over fast."

Once Michael and I were in the privacy of our car, we held each other and cried over the loss of our baby. I told Michael that the night before I had stayed up long after he had fallen asleep, praying about the baby. I said that I had asked God to forgive me.

"Forgive you?" he asked. "Forgive you for what?"

"Forgive me, first of all," I said, "for the terrible attitude I've had about Sarah lately. I don't love her like I should, or even like I thought I would. I'm really ashamed about it. I also asked God to forgive me for the way I slandered this baby by saying stupid things like 'That's all I need, to be pregnant now.' I've taken so many things for granted. I guess I thought I could get away with acting so ugly. I see now that I can't. I don't have that right. God never had to allow me one single child, Michael, but in His goodness, He gave me six, almost seven, for which I have been very ungrateful. He needed to show me that He can take a child away as well as give one. I deserve every bit of this punishment."

Michael was alarmed now and grabbed my arm. "God is *not* punishing you, Sally. I struggle with Sarah, too, and I feel guilty. I don't love her the same way I do the boys. You have had a lot on you lately, Sally. We both have. But please believe me: this is not God punishing you."

I sat beside him quietly then, resting in his arms while he rubbed my back. I wished so much that I could fully believe in the less punitive God that Michael was beginning to embrace. As I thought about it some more, Michael *did* seem sincerely convinced that God would not have taken our baby in punishment, but it still sounded too indulgent for me to believe it. Not *hard* enough, I thought to myself sardonically. Yet Michael's tempered words *had* left an impression on me. My feeling of guilt, I found, did not seem as abysmal as it had before.

As I later learned, Michael was not as sure of God's grace for himself as he wanted me to believe. If he was so vehement in assuring me that the baby's death was not an act of divine punishment directed at me, it was mainly because he believed it was an act of divine punishment directed at him. As he would explain to me years later, his agreement to adopt Sarah had been an act of penance; he had hoped that if he willingly took on the challenge of raising a special-needs child, God would deliver him from the sin of homosexuality. Secretly, however, he feared that God *had* taken our baby—as punishment for that sin. Yet, though I was able to share my fears with him, he was unable, as yet, to share his fears with me. He was caught in a complex web of secrets and lies, and he hated to see me bearing the brunt of them. For my part, all I could see at the time was that he was being extremely thoughtful and sensitive to me. I felt that he and I were closer than ever.

Monday came much too quickly. All weekend, I had struggled tremendously. What if it was a mistake, I wondered, and the baby was still alive, with a weak, undetectable heartbeat? If the baby was dead, why hadn't God allowed my body to abort naturally? When I went to the hospital, I shared these concerns with the doctor on call. Somewhat exasperated, he ordered another sonogram. Only the nurse, a woman, seemed to understand my feelings of maternal responsibility. I lay quietly on the table and watched the sonogram screen. As much as it broke my heart, I was convinced by the fuzzy image that the perfectly formed baby was not moving or breathing. Once the screen was turned off, I was able to allow the inevitable procedure to begin.

Apparently Jean had chosen to spare me many details, because delivery was even worse than I had imagined. An hour after the drug was administered, I was completely engulfed in nausea, vomiting, and a fever that continued throughout four hours of insufferable contractions with barely a minute between them. After five births, *this* was a pain I was not sure I could endure. Once I delivered our very small, lifeless son and he had been taken away, I thought about the many times I had longed to deliver a baby naturally, rather than by cesarean. To have to do so now, in such a horribly painful way, without the joy of a baby to hold afterward, seemed cruel. Empty arms, I kept thinking; my arms felt so pathetically empty.

Michael took the baby's remains home and, with our neighbor Stu, buried them in a tiny box in a beautiful spot he and I had chosen. Marked with a large stone, the grave is on top of a hill, surrounded by a patch of wild ferns, only a stone's throw from the cool waters of the creek. In the year that followed, Michael and I and the boys always paused there during our walks in the woods. Even in a freshly fallen snow, we always managed to find the small grave of the baby for whom hello had also meant good-bye.

The stillbirth spelled the beginning of a difficult period. When I returned home from the hospital, I discovered that the tension between Michael and me had grown. Fortunately, the Shores's house had been completed, and they had moved into it while I was in the hospital. I had assumed that their leaving would relieve some of the pressure in our home, but quite the opposite proved to be the case. During the weeks that followed their departure, Michael became unusually curt and impatient with both me and the children, especially Sarah. It was as if the closeness he and I had experienced after the loss of the baby had vanished overnight.

On a particularly bad Saturday, Michael said he had to get away for a few hours—alone. I understood his need, or thought I did, and was relieved to hear him acknowledge that a problem existed. He returned home late in the afternoon, and though his mood had softened, he was pensive. That evening Michael handed me a letter, which I read immediately. I was surprised to discover what a hard and calloused place Michael had come to. As I go back over its contents today, I find Michael's words to be incredibly candid and revealing. If only I could have had the sense to understand what he was trying to tell me then. Michael wrote:

> I hope you can make some sense out of all of this because it will
> be pretty mixed up (because I am). . . . I've not felt the Lord in
> my life for at least two years. I've not felt love or friendship
> from Him, so it's hard to give something out that you don't have
> within you. I hate the last two years and life like it is now. . . . I
> know time is going on and I am *not*. That gets terribly frustrat-
> ing to me so I try to find other outlets in life, like work, or build-
> ing a log house, or my own little world. . . .

Then he wrote about us:

I realize life with me has not been a piece of cake and that the countless, repeated arguments and reconciliations have worn you down and also worn me down. . . . I may just admit defeat in my own ways and go on living with them—or I may go the way of the Lord—easy choice? No, not really. There's too much invested in both, so I'll probably continue to walk the tightrope I've been on, and wait for it to break again. I just don't know. Sometimes I can see where a Darin [Charlene's ex-husband] finally said 'the hell with this Christianity' because it was getting him nowhere.

Sally, I've tried to hang in there with the Lord for whatever reason, pride, love of the Lord, appearance' sake, you, whatever . . . but right now I've just felt like letting go. If the Lord is a reality then He better hold on to me and let me feel his love for me. Seems like a small request for a mighty God.

In the final paragraph, he wrote about friends:

I don't have much to offer. Superficial friendships will do for a while. . . . I've always seen you as my best friend anyway, and probably always will. . . . Sorry! Maybe God can do something in this area—like change my heart?

At the time, I had no idea what Michael was struggling with here, only that his words made me sad. Later I would understand that if he didn't have close friends, it was because he didn't want to develop a closeness to someone who, if he or she discovered Michael's secret, might turn on him in a flash.

One day Michael would tell me about a time, earlier than this, when he had confessed to Stu about his struggles with "occasional bouts of homosexuality." Stu had reacted calmly, advising Michael not to worry, but to simply resist Satan. "Just rise above it, Michael," Stu had said. Ever since then, and especially when "resisting Satan" did not work, Michael had felt awkward around Stu, feeling sometimes that Stu regarded him reproachfully.

The letter's closing sentences were what allowed me to keep my head buried in the sand. He wrote: "My problem is not with you per se. But it seems like all my problems reflect back on you—I'm sorry. I love you." In reading those words my main concern was alleviated. Michael's problem was not with me. He still loved me. If I clung to that, I could fully trust God to work out anything else, couldn't I?

Besides, I was glad for any time Michael opened up to me, so my heart went out toward my husband more than ever. I promised myself to love him more and protect him better. I would pray more fervently for God to do the work in his heart that Michael said he desired. I believed with all of my heart that God would do so, because I believed that He saw Michael's heart and how hard he had been trying. Everything would be fine. It had to be.

As soon as I laid the pages of his letter down, I went to Michael and, wrapping my arms around him, told him that God would be faithful in completing all that He had begun in him. Having gotten his problems out on the table, Michael felt better, even if what he had put on the table had been only enigmatic half-truths. For a while things were better. But the peace lasted only until Michael's level of stress became unbearable, at which time we found ourselves at odds all over again. This situation developed into a destructive cycle that would worsen with each rotation over the next six years.

One morning in early March, I suddenly had an unexplainable need to see Mother and Daddy. Sure that Michael would think it ridiculous to take a trip to the island now, I finally tried to tell him how strongly I felt. He was puzzled at my urgency but agreed to go. When I called Mother and Daddy and told them that we planned on coming for a long weekend, they were very pleased.

The weekend on St. Simons was pleasant, though it was still too chilly to enjoy the ocean. Mother seemed unusually interested in talking to me. One morning at breakfast she began telling me things I had never known about her past, such as the details of her parents' divorce. At the same time, she seemed more anxious and frayed than usual. She had lost a good bit of weight, insisting it was "nothing, just an upset tummy." I also noticed that Mother and Daddy were even more impatient with one another. He was irritable and short with her. I attributed their stress to Daddy's recent diagnosis of a slight heart problem. But Mother did not seem happy, and that bothered me. Throughout the whole weekend with her, I had the distinct feeling she wanted to tell me something but could never bring herself to do so.

One windy afternoon, Mother, Daddy, Michael, and I took the boys, along with Sarah in her umbrella stroller, down to the pier for a walk. Granddaddy Bop had his camera and was taking pictures of little Michael entertaining himself chasing seagulls when suddenly the boy surprised us all by catching one of the birds in his hands! As soon as his granddaddy took a picture, little Michael let the squawking bird go. Afterward, Daddy took a group photo of us on the pier that day—the last one ever taken of Mother with my family. Now, reading and rereading that picture like a mystery novel, I still search for signs of illness and wonder whether, if we had noticed such signs, we would have been able to save her life. I'll never know for sure. But I do know that, at least to some extent, Mother chose when and when not to fight for her life.

Michael and I and the children enjoyed the weekend with Mother and Daddy. On Sunday, I found it especially hard to say good-bye. Soon, however, we were crossing the bridge back to the mainland. "Thank you again for taking us down to the island so spur-of-the-moment like that," I said.

"No problem . . . but why do you think you got so upset when we were leaving?"

"I don't know. It's just that I'm going to miss them." I was starting to cry again. "I really can't explain it."

On the way home from the island, I settled down in the car to read a book that my friend Scarlett had given me. The book was *A Wrinkle in Time,* and the author was Madeleine L'Engle. Many fundamental Christians did not allow their children to read it because it contained references to witches and because one of the characters was a medium; their fear of their children's being deceived by such things was very strong. A few years later I would hear Madeleine L'Engle speak, and she would brilliantly explain, "Oh—but I always tell them that she's a *happy* medium!" I was ashamed to admit to my less inhibited friend that even though I was an adult, I was a little afraid to read the book. Yet I had finally made up my mind to ignore my apprehensions. While Michael drove for seven hours and the children slept, I read *A Wrinkle in Time* in its entirety.

I was so engrossed in what I was reading that when Michael looked over at me and said, "The book's really good, huh?" I could only smile and nod my head yes. When we were not too far from home, I finished the book, laid it down on my lap, and began to cry.

"What's wrong?" Michael asked. "Did it end sadly?"

"No," I told him. "I just realized what a tiny box I've been keeping God in. Madeleine L'Engle's book was full of so many spiritual possibilities I never would have imagined had I not read it. We really are such a small part of a much bigger picture, Michael. It makes me feel foolish that I think I know so much when—in fact—I don't know much at all!"

Puzzled by my impassioned answer, Michael smiled and said, "Yeah, I guess that's true," then patted my knee reassuringly.

I was entirely serious. Madeleine L'Engle's book had presented me with a new perspective on God. Though a work of fiction, it had enlarged my view of possible goings-on in the vast universe created and sustained by God. In the book, evil was present and powerful, and though it was terribly frightening for the characters in the story to be caught in an unknown spiritual realm, the fact was that each time evil deceived or hurt them, the enormous power of love always prevailed. It would still be several years before I would be liberated entirely from my fear of deception, yet after reading *A Wrinkle in Time*, I felt that I had at least begun to "set God free." And, in the process, I had also opened myself up to discovering things about Him that would both surprise and delight me. Though unaware of it, I was very close to experiencing the real power and truth in Christ's assurance that "you shall know the truth, and the truth shall set you free" (John 8:32).

Mother's first signs of illness seemed innocent enough. When at first she complained only of pain in her back that ran down her left leg, her doctor diagnosed it as an inflammation of her sciatic nerve. That was the end of March. By the first of April the pain had become so intense, and Mother so unstable on her feet, that she was hospitalized. She was extremely disoriented and had severe vomiting.

Whenever Camille or I called Daddy to check on Mother, he assured us both that she would be home from the hospital any day. So I was completely taken aback one day when my niece, visiting my parents from Australia, called in a panic and said, "Grandmother's really bad off, Sally. Either you or Camille must come down here. Something's not right. She's not getting any better and I don't know what to do." I told her not to worry. Camille and I would be there as fast as we could.

After making some hasty arrangements for the children—Michael was away on business—I picked up Camille and we headed to St. Simons late that afternoon. Neither Camille nor I was prepared for the frightful state in which we found our mother. The closer we got to her hospital room, the more oppressive the air became in the hallway, until finally we stopped and prayed for strength before seeing her. As we slowly pushed the door open, Camille and I could see Mother on her bed. Curled up in a fetal position, with her fingers tightly clasped around the side rails, she barely resembled the woman either of us had last seen.

As Camille and I leaned over to give her a kiss, Mother slowly opened her eyes and attempted a smile. "How are you, girls?" she asked, her voice a small, birdlike one that seemed to fit her emaciated body. "You girls didn't need to leave your families to come down here." That was a comment to be expected from Mother, who considered imposing on anyone despicable, and who hated to be caught without her lipstick on. How much she must have despised being seen in a tacky hospital gown with her hair not done. Camille and I told her that we loved her, that our families were fine, and that we wanted to be there. She was asleep in seconds.

Later that night, I called Michael and tried to explain what we were up against. I told him I wasn't sure when I'd be back. I couldn't think of another time when I had dropped everything at home in Michael's lap without warning. Promising that I'd call the next day, after we had spoken with Mother's doctor, I said, "Give the boys and Sarah my love. I love you."

"I love you, too. Hurry and come home."

At the hospital the next day, Mother and Daddy's family doctor took Camille and me into the hall and shocked us by saying that it was our *father* we needed to worry about. "Bob has angina, an aneurysm in his aorta, and some cirrhosis of the liver. He is a walking time bomb!"

"Well, what about Mother?" I asked the doctor.

"Oh," he said much too nonchalantly, "your mother will be fine. Lucy's a strong woman." Strong woman? I almost laughed. Were we talking about the same Lucy Lowe? "She may have had a slight stroke," he continued. "Now—go on and take care of that father of yours. Just leave your mother alone and let her get some rest." He strolled away then, leaving us to stare at each other.

Camille and I could read each other's minds easily. We were both wondering: is this doctor crazy? What he said about Daddy was true—but we couldn't accept the verdict that Mother was fine. Slowly we walked back to her room, where we spent the day. Mother mostly slept, and Daddy mostly read the newspaper. That night, as early as we could, we persuaded him to go home. Then Camille and I settled ourselves down on the surprisingly filthy carpeted floor to spend the night beside Mother's bed. Before trying to get some sleep, Camille and I agreed that the doctor could forget one thing for sure: we would not leave Mother alone.

The next thing we knew, Mother's doctor called in a specialist, who at once determined that Mother had had a stroke and told Camille and me to just wait it out. "Try to encourage her to do normal things," he said. "Encourage her to eat!"

After our niece returned to Australia, Camille and I began to work on Mother. Since we'd been there, Mother had refused anything more than a few bites of soft food. She had also made it clear she hated riding in a wheelchair. Though she said it was because it hurt her stomach to sit up, we assumed she didn't want anyone to see her. So Camille and I came up with a bribe. After making one trip with her around her hospital floor, we would offer, "Mother, if you promise you'll eat, we'll take you back to your room." It worked every time. However, after every forced bite of food, Mother would cry that her stomach hurt and beg us not to make her eat.

For several days we continued to think we were doing a good thing, coercing our frail mother to eat. It was only when her bladder and bowels began emptying onto the floor every time we held Mother up that we began to think we had made a mistake. Slowly Camille and I began to discuss the disturbing possibility that maybe this was not a simple stroke. When we mentioned to Daddy that perhaps Mother needed more-qualified doctors and should be transferred to Emory Hospital in Atlanta, he became irate. "Savannah has the best research doctors around. As good as the Mayo Clinic!" he proudly informed us.

"Fine," I sighed. I knew one thing—any place would be better than the hospital we were in.

The night before Mother was to be moved to Savannah, she awoke at about two o'clock, looked at Camille and me, and said, "Let's split, girls! Let's get out of here." Camille and I laughed so hard we had to bury our faces in the grimy carpet. Who was this woman who used words like *split*? Surely not *our* dignified mother. Had we known then that the disease that was eagerly ravaging her body had already begun its assault on her neurological system, her odd words would not have amused us so. Sadly, we would never know Mother to be any more lucid than she was that night.

At St. Joseph's Hospital, in Savannah, Georgia, Mother underwent a myriad of tests, each of which took a toll on her kidneys and other organs. After several weeks, we all began to wonder if she would die from her illness or from the grueling search for its cause. Though her condition never improved, my sister and I tried to find encouragement in even the smallest thing.

Night after night Daddy would sit by Mother's bed in the intensive-care unit, badgering her loudly, "Squeeze my hand if you love me!" Mother was so weak by then, but Camille and I wondered if she didn't summon up one slight squeeze just to hush him. After she obliged, Daddy would fall completely apart. We would have to pry him, sobbing, away from her bed. When, in a few weeks, Mother eventually slipped into a coma, Daddy sat by her bed repeating angrily, as though she were betraying him, "Wake up, dummy. Wake up!" My sister and I looked at each other then. She asked me, "If your husband was sitting by your bed while you were in a coma, saying 'Wake up, dummy,' would *you* wake up?" We both knew the answer.

Toward the end of May, the doctors still had not come up with a diagnosis and Mother's condition had grown even more grave. Our sister flew in from Australia and joined our round-the-clock vigil. We did not have much of a chance to talk about the last ten years of separation; there were many important decisions to be made about Mother, especially as Daddy became less and less able to cope with what now seemed inevitable.

One morning early in June, as my sisters and I were getting up from the recliners we had been using as beds in the ICU waiting room, we saw Mother's kind doctor approaching with a smile on his face. "I have some cautiously good news for you!" he told us. "I cannot give you a reason why, but your mother is awake and she seems to be fairly alert. We have no idea what caused this, nor do we know how long it will last, but I have left instructions for your family to have unlimited visiting time today." He shook our hands and walked away with decided enthusiasm in his gait.

We ran to the motel to get Daddy, then returned as quickly as possible to begin visiting Mother. Daddy was first, of course, and he visited her alone. After he stepped out my sisters and I entered, one person at a time. Finally it was my turn to go in and join my sisters. As I slipped in behind the closed curtains surrounding Mother's bed, I felt almost timid. But as soon as I saw her I was filled with awe. As I stood at the foot of Mother's bed, my hand just barely touching her covered foot, everything seemed to be moving in slow motion. Was this a dream? I wondered. I looked at Camille, who smiled knowingly at me then, as if to say, "It's okay to move closer; she's real." I took one step and Mother's eye caught mine. Her face lit up instantly, like a beacon lighting my way home. "Sally," she cried out to me in greeting, her voice a raspy whisper but still filled with incredible love. "How *are* you? How are Michael and all of the children?" I was quickly drawn to her then.

I felt I had to kiss her cheek, breathing tube or not, before she—what? Vanished? It was ethereal. Magical. I bent down, and as I smelled her skin and felt its dewy softness, I knew that, despite all of the absurdities she had endured, she was still *distinctly* Mother.

I will never forget the sense of peace that emanated from my mother, a woman whose countenance had always been marked by stress and anxiety. Her tranquillity was real, almost tangible, and it filled the room. Mother had an aura that I can only describe as blissful. This was what Camille and I had prayed with Mother for, a peace that passeth all understanding. Now she had it and was passing its goodness on to us.

On the morning of June 10, Camille and I were having coffee in the cafeteria before we began our daily vigil with Mother. It had become imperative to Camille and me that we be with Mother when she died, so now we were never far from her room. We saw the nurse approach, and we knew what her words would be before she reached our table. "It's time," she said. "You'll have to hurry."

Holding each other's hand, Camille and I entered Mother's room more boldly now than we had that first time a little over two months before. Gradually, we had become accustomed to the feel of death, and the fear of it could no longer shock us. We had been there for only a few minutes when we both suddenly knew that her life force had slipped from her body, just like a vapor, and that the essence of Mother was not there. Only the shell of her life, her visual body, was left behind. Knowing it could no longer feel any pain, we each laid our heads upon her chest one more time, just to feel our mother, and then we left to go to our older sister and Daddy.

It was a holy thing to be with my mother as she breathed her last breath, even as she had been with me as I breathed my first. We had completed a circle, and now I felt intricately tied to her as I had not before. We had shared one birth and one death together. My only regret would always be that we had not shared a lot more of life.

Michael was in a dark mood when I returned home. I assumed that it had to do with my absence, or perhaps with his professional situation. One of the companies for which he was a manufacturer's representative had decided to let him go. That meant a loss of one-third of our income, which meant added pressure on us all. My return home did not seem to make him any happier. Michael and I finally talked to each other and agreed that neither of us could understand any longer what God was doing in our lives. We had spent so many years expecting

James Smith to speak to us on God's behalf that we didn't recognize His voice anymore ourselves. I told Michael that I no longer knew what to believe about God. Our relationship with the Shores had become even more stressful. And both Michael and I felt ourselves at an impasse with Sarah. All in all, we both felt we were approaching the end of ourselves.

My friend Jean and her husband, Pat, had recently received counseling from a place called Grace Fellowship International. The counseling center had no denominational affiliation, and the counselors, though not certified therapists, had each completed an extensive Christian counseling training session. Jean and Pat insisted that the counseling had completely changed their lives and begged us to try it. It was obvious we needed something. I made an appointment for us to go together that very week.

As Michael and I poured out our past spiritual journey, Glen, our counselor, listened intently, often looking as though he were in pain. Afterward, he said, "You guys are in desperate need of reprogramming. We need to get rid of those 'old tapes' you're listening to over and over in your heads and replace them with a completely new set. It sounds as though you know very little about God's unlimited grace and even less about His unconditional love."

Michael and I looked at each other. Then Michael said, "We know something—though not much—about God's grace. But, from what we know about God's love—it's *definitely* conditional."

During our months of relearning with Glen, Michael and I often spoke about the new revelations we were experiencing about God. One day I said, "I don't see God as being nearly as punitive as I used to, Michael. In fact, I think a lot of what we used to beat ourselves up about as sin was really just part of being human. I don't think God made nearly the big deal out of it that we did!"

"I agree. What we're learning now *feels* more right than anything we've ever been taught in the past—besides the fact that it makes a lot more sense, you know?"

"Yes, and it makes me mad that we bought into it *all*—hook, line, and sinker!"

"Especially the *sinker* part," Michael added sarcastically. "James really did mislead us for a long time."

"Well, at least it feels like we're growing again spiritually, you know? Sometimes I think I can almost hear God's sigh of relief," I said hopefully. "I still believe that old saying is true: 'God takes us the easiest way *we* will go.'"

Even though in our ignorance we sometimes chose difficult paths for ourselves, I had seen that God still works out His plan for our lives along the way. As Michael and I became more tolerant with ourselves and loosened our tight hold on life, we enjoyed life, and each other, more.

Yet though Michael had eagerly accepted the teachings of Grace Fellowship, he still seemed so full of unexplainable discontent. At this point, I felt only saddened and worried for him, but before long my feelings would change to resentment, then to rage.

In September, Michael and I went away on a weekend trip together to Williamsburg with our old friends from Lambs' Chapel, Chuck and Lou Ellen. We had a wonderful time together shopping and touring Old Williamsburg, but on the way home I watched as an unhappiness seemed to unfold over Michael. I hated to see this happening and could not understand what it was about our life that he found so unbearable. I wrote in my journal:

> Where is the Michael that I glimpsed this past weekend away together? He was so neat, and I felt so in love with him. But the "Michael" that began again as we drove home (the headache, the uptightness, the anger, the nervousness, etc.) is the one I am really afraid for. I don't know how much longer I can watch him get worse and worse—so unhappy, so miserable. No joy. I'm afraid that he feels hopeless again.

Not long after that, I discovered that I was once again pregnant. As seemed to happen, every time I learned I was pregnant, Michael was immediately returned to his old smiling self. The responsibility, as well as the joy, of having another child always anchored Michael and, and I was later to discover, gave him the incentive to abstain from his secret life . . . at least for a time.

Michael and I were at last enjoying our faith more and had begun to look for a church that would be a joyful place to worship. We had heard about a church, Calvary Chapel, one of many nondenominational chapels that had been founded in California by a pastor named Chuck Smith. Calvary Chapel also had a small Christian school. Michael and I were thinking of entering little Michael into the school

in eighth grade the next fall, so we decided to attend a Sunday service
at the church.

We were impressed. The pastor, Norman Jones, proved to be an
unassuming man of about forty with a pleasant, ready smile and a
head of white hair. We were pleased by his sermon, in which he used
several of the diagrams that were also used in Grace Fellowship counseling to illustrate God's unconditional love and grace. After the service, Michael and I spoke with Norman, who told us he had also gone
through Grace Fellowship counseling. We appreciated his sharing
openly with us. Norman assured us that he believed so strongly in the
message being taught at Grace that he planned to incorporate it into
many of his sermons at Calvary Chapel. Michael and I were happy to
hear that. Though we both agreed that the congregation lacked enthusiasm during the worship time, we still thought Calvary might be a
good place for us, at least for now.

So we began attending Calvary regularly. One Sunday, Norman
asked, "Where were y'all last involved in church?"

"Have you ever heard of James Smith?" Michael asked in return.

To our surprise, he frowned and said, "Yes, I know him."

Michael went on to tell Norman we had been involved in the
Hebrews Six Fellowship for eight years and that it had done quite a bit
of damage to us spiritually. Norman laughed sympathetically: "Yeah, I
would imagine that a steady diet of James Smith would make anyone
sick!" Michael and I looked at each other and smiled.

As a result of our Grace Fellowship counseling, Michael and I had
found a considerable amount of freedom from the legalism we had
operated with for so long under James Smith's authority. It felt great
not to be as concerned with measuring up. Calvary Chapel was still
strongly fundamental in its beliefs, but that suited us fine as long as it
operated without the constraint of a pastor like James.

Soon Norman had Michael leading a home-group meeting (which
was set up in much the same way as the cell-group meetings Michael
had led in Hebrews Six) in our home every Friday night. The group
started with about four or five couples and quickly grew to twenty-
four people strong. The Shores began to come to the home-group
meetings, though it was several months before they joined Calvary
Chapel as well. With Stu and Becky there, it seemed like old times—
except better. In home group, we spent a long time in worship, which
was led by a new friend from Calvary Chapel named Blake. Something—I didn't know what—had drawn me and Blake's wife, Joy, to

each other during one of our first Sundays at Calvary. Michael seemed to like Blake and also seemed happy to be leading a group again. He led very loosely, which sometimes upset Norman, who tended to like to lend a little more structure than Michael did. But Norman laid his personal expectations aside and was, at first, able to give Michael pretty much a free rein. We began spending a lot of time with Blake and Joy, talking about the Lord and sharing about each of our past spiritual experiences. When Michael and I described the worship at Lambs' Chapel to our new friends, their faces lit up. How much they longed to worship God freely, they told us. Maybe, we suggested, Norman would be interested in allowing more freedom in the worship at Calvary Chapel—allowing the songs to be started spontaneously by anyone in the congregation and more freedom to clap and move with the spirit. Michael and Blake agreed to talk to Norman. When they did he was cautious but said he was "open to whatever God wants for Calvary."

Summer came at last, but our baby was not due until August. I thought that between the gross, muggy Georgia heat and my huge belly, I might suffocate. Michael and I had decided that this baby would for sure be our last. However, my doctor did not believe we were serious and laughed every time I reminded him I wanted my tubes tied during delivery.

August 13, 1985, finally arrived, and with it came the birth of Frank Samuel, who weighed seven pounds, eight ounces. Michael and I had decided to name him Samuel, which meant "consecrated to God."

We were in the delivery room and things were moving along in routine fashion until I heard the obstetrician, who was opening my uterus at the time, suddenly let out a *whoops!*

"Why did you just yell *whoops?*" I asked, ridiculously trying to lean forward to see. Michael put his hand on me gently.

"Oh, it's nothing," the doctor said, not wanting to alarm me. "My finger just slipped through the wall of your uterus, that's all. No big deal. The wall's a little thin from all of the births you have had. Good thing you decided on a tubal ligation. This uterus wouldn't make it through another pregnancy."

Michael and I looked at each other, both thinking that God had confirmed our decision not to have any more babies. It helped a lot to know that I couldn't carry another one even if I wanted to. Michael brought Samuel to me now. "He looks a lot like Timothy," he said. All I knew was that God had given us yet another beautiful son. I was, as always, in awe of that fact. I could see by the way Michael looked at him that this last son was going to be particularly special to him.

At my six-week checkup the nurse told me what had really happened in delivery: "Sally, the doctor put his whole *fist* through your uterus! It's a miracle that you carried Samuel to term." I was shocked.

In a moment, the doctor came in and confirmed the nurse's report. "Sally, you'd better be glad you and Michael decided to stop with this one," he added. I assured him that I was. I looked down at my precious little son asleep in his infant seat. "Thank you, God," I prayed silently, "for blessing us with one last baby boy."

chapter 8

More Than One Answer to These Questions

"Can I *please* watch *A-Team* on TV tonight?" little Michael asked.

"I've explained to you how un-Christlike violence is, son," his daddy answered. "Let me ask you a question: would Jesus want you to watch that show?"

"No, sir, He wouldn't."

"Okay then, let's not ask about it again."

"Yes, sir."

While our sons occasionally questioned a specific regulation, they accepted everything we presented to them as spiritual truth. Each of them had made a personal commitment to Jesus as Lord and Savior (by praying the "sinner's prayer"—either with their father or me, or during an "altar call" at church camp, or, in the case of little Michael, with his fourth-grade teacher), and as a result, the conflicts that came up were usually easily resolved. Whether or not our sons' beliefs were purely imitative or the result of sincere commitment—or perhaps a combination of the two—they usually lived their Christian lives out just as zealously as their parents did.

For the most part Michael's and my brand of Christianity, with its narrow boundaries and tight restrictions, gave our children the same false sense of security that it gave us. That sense, combined with the blissful ignorance all children operate in, led them to believe that if you are a Christian, none of the "bad things in the world" can happen in your life. Believing that we should spare our children from the spiritual disillusionment we faced, Michael and I didn't tell them that we now seriously questioned the legalism we had embraced as the only truth for so long. Our decision to keep that a secret from them would only make it more difficult, of course, when we were forced to tell them later.

I took a special delight in Samuel during those first few days and weeks, even staying home from church longer than was necessary to spend time alone with him. Michael spent a lot of time holding and talking to Samuel, too. Together, he and I talked about how much we were going to miss having babies.

Eventually the time came when I had to begin school with Daniel, Matthew, and Timothy, all of whom were still being home-schooled. I had decided to move slowly during the first few weeks, in order to give everyone time to adjust to a new schedule—especially me.

On September 4, however, our unhurried days were abruptly pulled up short when I answered the phone and heard Mac, Michael's oldest brother, telling me that their youngest sister, Margaret, had died suddenly at work.

"What?! How? I can't believe it, Mac."

"I know," he said, his voice dropping. "It doesn't seem possible, does it? Apparently, she told her boss she didn't feel well, and that she thought she would sit down for a minute—and then she fell over and died instantly."

Still very shaken and dazed, I hung up the phone and told the children now looking at me intently from over their schoolbooks that their aunt Margaret had died. Seeing the disbelief and sorrow on their faces while they cried and hugged me, and each other, I worried about how much worse it was going to be to tell little Michael. He and Margaret had always had such an exceptionally close relationship— more like brother and sister than nephew and aunt. Over the years, the two of them had never lost their uncanny ability to enjoy each other's silly antics. He would be crushed to hear of her death.

I finally managed to locate big Michael, who was away on business at a store he sold to, and told him about Margaret. He came so completely undone that I now worried about him driving safely home. As soon as he came in the door that afternoon, we held each other close and cried.

I later learned that from the time of Samuel's birth until about six months after Margaret's death, Michael was in one of the periods where he was able to deny himself gay sex. Although he had long ago moved beyond his first timid flirtations with gay life and had, both with Don and the former priest, experienced gay life on a fuller level, Michael still was not about to throw away our secure life together in order to claim another. Instead, he had promised God once again that he would stop his secret life. After hearing about God's unfailing love through Grace Fellowship counseling, Michael felt that he had true reason to hope that a God of unconditional love would not condemn him to an entire life of inner conflict. There had to be a way out. He would come to see that there was a way out—but not in the way he expected.

As for me, I had come to the conclusion that I really needed to love my husband for who he was.

> September 15, 1985: For some time now the Lord has shown me what a wonderful man Michael is. In fact, if he never changed "for the better," or never "grew" anymore at all—he'd still be wonderful just as he is. I want him to feel secure, and to know that as least his life at home is stable and under control.

Having recently read and reread Madeleine L'Engle's poem "To a Long Loved Love: 7," I had quoted Michael the first two lines— "Because you are not what I would have you to be / I blind myself to who, in truth, you are"—and then promised him that I was going to try to love him for exactly who he was, not for who I wanted him to be. I had no idea then just what that would come to mean.

Before long, however, I began having what I thought were irrational fears about Michael.

> November 30, 1985: Lately I find my mind dreaming up fears, stupid fears. Sometimes I feel like I'm on borrowed time with my husband, just "knowing" that one day something will take him from me! The other night, I could not sleep because of my fears, so I asked God to put a "hedge of protection" around Michael (just in case any of my fears were grounded)—especially while he traveled. I was able to sleep then.

I was beginning to feel that maybe I was crazy. One minute I felt great about Michael and was certain we were going to have a wonderful life together. The next minute I felt totally insecure and wondered whether we would be together forever or not. I could not understand why I had these mood swings. It had not occurred to me yet that my moods were directly related to his. I blamed them on myself and my inability to be consistent. And of course I prayed for God to do a work in my heart—again.

By the spring, however, certain problems seemed to be approaching a crisis point. Our relationship with the Shores had deteriorated to the extent that we were strongly considering moving away from them. One afternoon while sitting on the front porch talking about where we might move, Michael proposed an amazing idea. "Why don't we just sell the house, buy a Winnebago, and travel across the country for a year with the kids?"

"Uh-huh," I said. "Wait—are you serious?"

"Yeah, I am sort of. Just think what a great education it would be for the boys!"

"You know . . . I really want to support you and be excited about whatever you decide is good for our family. But this time I really think you've gone around the bend! Do you honestly think that would be a good plan—even with Sarah? Michael! Nine people in a Winnebago?"

"Okay, so it'd be tight. I still think it'd be great to travel around the country like that. And I just do not like where we are now. I don't know, Sally." He stopped and then added, "I just want to do something that's really *right* for us, you know?"

I was immediately worried that he was running away from God. "Okay, but how do you know it's what we're *supposed* to do, Michael? Have you prayed about it?"

"No . . . I don't know. Can't I simply have an idea without it having to be a major spiritual decision?!" Suddenly the tension between us was heavy. We both knew an argument was about to erupt, so we let the subject drop.

Fortunately, Michael soon completely dropped the idea of traveling around with nine people in a camper. Yet his unrest and dissatisfaction remained.

Even though Michael and I were happy at Calvary Chapel, the worship there was still not as free as we had hoped it would be. Joy and Blake, who had become close friends, shared our desire for freer worship.

At about that time, Michael heard about a workshop on worship that was being held at a church in the North Carolina mountains. After we told Blake and Joy about it, the four of us enthusiastically decided to attend. The workshop was wonderful. Joy and I were absolutely entranced with something called "interpretive dance." We stood together and marveled as dance teams put on performances that combined ballet with drama in a godly, passionate way. We could easily see how having interpretive dance as part of a service could deepen the congregation's worship time with God. The stirring music and dramatized lyrics, together with the simple abandonment of the dancers, all moved me toward God in a way I had not experienced even at Lambs' Chapel.

Joy and I—both of whom shared a background in ballet—believed that together we could choreograph and write a script for interpretive dance. Michael and Blake were just as eager as Joy and I were to persuade Pastor Norman Jones to allow us to form a dance team at Calvary Chapel.

With some reservation, Norman gave his permission, and Joy and I wasted no time in announcing to the congregation that we were forming an interpretive-dance team. Soon we had six or eight women who were interested, and Joy and I began meeting together one night a week to work on the dances. The church gave us enough money to purchase material to make costumes, banners, and streamers. We took yards of brightly colored satin and cut them into long strips, which the dancers drew gracefully through the air as we danced. Most of the time we danced barefoot, and our costumes were simple: white shirts with loose slipover jumpers.

The first time we danced before the congregation it was magical. Still, we were all anxious as to how the congregation would respond. And at first there was resistance from some members, who preferred a quieter, more orderly style of worship. After they had experienced the gentle power of interpretive dance a few more times, however, most of them changed their minds.

In dance, Joy and I were kindred spirits. It was something that had been in both of our hearts since we were small, and now we had found a way to use it to worship Jesus. Neither of us could have been any happier than we were when we choreographed dances together and then shared them with the enthusiastic women who had joined the team. She and I continued to enjoy the Lord in dance until, as all too often happens, "man" (as opposed to God) decided that he had to control it.

I didn't want to see the first sign of that happening. As the worship leader at Calvary, Blake (the authority having been delegated to him by Norman) had the final say-so over all matters pertaining to worship. One day, out of the blue, he said, "I think I'm going to have to have the last say about what is and isn't proper for women to wear while dancing before the body [i.e., the church]. I'm going to need to see each dancer in costume before she will be allowed to dance."

"I think you are absolutely wrong, Blake," I said. "Why on earth shouldn't Joy and I be completely entrusted with knowing what's appropriate for the dancers to wear?"

"Well, Sally, I can probably trust you to decide what's too short or too tight, or what material can be seen through, but to tell you the truth, I'm not sure I can trust Joy in the same way." He had said this in front of his wife, and the hurt on her face broke my heart.

Not only was Joy hurt by her husband's lack of trust in her, but worse, she knew that I was right. Nonetheless, she believed she had to be submissive to her husband, which, in turn, meant I had to be, too. Joy hated the conflict that her submissiveness to her husband produced in me, but even worse she hated the wedge that had been placed between Blake and me.

"Why, Joy?" I asked her later when Blake was not around. "Why does Blake feel like that? I can't imagine Michael ever not trusting me, and certainly not thinking he would know better than I would what a woman should wear to dance in before God!"

Joy told me then, tearfully, about her "wild life before coming to the Lord." She had been married once before, had divorced, and had been into drugs. Her dress then, she said, had reflected her lifestyle. After becoming a Christian, she met Blake, who had led a strict Baptist life and who, though he loved her and wanted to marry her, was very taken aback by what she told him about her former life.

"When we decided to get married," Joy said with an embarrassed laugh, "Blake literally went through my closet and threw out all of the clothes he thought were inappropriate for me to wear as a Christian."

I was sick with humiliation for my friend. "But Joy, that was a long time ago. You have two children now, and you dress both them and yourself completely modestly! I still don't see why Blake doesn't trust you now."

"Well," she said, "I guess I really don't either, except that I think Blake is afraid that if I am given a little bit of freedom, I'll backslide into my old 'wicked ways.'"

Having no idea where my sudden furor and boldness came from, I said, "That's totally ridiculous!" Joy didn't say anything, but her message was clear: ridiculous or not, she was going to remain submissive to Blake. I feared the consequences, but for the time being I didn't argue with her any further.

I did, however, discuss it with Michael. "Blake's attitude makes me wonder what I even think about total submission anymore—both in marriage and to spiritual authority," I said.

"I know it does, and I feel the same way. From all we went through in James Smith's group, and then after the counseling at Grace Fellowship, my views about it have changed a lot."

"Michael, it makes me sick to see the terrible mental and spiritual anguish that kind of raw submission is creating in Joy! Why is Blake doing that to her—and why is Norman allowing it?"

"I'm afraid it's a lot about power and control," Michael said. "And I think it was *man's* doing, not God's. Now that we see how wrong it all is, we've got to be careful not to buy into the idea of extreme submission again ourselves."

"I agree," I said, and I meant it. Once again, however, disregarding an old principle felt "loose" and scary to me. But I had only to think about my beloved friend Joy to remind myself of why I *had* to let it go.

Michael and I soon asked Norman if he did in fact agree with Blake's decision about the dance team, and one evening the five of us all sat down to discuss the problem together. After Michael and I strongly protested Blake's decision, Norman, who looked a little surprised at Blake's demands, said, "Knowing Joy's past, I can understand—though not necessarily agree with—Blake's concerns."

"I just think we need to be very careful," Blake said. "The dancers are a part of the service to worship and please God. The last thing we want is for their dress to be such that it could cause a man to stumble into lustful thoughts!"

"I agree with you, Blake. But I also need to remind you of what a submissive and godly wife and mother Joy has become. I do think that, along with Sally, you can certainly trust her in this." Michael and I kept quiet while waiting for Blake's response.

"Well, Norman, I'll *try* delegating the dress decisions to Joy and Sally. We'll see how it goes, okay?"

That last comment infuriated me all over again. Blake was being completely patronizing, and I felt as if Joy and I would be laboring with Big Brother constantly watching over our shoulders. Knowing how I was feeling, Michael said, "Well, Blake, I hope you can see your way clear to trust your own wife. I certainly know I could."

Big Brother did watch, and never for a minute did he let us forget he was in control.

As a result of our discussions about submission and because we heard he was starting another discipleship group, Michael and I decided we needed to talk to James Smith. We felt we needed to let him know how much damage our days in Hebrews Six had caused us. We wanted to try to do so before James inflicted the same harm on another group. Since the disbanding of the Hebrews Six Fellowship there had been at least two divorces among former members, and there were many others besides us who had had to undergo some sort of extensive spiritual healing before they could have a healthy relationship with God. Michael and I still loved James and Laura very much, but we felt compelled to "risk the relationship," just as James had taught us long ago to do, in order to tell him how we felt.

Michael and I first wrote James a letter outlining our feelings, in which we said, in part: "James, while we were under you in Hebrews Six, no doubt God accomplished some very good things in our lives—such as a strong commitment to Christ, to our marriage, and to the fellowship. But, at the same time, believing your word to be God's for so many years crippled us in our ability to hear God for ourselves." After receiving the letter James called us, and we met with him and Laura over dinner to discuss its contents.

James maintained a coolheaded, defensive attitude throughout the evening. I found myself thinking, however, that he looked completely worn-out and tired of life. This man who once seemed terribly intimidating to me now seemed harmless—almost vulnerable—and for some reason that made me feel uncomfortable.

James listened intensely, but quietly, as Michael spoke candidly to him: "There was always such an absence of any reference to God's love and grace in your messages, James. Sally and I have come to believe that His love and grace are much more plentiful than His wrath is. Your messages were always so full of doom and gloom, and we just don't see it like that anymore. You may not have known it, but in the last days of Hebrews Six, people often commented that when you spoke it seemed as though a dark cloud surrounded you. It was oppressive, James."

At this point, Laura broke down in tears and cried out to James, "How many lives *have* you ruined in the last ten years?!"

Under the table, James reached over and squeezed his wife's knee in an effort to quiet her. "Well," he said, "I never pretended that my messages were easy to receive—or to give, for that matter." Laura continued to cry softly, but in a moment I saw that she had placed her hand on top of his.

Laura must feel awful, I thought to myself, to love her husband as much as I knew she did and yet know in her heart that his "words" were far too morose for anyone to endure anymore. Looking at James, it occurred to me that even James himself would not be able to endure them much longer.

"I can't agree with what you say God has shown you about his love and grace, though both are certainly available for us," James said. "I still fear that many use that fact as an excuse for sin, and it is to that that I have to speak. However, in an effort to instruct you as I believe God had me do, sometimes I might have been too harsh on you and others. For that, and for ever having hurt you, I am truly sorry."

"We forgive you, James," Michael said softly. "And if we've ever hurt either of you, we apologize too." We sat there quietly for a few minutes; then someone finally said it was time to go. On the way home, Michael said, "Well, that was sad."

"Yeah, it was. And you know something? I will always wonder if James really believes what he preaches or if he knows darn well it's not true."

Summer came at last, and with it our yearly weeklong vacation to St. Simons Island for a week. The weather on the island was perfect that year—not too hot, but no rain either to spoil days on the beach. Everyone, including Michael, seemed to relax more that year. Besides which, he and I had one of our nicest times ever on the island, playing with the children and lying on the beach reading and soaking up the sun.

Once home, Michael and I faced the need to make a decision about the children's schooling. Little Michael, now ready to begin high school, was begging us to let him attend public school. Our only worry was that he might not yet be ready to stand firmly on his own. One day little Michael came to his father and me to pose a serious question: "I believe that I'm a strong Christian and that I know who I am, both in Christ and in this family. Would you please give me the chance to prove to you and to the Lord that I can be strong even in public school?" It was a remarkably mature speech, and after hearing it, we agreed to let him give it a try.

Daniel and Matthew were now clamoring to be allowed to attend public school as well. After checking out the elementary school, Michael and I discovered that we liked it very much and decided to place Daniel in sixth grade and Matthew in fourth grade.

We also found that Sarah was eligible for kindergarten as a part of the school's "mainstream" program. That news came as a relief to me, as I had long since realized I could not possibly teach Sarah at home.

That fall, when the yellow school bus stopped at the foot of our driveway, Michael and I watched Daniel and Matthew and Sarah climb on board. Big Michael then took little Michael and registered him for high school. I watched them all leave, and of course I cried. After which I pulled myself together and began the first day of teaching Timothy. Watching him that morning as he worked assiduously on his phonics at the dining-room table, I thought to myself that if Josiah and Samuel would allow me to, I would enjoy getting to know this particular child of mine who, so far, had been so undemanding. Ever since he was very small, Timothy had always hatched the most unbelievable stories, including ones about his imaginary friend John

Peter—who, of course, was always to blame for any of Timothy's misbehavior. I hoped that his spontaneous creativity had not been lost.

Little Michael had very few problems adjusting to public high school. True to his promise, he did not compromise his Christianity even if it made him unpopular. Daniel adjusted well to sixth grade, except that, like me, he was sometimes told he asked too many questions.

Matthew went to school with bold Christian buttons pinned onto his shirts. One read, Choose Life; another had the word *Devil* with a slash through it. Sometimes he wore a T-shirt that had God Is Awesome printed across the front. At first I wondered if Matthew's zealousness would make it more difficult for him to make friends, but that was no problem. Matthew made several really nice friends in fourth grade who would remain his friends through high school.

At bedtime Matthew would be full of questions about matters that, because of what he had heard about them in school, he found deeply troubling. One night, as his daddy and I stood by his bunk bed, having just heard his prayers and told him good night, Matthew said, "A lot of the kids at school have parents that are divorced. Will you ever get a divorce?"

Michael and I had always taught the children that, for a Christian, divorce was contrary to the will of God and was therefore wrong. When our good friend Charlene and her husband, Darin, had divorced, we had told the children that it was Darin who had wanted the divorce. Neither Michael nor I had told them that, in fact, after a long, exhausting battle, Charlene had wanted it too.

"Matthew," I said to him now, "Daddy's and my commitment together is also a commitment to God. As long as we stay close to the Lord, He will make certain that our marriage lasts forever. I promise that you don't need to worry about us ever divorcing, okay?" Those were my words to Matthew, and I believed them.

"That's right, son," Michael added. "Your mother and I are committed to each other and to the Lord. Divorce is not an option, okay?"

Matthew turned over and snuggled down in his bed for a good night's sleep—secure in the knowledge that his mama and daddy would be together for always. Michael and I walked downstairs side by side, each lost in a private world of thoughts.

Michael and I had changed our views about submission, and we both felt more free to search for a deeper and more personalized relationship with God. I even felt freer to speak my mind to those in authority over me—specifically, Norman and Blake. Yet I still believed what I had been told in Hebrews Six: that I should not move ahead of my husband spiritually. I could not see God ever blessing my doing so. Even with the positive changes I saw taking place in our Christian lives, I still believed there was something that kept Michael from totally giving himself to God. All I knew to do was to encourage him to put more effort into his spiritual growth so that we could be "one in the Lord."

In doing so, however, I placed high expectations on Michael—expectations that he struggled to meet, and sometimes grew sick and tired of and set aside. Though he had asked me many times to prod him whenever he grew lax in his efforts to have a deeper, closer walk with the Lord, I knew he often wished that I would just leave him to himself. Deep down, I knew that that was what he wanted. But how could I leave my husband to himself when I was sure that something within him was giving him hell?

In those days, Michael was so sick of himself—of his own spiritual stops and starts—that he had lost almost all hope. It seemed to him that no matter what new truth he discovered in his walk with God, it never answered his most critical questions—why he still struggled with homosexuality, and what he could do to stop. It was getting harder and harder for him to believe he would ever attain the relationship he wanted with God. It seemed as if God were teasing him cruelly. So all he could do was to encourage me to move ahead in my spiritual journey without him. But then, because of my fears of God's disapproval should I do so, he was met with my resistance and my insistence that we journey together.

January 17, 1987: Somehow I began to feel myself losing Michael beginning on Christmas Eve I think. We had had two such good weeks—he was so relaxed. But then it seemed to slowly ebb away. I tried to do things to pull him back, anything to keep him the way he was. He is so easily provoked, so irritable. I've tried to make him smile, laugh, calm down—whatever! The children are even afraid of him—his temper flares up so much at them. Am I exaggerating? I hope so. But I think not.

February 20, 1987: The other night I told Michael that I think I must be filled with more desires than he is. I do not know what else to think. Michael acts like a man who cares, yes, but just not enough. I want so much for us to have a deeper relationship with each other and with God. He says he wants more as well, and that we'll have it together—though I see little action. Michael eludes me. And now, as a result of our arguing about these matters, he has grown defensive and offensive with me. He refuses to communicate—which, of course, he knows is, for me, the ultimate form of rejection. All day yesterday I tried to talk to him so that we could understand each other and find a way to make up. He completely shut me out. Last night I spent hours awake, thinking, on the sofa while he was able to sleep in our bedroom. How could he sleep with all of this unresolved between us?

He nervously cleans up constantly—not only a slap at my homemaking, but also a statement, I think, that he cannot just relax around here and enjoy his children—or me. And our arguments do not go unnoticed. Just the other night we were talking to the boys about their fighting with each other, when Josiah, who is six now, piped up and said, "It's like when you and Daddy fight." I picked him up and put him in my lap and asked, "Then what happens?" He answered thoughtfully, "Well, then you stop, and it's kinda like a miracle!" Michael and I were both convicted by his words. I think we both know our relationship is in real need of a miracle.

It was growing apparent to me that my own feelings of discontent were rapidly catching up with Michael's. Together, we were an accident waiting to happen. And happen it did.

Things only got worse between us, and in May we had a terrible fight. "Why do you have such a negative attitude toward our friends?" I shouted at him in our bedroom. "It seems like you have something negative to say about almost every man in our Friday-night home group! You don't trust anyone, so you're not close to anyone. How can you stand to live that way?"

Without answering me, Michael turned and left the room. In a minute I heard the screen door slam. Looking out the front window, I could see him heading down the hill toward his vegetable garden. I knew that that was where he worked out a lot of his problems. Maybe he'll see things more clearly when he returns, I hoped.

When Michael came in, he asked me to come into the back room with him. Once we were there, he closed the door; then, pacing back and forth, he erupted like a volcano, spewing a lava of angry words all around the room, and at me.

"I quit!" he shouted. "I don't have it inside. I'm a phony and I have no more motivation or desire to even try to be real. I'm tired of making promises I don't keep, and I'm not going to do it anymore. I don't want the 'deeper walk.' It doesn't work for me. If I can do well in my job and be a good husband and father, I'll just be content where I am. I'm not forsaking God, but I give up on trying to live up to any more expectations. I don't want to argue and I don't want to talk about it anymore. *I* can do just fine right where I am, and if you can, too, then that's fine also."

"What is that supposed to mean?" I asked.

"It means just what I said. I don't know whether or not you can be happy with where I am."

I heard a challenge in Michael's words—a challenge for me to leave. And so, feeling angry and scared, I packed a small suitcase and left for my sister's house for the night.

When Camille and I sat down on her bed to talk, I told her I felt as if I had a new husband—one I didn't like and would not have chosen. My own words terrified me, and I began to cry. Richard knocked on the door softly. Seeing me upset, he came over to the bed. Both he and my sister wrapped their arms around me.

In his most brotherly way, Richard said, "Sally, it can't be all that bad. Michael's a great guy, and he loves the Lord. You guys'll work it out." Maybe Richard's right, I thought, taking in a deep breath. I looked at Camille, and she gave me a hopeful smile.

Driving home the next day, I did a lot of thinking. I hated the way I had been acting lately. I had flown into some dreadful rages during fights with Michael, and he had looked at me with contempt. How could I blame him? The way I had acted was disgusting.

May 18, 1987: Sometimes I see Michael as wonderful. I love him, and think I can be content with our life just as it is. Then, he comes home irritable, or else I think about parts of our life that are not "wonderful," and I am suddenly consumed with a dark despair. Maybe I'm crazy, but I know I can't stay like this. Our Christian lives can't suddenly be headed in the way that Michael seems to be headed—dispassionate and mediocre. If I give in to this apathy of his, I will end up hating him. Michael keeps saying he has to be himself. I thought he was himself in Christ. I am so confused.

May 19: Last night Michael and I talked better than we did before I went to Camille's. He let me in a bit more, and pride and doubt out a bit more. He seemed to understand what I meant when I calmly asked how it was that he could he just stop trying. I told him I didn't care what he did, as long as he did *something* toward his further growth in the Lord. To do nothing, to give up—that would be the worst thing to do. He agreed and has decided to counsel with Norman Jones.

While counseling with Norman, Michael told me more than once that he felt as though he were taking one step forward and five backward in his spiritual growth. I had decided that Michael was in bondage to Satan, and I was angry, both at Michael for allowing it and at the enemy for oppressing my husband. When I told Michael I believed it was Satan's lies that were largely responsible for his present state of doubt and discouragement, he looked at me long and hard before saying that he agreed.

Meanwhile, I was struggling horribly with Sarah. More than ever it seemed that the more uptight I was, the less energy and patience I had for her. Sarah placed great demands on whomever she was with. She rarely did anything of her own volition; I had to give her instructions in order for her to eat or to play. Sometimes she might stand in the same spot for an hour unless she was instructed to move. As she was too big to carry now, and as she walked so slowly on her own, to go anywhere with Sarah meant taking a lot of extra time, which often I simply did not have. I prayed about the situation with her in every way I could think of and asked for prayer from others as well. Much like Michael, in my progress with Sarah, I felt as if I were taking one step forward and five steps back.

One rainy Saturday, Michael said that he had business in Atlanta and would be away for the day. The children were bored and exceptionally disagreeable with one another. I made the mistake of choosing this time to work on potty training Sarah. Although she had done well in kindergarten, Sarah's teachers had felt that she needed one more year to prepare for first grade. And though they had been gracious all year about having to change Sarah's Pampers, they had understandably requested that I try to have her potty-trained by fall.

After several unsuccessful attempts at getting Sarah to understand what I wanted her to do—wet the potty and not her panties—I became exasperated. I put her back on the potty much too hard. I turned to leave her, then heard her crash to the floor and begin screaming at the top of her lungs. She had landed on her head, on the side with the shunt. Terrified, I picked her up and carried her downstairs to my bed.

There I sat, feeling miserably guilty and utterly defeated. Upon examining her, I could tell she was physically fine. Still, the ordeal shook me up dreadfully and left me feeling all the more that my heart was exceedingly wicked in regard to my helpless little girl and that surely God had removed Himself far from the likes of me.

Michael came home later that afternoon and we had dinner with the children, during which I watched Sarah carefully to be sure she was still all right. Later that night, after the children were asleep, Michael and I settled down on the sofa to talk. I told him exactly what had happened with Sarah that day, hoping all the while that he wouldn't think too badly of me. Holding me close, Michael listened to the story, and when I finished, he said he understood both how awful I must feel now for having hurt Sarah and how easy it would have been to lose patience with her. Michael tried hard to relieve me of some of my guilt, but there was no way for that to happen anytime soon. Every time I thought about how intolerant I had been that morning, over something as insignificant as potty training, I felt sick. I told Michael how much I hated the fact that I still struggled with Sarah. He said he hated that he still struggled with her, too. We agreed to drop the potty training for a while. We'd try again closer to school time. Michael couldn't have been any kinder to me that day, and I was deeply touched by how understanding he was and how much he cared about my feelings.

Changing the subject, I asked Michael about his day in Atlanta. Looking pensive, he said that, after his appointment, he had driven around for a long time and had finally stopped in a park for a while just to think.

"Did you feel any better afterward?" I asked him hopefully.

He smiled and said, "No, not really, but it's okay."

I didn't understand what he had meant by his last comment, but suddenly I was so tired that I couldn't keep my eyes open. "Come on," Michael said, helping me off the sofa. "Let's go to bed. We both need some rest."

As I would not learn till years later, Michael's appointment in Atlanta that Saturday had actually been at a so-called gay ministry located in a house near Piedmont Park. For the last six months, he had attended counseling sessions. The ministry had a process intended to break a person from the gay habit. First the person had to confess homosexuality as sin and repent. Then he or she had to resist Satan (James 4:7: "Resist Satan and he will flee from you"). Finally, the person had to restrain himself or herself from further sin. The three Rs—repent, resist, and restrain. Believing that God would surely reward his determination by giving him the desire of his heart—to be straight—Michael had followed the requirements faithfully for six months, even undergoing a time of deliverance (the exorcising of demons) much like the ones I had gone through with Janet and Suzanne many years before.

After six months of this earnest striving, Michael had asked his counselor why he still had desires for men. Why, he asked, after prayer and deliverance and willingness and obedience, had God not taken that desire from him?

The counselor's answer was for him to do more of the same: "Repent, resist, and restrain, Michael. And you're going to have to do so for the rest of your life."

Having decided then that the counselor had no real answers for him, Michael had left his office that Saturday knowing he would not be back again. All they had to offer him, really, was the advice that he exercise willpower—mind over matter. It was the same thing he had been trying and failing at for years.

Michael's main issue had still not been resolved: if God wanted him free from this sin, why did He not take the sinful desire away from him? Believing now that it was of no avail to keep asking God to change him, Michael had given up believing that God would ever effect such a change. At this point he was too exhausted from his battle with homosexuality to consider that there might be another reason—other than personal rejection—why a loving God might not answer his prayer in the way that Michael had asked Him to for many years.

Coming home that Saturday to find me distraught over what had happened with Sarah had only disillusioned Michael even further. Sarah was a reminder to him of yet another attempt to gain God's deliverance from sin—his own personal form of penance—that he was failing in. To see me suffering because of his "curse" was becoming unbearable to him.

That year, Michael had become involved with the local Republican Party. When Pat Robertson announced his presidential candidacy, Michael became an alternate party delegate. Now he decided to campaign for a seat on the board of commissioners of Forsyth County. At the time many of its members were good old boys who had been on the board for several four-year terms apiece. Rumors of corruption had surrounded the board for years, and at last several incumbents were being challenged. If Michael won the election, he would be the first Republican to be elected on any local level since Reconstruction days.

Michael and I and our seven children launched the campaign from the back of Stu's pickup truck during the Cumming Fourth of July parade. Along with the other candidates, who were also in cars and trucks, we had a great time throwing candy and gum and campaign cards to bystanders. Campaigning as a family was exhilarating, but my greatest delight was seeing Michael so full of life.

Michael was widely attacked for being both a newcomer in the county and a newcomer to local politics. "Who is this high-powered guy from Atlanta?" one of the local newspapers wrote. Some people in the county, moreover, were committed to the "If it ain't broke, don't fix it" ideology. So Michael had to work extra hard to convince voters that a change was needed on the board of commissioners and that he was the right man for the job. He got out and met as many of the people in Forsyth County as he possibly could. He went door-to-door, and he stood in front of Wal-Mart introducing himself to shoppers. Everywhere he went, Michael listened carefully to what people had to say and learned what they were most concerned about: namely, the need to wisely plan for county growth and to stop the corruption in local politics. Michael promised that a vote for him would ensure that both of these needs would be met.

I told myself that Michael had found an important part of his identity that completed him and that he could commit himself to. Michael told himself the same thing and for a while even believed it might be true. But for all of the identity Michael was finding, I was slowly losing mine. Or, rather, I wasn't sure if I had ever had one in the first place.

> June 20, 1988: I feel so out of place with myself. I "don't know who I am" . . . sounds like the seventies. I find myself feeling so unsure of myself . . . of what I even believe . . . so uncreative and insecure. It's all wrapped up in: I don't fit . . . like if I disappeared I'd go unnoticed for quite some time, except maybe for not being somebody's mother anymore.

Later that July, Michael and I and the children joined Camille and Richard and their children for a week's vacation on St. Simons Island. Our rental house overlooked a rough part of the ocean called Gould's

Inlet. Sitting out on the deck in the early morning, I was able to find the rare sense of peace I felt I had lost.

As was our routine, Camille and I arrived on the island a few days early to spend some time with Daddy, who was having health problems. He had lost a considerable amount of weight, suffered from dreadful headaches, and had become so physically weak that it was painful to watch him walk across the room. It broke our hearts to see a brilliant and creative man stay closeted on one of the most beautiful islands on earth and waste away in the process. And in addition to his poor health, Daddy had also become very cantankerous.

Camille and I could handle a lot, and over the years we had laughed off many of Daddy's insulting remarks. But every now and then we decided that if we were going to survive caring for him in the years to come, we would have to call him on some of those comments. One day, I walked by Daddy and he said, "You're getting fat! You need to lose some weight."

He was sitting at the kitchen table, and I sat down trembling with anger and fear of what I was going to say. "And *you* do not need to speak to me that way, Daddy. You should keep those kinds of thoughts to yourself."

"Well, I'm your daddy—so I can say that to you."

"True—you are my daddy. That fact does *not*, however, give you the right to speak to me like that," I replied calmly. But then my voice rose as I said, "You know something, Daddy? Camille and I come down here every year to spend time with you not because we have to, but because we want to. But you know what? We *can* go home. And if you continue to treat us the way you have been this week, we will." Having spoken that way to my father, I wanted to throw up.

I was shocked to hear his response. "I'm sorry," he said and hung his head in remorse. "I won't do it again."

My sister had stood by and, seeing that I was holding my own, had watched the scene without interrupting. When she and I spoke about it later, we agreed that though we both found it extremely uncomfortable, we would have to stand up to Daddy. Otherwise he might wrongly think he could treat us the same way he had treated our mother.

By fall, Michael was gaining in popularity and support. While I was glad to see him become passionately committed to something again, I was concerned about what was happening in the rest of his life. I had hoped that getting outside of himself and into community involvement would help Michael loosen up and feel more positive about his life, but instead he had become more critical of our friends and less interested in church activities—and, sometimes, less interested in me. And, of course, the more I said about it, the more he withdrew.

Election Day finally arrived. When I voted that morning, several elderly people stopped me to say that in voting for Michael, they had voted Republican for the first time in their lives. That night, along with little Michael—whom we now called Michael Jr.—and many of our friends and supporters, Michael and I waited at the courthouse for the election results. To our delight, Michael won the race by a flattering margin. Some said Michael rode in on the coattails of George Bush, while others argued that the county had finally recognized its need for new blood.

Michael was so thrilled and happy to have been elected and so sincerely eager to do his best for the community that had shown its trust in him. He had run on his image of having a model family with traditional, conservative values and, as I later learned, was so scared of being caught in any sort of gay-related activity that, for the time being anyway, he was "keeping straight." Besides, his business was going well, and though he sometimes felt overwhelmed with the responsibility of leading home group each week, even church life seemed all right. Although Michael had given up believing that God would ever take the desire for other men away from him, he thought now that maybe God had made his days so full that he wouldn't have time to act on his temptations—at least for a while.

I found that I enjoyed being a commissioner's wife, and our boys enjoyed the benefits that derived from being a commissioner's sons. When the Sawnee Women's Club (Forsyth's version of the Atlanta Junior League) extended to me an invitation to join, I accepted, knowing that this indicated Michael and I had been accepted, socially speaking, in Forsyth County. When I attended my first meeting I was surprised that clubs still existed in which the members were listed on the roll not by their first names but as Mrs. so-and-so. I was even more surprised to find that a prospective member could be blackballed by a member when her name was suggested for membership. Shades of my old high school sorority! Still, I told myself, it felt good to "fit" somewhere, even if it *was* the result of being Michael's wife.

It was at about this time that I read another of Madeleine L'Engle's books. *Two-Part Invention* told about her forty-year marriage to an actor named Hugh Franklin, who had recently died from cancer.

While reading the book I found out that Hugh Franklin had played the part of Dr. Charles Tyler on *All My Children*, a soap-opera father I had thought was wonderful in the 1970s. Reading now what Ms. L'Engle had to say about their marriage, even with its imperfections, had given me a new inspiration about my own. I wanted Michael and me to share the same sort of devotion that she and Hugh had shared for so many years.

> January 10, 1989: Madeleine and Hugh truly shared life together, though they each had a life of their own as well. I so want this for Michael and me. I have no set pattern or rules, anymore, which we must fit into. I want our life to be ours alone. I don't care if it fits no one else's style. I do, however, want it to fit God's plan for us. But there seems always to be some sort of obstacle in our way—something that is keeping us from attaining what I want for our marriage. I do know that there needs to be a healing in my husband. Right now his love for everyone is so controlled. Did he perhaps inherit this from his father? I absolutely do want to discover the secret that breaks what binds his heart so that it can be free to soar and free to love. But how, Lord?

Further along in *Two-Part Invention,* I read this sentence: "Our idea of a pleasant evening was a small group of people eating a well-cooked meal together, and talking about art and the world and life and the theater and what it was to try to be human and all the many topics of conversation that make for a creative and stimulating evening."

Except for our Christmas dinner parties (which were by no means small) and our infrequent evenings with either Russell and Scarlett or two new friends, Robbie and Patty, I felt a tremendous lack of friendship. Though Michael said he wanted the same thing in our friendships that I did, when I observed him with company, he sometimes reminded me of our children when they were toddlers: they had enjoyed playing around their friends, but not with them. Then I remembered that, as toddlers, they had not yet known *how* to play with a friend. I wondered what kept Michael from knowing how to enjoy being intimate with his friends. What was it that he feared about getting close?

> January 10 [continued]: Michael and I have lost something that we once had the beginnings of together. I hope we can find it. So many times I feel that I am scrambling to find the pieces to a puzzle. Then I wonder—when I do find them, will they even fit?

"Everyone take your seats," Pastor Norman began impatiently. Adults and children quickly scattered themselves into seats around the room, abruptly ending the usual Sunday-morning greetings. The musicians, who had been warming up for worship, quietly laid down their instruments. "People," Norman continued, "if you were not present at the financial seminar yesterday, you need to know that you were *not* where *God* would have had you be!"

He spit his words out with such unusual harshness that I looked at Michael and whispered, "Why is he so upset?" He shrugged his shoulders.

"Last Sunday I told this entire congregation that it was your responsibility as stewards of God's money to attend this seminar, but many of you still were not there." He gripped the podium tightly and looked around the room gravely. "I am very disappointed, and I do *not* want to hear your excuses, because, as your pastor, I *told* you to be there!" With that, he sat down beside the flustered musicians—who did not know whether to play or maintain silence—and folded his arms across his chest.

I felt like my clothes had been suddenly yanked off and I was forbidden to cover myself with my own hands. I didn't dare look around the room for fear of reproachful looks from those who had attended the seminar. I did, however, look over at Michael, who sat perfectly still—with the exception of his jaw, which he was working back and forth.

There was a church picnic following the service that Sunday, whereupon Michael ignored Norman's warning about excuses and pulled him aside to talk. "Norman, the reason Sally and I weren't at the seminar yesterday was that we had already attended the same seminar in James Smith's group. And I think it was terribly unfair of you to rebuke the whole congregation like that, without giving us the opportunity to explain."

Having calmed down considerably since earlier in the morning, Norman said, "Oh, I understand. All right, perhaps I was too harsh this morning. However," he quickly added, "I am sick and tired of Calvary Chapel members picking and choosing which of my instructions they want to comply with."

When Michael told me later about his conversation with Norman, he said he believed he and Norman had parted on good terms, but I was still concerned. "Norman seems unusually uptight to me," I said. "Why do you think that is?"

"I really don't know, Sally," he answered, looking worried. "I just hope it's not what we're both afraid it is. I hope he hasn't become another leader who loves his power—like James Smith."

Before I could respond, Michael held up his hand and adamantly said, "I'll tell you right now . . . if that's the case, we'll be out of that church! I can't take much more of this legalistic junk, Sally." I was surprised at his tone, though not at his words, and nodded my head in definite agreement.

The cycles I saw, cycles that I and others had moved in for so long as Christians—striving to please God, failing, feeling guilty, then striving again—had become depressing, monotonous, and even ridiculous to me. I hungered for more of what I now called the mystery of faith, though I knew little about what it was I was seeking, and less about where to find it. Once again, I had a strong sense that something vital was missing from my spiritual life.

Maybe, I mused, Michael and I are no longer as far apart spiritually as we seemed to be. I had lost my incentive to read the Bible, as I knew he had; for to read it meant hearing James's heavy interpretation along with every scripture. Thank heavens, I thought to myself, Scarlett has introduced me to the works of Madeleine L'Engle and C. S. Lewis—both of whom encouraged readers with their examples of upbeat, down-to-earth relationships with God.

Ms. L'Engle, especially, had shown me new ways of viewing God. It had been while reading *A Wrinkle in Time* that I had caught my first glimpse of the mystery of faith. Now, in reading books such as *The Irrational Season* I understood for the first time that it was permissible to be angry at God. Or even to doubt His very existence and yet still believe. Gradually I let go of the idea that I had to have all the right answers to my spiritual questions and had to have the right way of living down firm. I began to grant myself the freedom both to think and to say, "I'm not sure what I believe about that," and to actually believe that God would not turn His back on me in fiery retribution. Slowly but surely, I was developing something that had previously terrified me—an open mind.

Though I felt that opening my mind to new ways of thinking would undoubtedly lead me into unknown—and sometimes frightening—territory, my present form of Christianity had become so lifeless that the prospective unknown felt more promising than it did foreboding. From the many discussions Michael and I had had together, I began to realize that what was *new* ground for me was the ground he'd been walking on for some time—ground that I had resisted. Spiritually speaking, there was less and less discord between us now. And, with that improvement, I theorized that perhaps our marriage relationship would be revived as well.

That fall Michael and I took Michael Jr. to college. The three of us walked all over the lovely old campus of Young Harris College until it was time for him to go to student orientation and for us to go home. Finally Michael and I hugged and kissed him good-bye, then waited until we were of sight before we both cried. I could not imagine home without my eldest son, whom I had shared life with since I was only a child myself.

Josiah joined his brothers in public school, leaving me with only Samuel to keep busy at home—which was no easy job. Samuel, who was now four going on ten, hated being at home without his brothers.

"I'm bored, Mama," Samuel said one morning while watching the yellow school bus drive away. "I think maybe you should send me to *board*ing school!"

"I don't think so, sweetie," I laughed, and hugged him. "I'd miss you too much!"

Later in September, Michael and I took off on a long-overdue trip alone, this time to the Bahamas. Michael had planned the trip, an indication to me that our relationship was on the right track. Before we left, I told myself that I would not allow any "old tapes" to spoil our time together. Having left the children with friends, we had a wonderful first time relaxing on the beach without having to keep an eye on several children. I delightedly threw myself into doing things I had never done before, such as snorkeling, going to casinos, sipping frozen daiquiris on the beach at eleven o'clock in the morning, and observing a pair of topless sunbathers. I found it quite amusing to watch whenever men tried to carry on a conversation with the two women—*without* looking down.

On our third night there, Michael and I went down to the hotel lounge late one night for a nightcap and to listen to calypso music. Suddenly I tugged at Michael's shirtsleeve.

"Look," I whispered.

There in front of us were two women dancing—together! At first I had thought they had had too much to drink and were just out on the dance floor being silly, but then, as their embrace tightened, I knew they were completely serious. Michael just smiled while we continued to watch the women dance, and I surprised myself by thinking, This doesn't even bother me that much—maybe I've had too much to drink!

The next morning we set our lounge chairs out on the beach, ready for another relaxing day. Laughing, I poked Michael in the side and quickly pointed to either side of our chairs. On one side were the two topless sunbathers, and on the other was the lesbian couple we had seen dancing together the night before.

Giggling, I whispered, "Which side do *you* want?" I didn't think twice about the fact that, blushing slightly, Michael smiled and chose the side next to the lesbians.

"I hate leaving the Bahamas and going back to the 'real world,'" I said on the way home from the airport.

"Me too. Getting away like that was great. What I hate is that our 'real' lives are too hectic," he said. "I've been wondering . . . do you think maybe we've outgrown some of the things we've been involved in?"

"Like what?"

"Like home group, maybe? I have so much going on in my life, Sally, that, honestly, I don't like *having* to lead the group every Friday night. What would you think about taking a break from home group for a while?"

Our home group had grown to twenty-four members, indicating that it still met the needs of a lot of people. I had reached a point, however, at which I not only was tired of fighting Michael about church matters, but had truly begun to share most of his feelings—and with a lot less fear of incurring God's wrath. Home group, especially with the many restrictions Norman had imposed on it, did seem more like a burden than a blessing.

"I think it would probably be a good idea for you to stop leading home group, and if you think we should take a break from it, that's fine with me. I think most of the home group will probably understand. As for what Norman will say . . . I'm not so sure."

Smiling gratefully, he leaned over and said, "Thanks for feeling that way . . . It really helps. We'll talk to Norman before we tell the group. I think he'll be okay."

As soon as we could arrange it, we met with Norman and his wife at their home.

"I completely understand," Norman said as soon as Michael had finished explaining our decision. "Ella and I have too much going on in our own lives. Let me assure you, I know what it's like to feel burned out."

"Thanks, I'd hoped you'd understand," Michael said. "Sally and I really appreciate both of you."

"I've been meaning to tell you that I want to be a greater support to you in your job as commissioner, Michael, both in prayer and involvement. I think maybe I've not been in the past. So please let me know what I can do, okay? Oh, and if you don't mind, I think Ella and I might come to your next home-group meeting to support you and Sally while you tell the group."

Touched by Norman's thoughtfulness, Michael said, "Thanks for your support, Norman. And of course I'd be glad for you and Ella to come on Friday night."

Norman and his wife did indeed come to our home-group meeting. While Michael carefully broke the news to the group, Norman remained silent. Everyone was upset, and many were quite agitated. One particularly troubled man protested angrily, "I feel like my parents have just told me they're getting a divorce and I'm supposed to be okay about it. Well, I'm *not* okay—and I won't be without you guys here."

The very emotional reaction of the group was so tough to hear that at one point I looked over at Michael and wondered how much longer he would be able to handle it. Then Norman suddenly broke in. "I need to interrupt here," he began. "While, to a point, I respect Michael and Sally's decision to take a break from home group, I have to tell you that there will be a breach between my spirit and theirs until they return. Furthermore, I am very concerned that if they leave, they might fall away from the Lord altogether—and may even take several of you down the road with them in the process."

Michael and I were shocked. Most of the group listened in submissive silence, but a few defended our decision, and one young woman even took exception to Norman's notion of a "breach" between us and him. After a while Norman closed the subject and introduced new guidelines that all home groups would now be required to follow. Meetings would have a specified amount of time set aside for Bible study, prayer, and worship and would end promptly at nine o'clock— putting an end to the relaxed atmosphere that our group enjoyed. A heated discussion ensued, during most of which Michael and I remained silent.

When everyone had finally gone home, Michael and I collapsed on the sofa. "I can't believe Norman did that to us," Michael began angrily. "The only thing I can figure is that he feels like he's losing his grip on Calvary Chapel—so he's pulling in the reins. I told you—I can't go this route again, Sally. I've got to talk to him." Though I agreed that he should talk to Norman, I also knew we both had the distinct feeling we had just come up against a brick wall.

The first thing Monday morning, Michael went to speak with Norman at his office. Before Michael had returned home, Norman called me: "I'm sorry, Sally, but I'm going to have to temporarily remove you as coleader of the dance team. I can't allow you to be reinstated until Michael shows proper acceptance of me as his spiritual authority."

And submits to your control, I thought. Though I was seething mad, I simply said, "All right."

I called Joy, my dance-team coleader, to tell her what Norman had said. She was almost as devastated as I was. I begged her to continue the dance team, but she refused, saying that as far as she was concerned, dance at Calvary was dead.

As soon as Michael came in the house, I told him what Norman had done. He turned and immediately went back to Norman's office to talk with him again. When he returned home once more, it was with the news that we would be leaving Calvary Chapel. Remembering our recent discussion in which we had agreed that we would never allow a pastor to control our lives again, I wasn't terribly surprised.

"What did he say, Michael?"

"Well, first I tried to explain to him that I did recognize him as my pastor—just not as my God. He said that it was obvious I had a problem with authority, and if I could not submit to what he believed was right for the whole church—which, of course, meant attending home group—then you and I should find another church to attend. I said I guessed that we should. Then I left. We don't have any choice except to leave, Sally. I'm sorry."

I could see that besides being furious, Michael was as deeply hurt as I was. I also saw that he looked exhausted from the whole ordeal. Resting my forehead on the kitchen table, I felt very tired myself. "I know," I said. "And, believe me, I've had it, too. We really need a rest from such intense churches—or something."

"Yeah, well, it looks as though we're about to get one," he responded sarcastically.

Later, when I thought about the serious impact Michael's decision would have on us both, as well as on the children, I was sorry, too, that things had to end this way. But, looking back over the last year, I saw clearly how things had progressed to this point. There was no denying the fact that we did not belong at Calvary Chapel, and, when I let myself, I felt a definite peace about moving on.

Despite that knowledge, I was thrown into a temporary time of fear and confusion. Fear because I worried that we might be being deceived by listening to our unreliable hearts (old James Smith tapes were obviously still playing in my head), and confusion because I couldn't really imagine where we did belong now. Sometimes I worried that Michael might drop the ball, spiritually speaking, and we wouldn't go *any-where*. At other times, when I felt more optimistic, I thought we might be moving ahead to a better place not only spiritually, but for our relationship as well. I strongly wished I knew which was the case.

As we expected, it was a difficult time for the boys. Though the younger ones were simply upset over having to leave their friends, Michael Jr. and Daniel were old enough to grasp what had happened and were angry at Norman. Michael and I told them that we would all have to find it in our hearts to forgive him and to pray for him and Calvary Chapel. We still wished we could insulate our children from the darker side of humanity and of life generally, and we hated for them to learn about some of the things Christians did to hurt one another, but finally we realized we were just avoiding the inevitable.

During the next few months I talked to Joy almost daily. We both missed dancing as well as seeing one another at church. I knew that she and Blake hoped Michael and I would see our way back to Calvary Chapel. Finally I had to tell her that that would never happen. Joy had been having a hard time lately and had begun counseling with Norman. Though I could not pretend to be happy about it, I tried to keep my opinions about Norman to myself.

One day Joy called me. "What's wrong, Joy?" I asked. "You sound so down."

"Listen," she began, "I'm really upset about this, but Norman said it might be a good idea if we didn't talk so much—at least until you and Michael work things out with the church. Blake agrees with him. I know you and Michael are not going to come back to Calvary, though, and the whole thing makes me sick. I have to do what Norman and Blake say is best, Sally—you know?"

I "knew" all too well, and, though I did not tell her why, it tore me up inside. Joy had been demoted to remedial submission class, and I was the bad influence that was keeping her from doing her homework.

"The whole thing makes me sick too," was all I said.

Over the next year our conversations became less and less frequent, until they eventually ceased altogether. For the last three years that I lived in Cumming, whenever Joy and I ran into each other in town, we would hug and one of us would start to cry. Then we would continue on our separate ways.

chapter 9

The Truth Shall Set You Free

While waiting to see what was next for us in the way of a church, I tried to concentrate on my growing sense of anticipation rather than on my angst. My anticipation was partially due to Michael's unwavering certainty that God would lead us to a church that would better suit our changing needs. It was also because I was beginning to believe that neither Michael nor anyone else was responsible for my spiritual growth—*I* was. And this new revelation felt more and more like something I was ready to explore.

"Whenever I think about a pastor," I half-jokingly said to Michael one day, "I find myself having a very radical thought—maybe I don't *need* one anymore!"

He laughed and said, "That sounds fine to me!" I laughed with him, though both of us understood the large amount of hurt and truth that had just passed between us.

As we talked about what we were looking for in a new church, we realized that we weren't exactly sure. What we *wished* for was a church with the style of worship we enjoyed at Calvary Chapel, but one that was not as dogmatic in its doctrinal beliefs. Both of us were ready to go someplace where discussion among people with differing opinions was permitted and encouraged.

For several Sundays in a row Michael and I and the children visited various churches in Cumming. We attended First Methodist Church for a month and were not satisfied that it was the place God wanted us to attend. We visited a local Church of God, and though the worship was slightly more to our liking, we held on to our seats when the nineteen-year-old preacher shouted out his hellfire-and-brimstone sermon.

A few Sundays later, at another Church of God, the pastor stepped down from the stage during the service and came over to our row. After a brief welcome, he unexpectedly clamped his hands around

Michael's head, closed his eyes, and shouted, "Brother! The Lord wants to baptize you in the Holy Spirit right now!"

There was a short pause before Michael firmly took the man's hands off his head and said, "I have already been baptized in the Holy Spirit, thank you."

Without missing a beat, the preacher moved to the next person down the line—with another word from God. At that point, Michael motioned quietly for me and the children to follow him. Not one child even bothered to ask if we would be back the next Sunday.

We tried the local First Christian church, where we found nothing to either excite or disturb us; we knew only that it was not the right place. We visited a Messianic Jewish church, which recognized Jesus as the Messiah but observed Jewish traditions as well. There we found worship and music we enjoyed, but after a few Saturday-night services we agreed that the pastor was too authoritarian.

By this point, I was getting very discouraged. I wanted a new spiritual home badly, and it looked to me as though we had just about exhausted our choices. Once again I began to wonder where God was in all of this, and whether he had abandoned us for leaving Calvary. Though Michael was frustrated, too, he always managed to hold firm to the notion that if we were just patient—and if I didn't panic—God would show us the place where He wanted us to be. One night during Christmas week, Michael and I took the boys to see a musical in Atlanta called *An Appalachian Christmas*. When, at one point, the cast sang "O Holy Night," I heard the words "a weary world rejoices" and felt my own shoulders wearily slump. After Christ was born, I mused, men and women were intended never to be slaves again—but I have yet to really feel free. Looking over at Michael, I knew he felt the same way, and tears welled up in my eyes.

The words "for yonder breaks a new and glorious morn" rang out with their promise for hope and freedom. *Something*, I mused, is not right in our lives. I tried to encourage myself with the thought that it was almost 1990—a new decade. Maybe it would bring us both whatever it was that we needed.

In early February I flew by myself to Raleigh to spend the weekend with my friend Bonnie. Over beers, we talked a lot about the years we had spent together in the Hebrews Six Fellowship, and about the damage it had caused us and our families.

"I remember the time I found beer in your refrigerator," I said, laughing as I reached for another piece of pizza.

"You bet you did! How do you think I survived all those years?" Bonnie said, chuckling at the memory of her and Jeff's small act of defiance.

"Yeah, well, you always were the rebel! Why on earth did we allow ourselves to be a part of Hebrews Six for so long, Bonnie?" I whined.

"I don't know," she whined back. "But—hey—at least we finally had the sense to get ourselves out of the 'lunatic fringe of Christianity'!"

"Here's to that stroke of genius!" I said, and we toasted with our beers.

March 13, 1990: I had a dream in which I had no idea where I was. A man called on the phone looking for someone, and when I told the man that the person he wanted wasn't there, he said, "Ma'am, I thought everybody was gone. Something is wrong, don't you know? Something terrible has happened. Somewhere, someone is really hurt." Something very serious was happening. All at once I knew what it was—it was the end of the world. I was filled with an awful fear of the unknown. I doubted my place in the Lord and I knew that utter devastation lay just outside the door. Then, slowly, from somewhere, the children began to come to me with looks of fearful wonder. They knew—we all *knew*. This was no tornado—this was somehow everything happening at once. No way to stop it. Finally Michael came in from outside and said, "It is *awful* out there." We all sat down in a circle and began to read the Psalms—waiting.

When I woke from the dream, it was morning, and I was deeply shaken. Still under its power, I looked at Michael sleeping beside me and wondered if he had had the same dream. Then I realized what a ridiculous thought that was. When, later that morning, I told Michael about my dream, he looked troubled—almost as troubled by it as I had been.

I had to remind him, "It's only a dream."

I learned later that while I was struggling in my more open—yet sometimes confusing—relationship with God, Michael was beginning his own new—and private—search for Him as well. When he left Calvary Chapel, Michael decided to totally discard his ties to fundamentalist Christianity—including the part that insisted homosexuality was a sin. With that new perspective firmly in place, he was determined never again to allow himself to be subjected to the false guilt he had suffered under for so long. Now he searched for a way to incorporate his new beliefs into his spiritual life as well as his home life. It was not easy.

In the midst of his search, however, Michael found a splendid means of serving God by helping to establish the Cumming chapter of Habitat for Humanity, an organization that assists families to build and finance their own homes, and, in no time, he had me involved as well. In a very real sense, Michael and I had come full circle, finding ourselves back at the place we were in our first year of marriage, when we had almost impulsively moved to Koinonia, where Habitat for Humanity was founded.

Our work with Habitat provided us with, in the words of Habitat's (and Koinonia's) founder, Millard Fuller, "a meaningful participation with God in His purpose for mankind." While we helped solicit funds and materials from local construction companies, labored to build the first Habitat house, and then watched excitedly as the first family actually moved in, Michael and I realized that the feeling we were having of truly and vigorously living out our Christian calling to love God and our neighbor had been sorely missing from our Christian lives.

March 19, 1990: The fundamentalist Christian's world is far too small to allow for the complete workings of the living, active God. Words like *social involvement* or *activists* scare them and conjure up images of lost hippies who "need the Lord" when, in fact, it is "finding the Lord" that should connect us back to mankind and society—not separate us from it.

Finally our world had opened up enough to enable us to see it and ourselves more realistically and humanly. So it was that after working together in this grassroots project, Michael and I added to our list of what we wanted in a church the same thing we now wanted in our day-to-day lives and had, in both respects, sought twenty years before: social involvement.

As it happened, Sam Candler, who was at that time the rector at the Episcopal church in Cumming, was also active in Habitat for Humanity. Michael liked Sam Candler and asked if I would be interested in trying the Episcopal church. I was surprised at his suggestion of a church that, for us, would be a step back in time. Still, I said I'd be glad to give it a try.

The next Sunday we loaded up the children, who protested a little and asked a few questions ("What *is* an Episcopal church anyway?" "Do they believe in God?" "Are they Christians?"), and visited the Episcopal Church of the Holy Spirit. After a half hour or so of scrambling through prayer books and hymnals and getting up and down what felt like an unreasonable number of times, I looked over at the befuddled faces of my family and wondered, What on earth are we doing in this church?

I took in one deep breath, then exhaled, after which I determined to give my worries a rest. Instead I looked out the high window over the church's simple wooden altar. There I saw a most gorgeous blue sky and low mountains thick with Georgia pines and hardwoods. The trees swayed slightly with the breeze as if teasing us all to come outside and play. All at once, a small flock of birds toured the sky and boasted a perfect V before they disappeared from sight. I thought that surely anyone who enjoyed this splendid view every Sunday morning would have to affirm the glory of God.

This blissful feeling didn't last for long, however, because during the Offertory, I realized that Holy Communion would soon follow. Having forgotten that Episcopalians take Communion every Sunday, I had neglected to instruct the children as to how to receive the Host properly. Nor had I told them they would be drinking real wine instead of grape juice as was the case at Calvary Chapel. I tried to send a softly whispered set of instructions down the row, but this resulted only in a series of "What?" "What?" "What?" Finally I put my finger to my lips, and then to my ears, signaling them to just be quiet and listen. Michael was quite amused by my efforts. I settled back in my seat then and smiled to myself. Who cares if they mess up? I reflected. Surely not God.

I listened carefully as Father Candler began the Communion prayers that I had at one time known by heart. "It is right, and a good and joyful thing, always and everywhere to give thanks to you, Father Almighty, Creator of heaven and earth." Hearing these words now after so many years, I was suddenly cognizant of their power. "In your infinite love you made us for yourself. . . . You in your mercy, sent Jesus Christ, your only and eternal Son, to share our human nature, to live and die as one of us, to reconcile us to you, the God and Father of all." I felt a deep settling taking place in my soul that told me unmistakably that God was indeed with me and with my family. I watched then as the priest broke the bread and lifted the cup of wine above the altar for the congregation to see. "After supper He took the cup of wine; and when He had given thanks, He gave it to them, and said, 'Drink this, all of you: This is my Blood of the new Covenant, which is shed for you and for the forgiveness of sins.'" At that moment a warmth came over me, a feeling of having finally come home. I began to cry, then quickly wiped away my tears, embarrassed. I had never before realized how strong God's presence was to me in the Episcopal Eucharist. That sudden awareness, along with the sure knowledge that

God in his goodness had brought me back to experience it again, gave me a tremendous feeling of gratefulness. With a renewed sense of reverence and awe, I followed Michael and the children to the altar to receive Communion.

Afterward, while kneeling in prayer, I thanked God for returning to me, that morning, that which I had lost—the mystery of faith. Familiarity doesn't breed just contempt, I thought to myself; it also breeds bitterness and cynicism. But mystery, I realized then, breeds wonder and expectancy and hearts open to a deeper level of trust.

After church, when Michael and I had climbed into the front seat of our van, I was almost afraid to look at him. I didn't know what he had thought about the service, and I wasn't sure what I even wanted his reaction to be. Finally he leaned over and asked me, "Well . . . what did you think?"

I choked back more unexpected tears. "I don't know. What did *you* think?"

"I really liked the service a lot—especially Communion." The look on Michael's face was soft and gentle—and hopeful.

"Me too. It felt like coming home."

"I felt the same way," Michael said. I could hardly believe that after all of our fundamentalist Christian days, Michael and I had found ourselves at home in an Episcopal church. But we had. And it felt exceedingly good and right.

Michael reached over and took my hand. "I think this is going to be a good move for us, Sally—in fact, I know it is."

Once Michael and I had made the decision to stay at the Episcopal church, I was both relieved and encouraged. Maybe now that the pressure to perform was completely off him, he could get down to the business of just knowing God.

We knew that the children would be more challenged than we were by the adjustment to life in an Episcopal church. On the one hand, we did not want our boys to lose what was real and valuable in their Christian lives; on the other, we were ready for them to be exposed to new ways of viewing God and Christianity.

The transition wasn't smooth. Daniel did not ever want to go back to Calvary, but he found the youth group at the Episcopal church something of an eye-opener. "Are the adult meetings different from the kids'?" he asked us incredulously one evening after coming home from the Church of the Holy Spirit. "I mean, at ours, lots of times we don't even talk about God! And I know some of these guys from school, and

I know they aren't Christians!" My, I thought with chagrin, haven't we taught him how to judge other people well?

Michael and I had met the youth-group leaders and liked them a lot. We understood that they had to find innovative ways to keep a very diverse group of young people interested in church-related activities; if they didn't succeed, the kids might not hear about God at all. It would take time for the wisdom of that concept to become clear to the children. In the meantime, with each Sunday that passed, Michael and I felt more relieved to be out of fundamentalist churches, and more grateful for the breath of fresh air we were experiencing at Holy Spirit. It felt so right to be where we were; we could only trust that God knew what He was doing with all of our lives, including our children's, and that, in time, they would understand and join in our enthusiasm.

That spring I saw an ad in the newspaper for a creative-writing class that would begin in May at a nearby community center. When I showed it to Michael he said, "Sally, I've been *telling* you to do something with your writing. I can be home that night with the kids. Take the class—please!"

It was true: Michael seemed to regard me differently these days. He had been after me to get involved in anything that I might find interesting; he had even suggested that I might want to work outside the home sometime in the near future. But that was not the only difference I had noticed about him; his appearance was noticeably different. His haircut and his dress had become very *GQ*, and he had begun to frequent the gym. He looked great. Only occasionally did I wonder why these changes had come about. As I learned later, Michael had become much more comfortable with his gay life and had found ways to be involved in it very discreetly in the Atlanta area. Still, any enjoyment he derived from it was consistently overshadowed by the constant lying and the guilt he had to endure. Regardless of whether he did so consciously or unconsciously, Michael was actively pushing me to become more independent, on the slim chance that one day he might discover a way for us to live apart.

So, while I was a little surprised at his unreserved enthusiasm, I nonetheless hurried and called my free-spirited friend Rosita, another aspiring writer, and suggested we take the class together. She readily agreed to join me.

On the way home from class one night, Rosita began insisting that a man in our class had been flirting with me. I told her, "You're crazy! He most certainly has not been. For God's sake, I told everyone the first night of class that I had seven children! What idiot would flirt with a woman with seven children?"

Rosita shrugged. "I'm *telling* you—the guy's been undressing you every week in class. Maybe he thinks 'doin' it' with a woman with seven children would be like conquering a fertility goddess or something!"

Blushing madly, I told Rosita to shut up—to which she simply shrugged and laughed.

One night several weeks later, Jeff and Bonnie, who had recently moved back to Atlanta from Raleigh, took Michael and me to an event called Paris on Peachtree, at which we tasted French wines and sampled cheeses and breads. At one point, while Michael and I were dancing, I noticed the man from my writing class—the one Rosita had sworn was flirting with me—dancing with a woman, presumably his wife. Laughing, I pointed him out to Michael and told him what Rosita had said.

"Oh, *really?*" he asked mildly, dancing the two of us over toward the man and his wife. "Come on, Sally, at least say hello to him. Better yet—let's go talk to him."

Forcing a smile, I stiffly waved at the man, who gave me a friendly smile and waved back. "No, Michael, I don't want to," I whispered into his neck.

I had not aroused the reaction I had expected or desired from Michael. So later that night while we waited outside for Jeff and Bonnie, still browsing in one of the shops nearby—and after a little more wine—I leaned against him seductively and asked, "Weren't you even just a little jealous of that guy?"

Instantly annoyed with me, Michael said, "No, of course I wasn't. Why would you think I would be?"

I was insulted. "Oh, I don't know—maybe I thought you *might* care if another man was interested in your wife! A little healthy jealousy *can* be exciting in a relationship, you know!"

"That's absurd," he said. "Jealousy is petty, and I refuse to resort to playing games like that."

"Maybe you just don't care. Maybe you'd be glad if someone else were interested in me."

"Now you're being ridiculous!" Jeff and Bonnie emerged from the shop then, putting an abrupt end to our argument.

That night, Michael and I went to sleep angry. In the morning, however, he seemed to be concerned that my feelings had been hurt. "I'm sorry, Sally," he said. "In all seriousness, I just did not want to get on that level with you. Don't you understand?"

No, I thought to myself, I really don't. But, tired of our being at odds, and *wanting* to understand, I said instead, "Yeah, I guess I do."

Even with the removal of fundamental legalism from our lives, the move to a refreshing new church, and the reduction in pressures, our marriage clearly had not improved. I had spent a lot of time thinking about what the problem might be, and, as of late, my thoughts had always returned to the same possible cause. Michael and I had at last come to a place in our lives where the children were growing more independent and were no longer in constant need of us. Since we had begun our family so young, I was excited at the thought that we could look forward to many years together, enjoying ourselves as a couple. I found myself thinking more as a woman and a wife, which further excited and renewed me, but with a drawback I couldn't ignore. Though Michael and I made love fairly often, I did not feel he truly *desired* me.

I observed the way other husbands looked at their wives from across the room—with obvious sexual desire—and I knew that that was not the way my husband looked at me. Increasingly, I felt a consuming need to be romanced—even sought after. And though I knew my emotions involved a degree of fantasy, I also knew that my longings were not entirely unrealistic.

One night, in an effort to explain how desperately I wanted his attention, I carefully told Michael, "I need to feel pursued, or something . . . I don't know. Maybe if you tried 'courting' me a little—made me feel that you *want* me. I really *need* that, Michael."

I ended—enticingly, I thought—by snuggling up close to him and saying, "I want all of this with *you,* my husband—no one else. But I'm getting to the point in my life where I've really *got* to have it."

I expected him to respond to my seductive invitation. His response shocked me: "Is that some sort of ultimatum you're giving me? And if I *don't*—what?"

"No, not at all." My embarrassment and disappointment turned to tears. After a few minutes passed, with me sniffling, Michael said, "I'm sorry, Sally, I didn't mean it that way. I think I understand what it is you want. I guess I've been depending on you too much to initiate things, haven't I? I promise things will be different. Okay?"

I wanted so much to believe him. "Okay," I said. "I really hope they will be, Michael. I know we could have a much better marriage, if we just try."

Wanting to get to know the Reverend Sam Candler better, in late July Michael and I invited him for dinner. After an enjoyable meal together, Sam settled himself down comfortably in a chair in the great room. About thirty-four years old, Sam was thin, attractive, with jet black hair and wire-rimmed glasses. He looked very much like the intellectual that he was. Yet he also had a playful smile that made it clear he was also capable of having fun.

Smiling, he looked at Michael and me after dinner and said, "So . . . tell me your stories."

Surprised at his request, I immediately became embarrassed. How could we tell an obviously highly intelligent Episcopal priest about the crazy course we had allowed our lives to take? I looked to Michael for help. He looked every bit as disconcerted as I was.

Laughing nervously, I said, "I don't think you *really* want to hear our stories. They haven't been all that much fun!"

"Oh, but I love to hear about other people's spiritual journeys. And," he added, "if you tell me yours, I'll tell you some of mine along the way." Since it was apparent he was waiting on us with great anticipation, Michael and I began sharing our "testimony."

About halfway through our tale, Sam took a deep breath and said, "Wow. You guys have really been through a lot. But . . . they say, 'To live is change, and to be perfect is to have changed much.' Now, how did you two get from *there* to where you are now?"

Once we had finished, Michael and I expected Sam either to be tongue-tied from shock or to announce suddenly that he had to go home to feed his dog. Both of us were amazed when, instead, he clasped his hands together in delight and, beaming, said loudly, "How *rich!* You two have lived such a rich life! What an evolution—such constant growth. This is fantastic!"

It was Michael and I who were tongue-tied.

Later that night, Michael and I talked about Sam's reaction to our lives. "Sam let me see our lives from a completely new angle," I began. "I couldn't believe how okay he was about everything! I feel better about our past. Maybe one day we'll both be really excited about our future."

"I hope so," Michael said. "We definitely have a lot of reason to be glad God showed us the way to the Episcopal church and to Sam Candler. It's a good start."

That night, thanks be to God, Sam's enthusiasm for life—all life— had opened the door to the possibility of healing and new life for Michael and me.

Our trip to St. Simons Island that summer was not one of our best. Not only was the house small, with no decks or even a porch, but there was no place to escape to be by oneself at all—and that summer, I often felt the need to escape. Still, once Michael and I were out on the beach, it was easy to allow the warmth of the sun and the rhythm of the waves to silence even the most pestering thoughts. Camille and Richard were there too, and it was fun to be with them and to watch how well the boys and their cousins interacted. On our vacations on the island, life always seemed more promising.

Though Michael and I were able to relax and have fun out or away together, I always noticed that his edginess and impatience rose again as we returned home. I also saw that more and more he withheld himself from friends such as Russell and Jeff and Robbie, who wanted to be close to him; from his sons, who needed him to talk openly with them as they grew into adulthood; and from me, as I longed to share dreams and know him more intimately.

I probed Michael more deeply for an explanation. "What's wrong with you that you can't seem to open up with your friends? They love you so much, and only want to become better friends with you."

In the past he would have cried when I asked that question and would have told me how much he wanted to be close with his friends but that it was difficult for him. Now he just shook his head.

"What about *me* then?" I continued. "I can't get close enough to you, either. And what about your boys? I can't tell you how many times I've heard them say, 'What's wrong with Dad?' What is your *problem?!*" I demanded.

Now he became angry. "My only *problem* is *you!* You expect too damn much! The only thing wrong with me is the crap I get from you about not pleasing you! Obviously I can't seem to make you happy. Why don't you go on and find out what would?"

Confused, frightened, and alarmed, I screamed back at him in a rage, "Why *can't* you be what I need? What's so impossible about being close to me—or to anyone else for that matter? And what do you *mean* by 'go on and find out'?"

He retreated then. "I don't know."

Those were insufferable times for Michael, who, even though he had finally made peace with the fact that God had chosen to leave in place his desires for other men, still labored under the maddening thought that he was trapped in his double life forever. At his darkest times he thought of committing suicide, or simply disappearing. He would tell me later how it had become increasingly harder for him to blame me for his distance and unhappiness; he hated leaving me with the impression that our marital difficulties were my fault. He told me that he had tried deliberately to push me away.

The children still went to bed comfortably secure in their parents' marriage, even as we were coming closer and closer to our day of reckoning.

Being in the Episcopal church and taking new classes—both the writing class and a new acting class—opened my world up to a more diverse group of people than the ones I had known in our narrow fundamentalist world. I found myself thinking and talking about all sorts of things I wouldn't have even considered before. I read books and listened to music that I would have banished as heresy a few years earlier. Out in the world at last, I began to dream my own dreams.

One morning in October 1990, I placed an impulsive phone call to the Cathedral of St. John the Divine in New York, where I knew Madeleine L'Engle was the writer in residence.

"Please, if you would be so kind as to send me Madeleine L'Engle's schedule, I would appreciate it so much. I'm trying to find out the next time she will be speaking in the South."

"Well, I can tell you. That will be in November, in Memphis, Tennessee," Ms. L'Engle's assistant informed me.

I called my friend Scarlett, who had introduced me to Madeleine L'Engle's books, and Rosita, who also admired Ms. L'Engle immensely, and the three of us quickly made plans to travel together to Memphis in November to hear our favorite author speak.

"Thank you," I said to the usher in Memphis as she handed me a one-page biography of Madeleine, and we took our seats in the large Episcopal church. "Look," I whispered to Scarlett and Rosita, "it says she also 'loves nothing better than to cook for her friends'—see, she's a woman after my own heart!" Knowing how much I loved doing the same for my friends, they both laughed. Suddenly Scarlett hushed us as Madeleine took her place on stage.

Madeleine L'Engle, tall and lovely, was seventy-two at the time. Her presence was magnificently strong and yet at the same time incredibly gentle. For about an hour she shared wonderful stories about writing and spirituality and told us a bit about her life. Until then, we had only read about these things in her books. Now the three of us sat spellbound by her every word.

After we returned from Memphis, I wrote Madeleine a letter in which I told her, among other things, a little about Michael's and my years in fundamentalist Christianity and about how reading *A*

Wrinkle in Time had enlarged my view of God. I received a very nice reply, which prompted me to consider attending her next writers' workshop, a three-day affair that would be combined with a three-day silent retreat at Holy Cross, an Episcopal monastery in upstate New York. Though I had grown up Episcopalian, I had never known that the Episcopal church had nuns or monks! For me, this would be a daring venture, and one I did not want to make alone. Scarlett agreed to accompany me, and together we made our plans.

Soon it was time for Michael and me to prepare our annual Christmas dinner party for our friends. A new fresh-air market had opened up that sold wonderful produce, cheeses, and breads and also carried a wide assortment of fresh and unusual flowers. Michael offered to do the shopping at the market while I ran other errands.

Arriving home after Michael and walking into our bedroom, I saw him bending over something on the top of a wooden chest at the foot of our bed. Startled to hear me come in, he looked up blushing, grinning widely, and asked, "What do you think?"

I took one look at the brilliant splash of colorful flowers arranged expertly and beautifully at the foot of our bed and surprised myself by shouting at him, "What are you doing? That's not what you're supposed to be doing!" A meanness arose in me such as I had never felt before. "That's *my* job—not yours! *I'm* supposed to arrange flowers—not you. Why don't you go and do something a man is supposed to do!"

"I'm sorry," Michael said, and he quietly left the room.

I regretted my words as soon as I had spoken them. Now they hung in the room like a reprehensible haze. Michael was crushed—both by what I had said and by what I had not. He had not gotten angry, though I wished he had. I felt awful for hurting him and also felt terribly angry and confused. I asked myself why seeing him arranging the flowers had bothered me so much. I got no answer.

I had reached the point where I wasn't making much sense to myself anymore.

After a while, I went into the kitchen and apologized to Michael for my horrible outburst. He forgave me. I knew, though, that I had deeply wounded his spirit and that it would take a while to heal.

January 8, 1991: Everything seems very surreal at this point. I don't want to remain in a dreamlike state at all. Rather I want to experience every part of this journey into "another world" to the absolute fullest.

Those were the words I wrote in my journal when—Scarlett being sick—I flew to New York alone.

I was awestruck when the driver let me out in front of the massive old stone monastery, and I felt very small when I knocked on the huge front door. The door was opened by a black monk in a hooded white robe who introduced himself and took my suitcases. As we walked along the hallway, which was lined with beautiful antique chests and an occasional chair, the monk told me that he was from Namibia and had been in the States only a short while. I apologized for my suitcases being so heavy. He smiled and, in his thick, beautiful accent, gently answered, "Why do you apologize? They are just your bags." His words spoke a simple truth of acceptance to me. I wished that I was as settled within myself as he appeared to be.

My room, or "cell," proved to be a small chamber with a simple bed, desk, chair, and chest of drawers; there was a shared bath across the hall. When the monk set my suitcase down and left, closing the door behind him, I sat down on my bed and, feeling suddenly overwhelmed by emotion, began to cry. Opening my journal, I wrote only four words: *Joy, fear, anticipation, holiness.*

Life at the monastery followed a steady routine. Every evening the monks and guests held compline (evening prayers), which was followed by the "Great Silence," which lasted through breakfast the next morning. After compline, I settled into my warm bed—where, surrounded by books and notebooks, I felt completely pampered.

When I awoke the next morning I was pleased to see that a light snow (enough that it would have closed schools in Georgia) had fallen during the night. Eating breakfast in silence was awkward and uncomfortable that first morning. My chair scraped the floor and my spoon hit the side of the bowl. No matter how careful I was, every move I made seemed to be *noisy*. But I was determined to try to use this opportunity to make silence my friend—or at least no longer my archenemy.

During the Eucharist that morning the celebrant had thanked God "for the wisdom He gives in the variety of His church." As I knew I would experience all kinds of people and ideas in the next five days, his words had touched me as being almost prophetic. Later, while waiting in the chapel for noonday prayers to begin, I was thinking to myself that I still could not imagine what sitting in a writing class and being taught by Madeleine L'Engle would be like, when suddenly there she was, entering the choir stalls with the monks, wearing an elegant black velvet hooded cloak. She looked regal.

Classes began after lunch. I was unprepared for the feeling of warmth and safety I quickly experienced there. The writers were urged to be serious about their work, yet Madeleine insisted that critiques, when they were made out loud, always be given in a spirit of gentle encouragement. The workshop went by much too fast, and before I knew it, only a few hours remained until the beginning of the three-day silent retreat.

That afternoon I sat in the parlor with a group of deeply spiritual women who were discussing books and teachers I had never heard of. I mostly just listened. At one point, however, I shyly said, "I would really *like* to learn more spiritually, but I'm so afraid of being deceived." Even as I said it, I suspected that my fear of being deceived was a part of my fundamentalist past that I definitely needed to jettison.

The woman next to me, who was around fifty years old and had the most peaceful countenance, calmly answered me, "If you live in a cocoon like that, Sally, how will you ever learn discernment? You don't learn by remaining isolated. Check things out. Then if you decide it's rot—toss it!" I wished so much that I really could stop being afraid.

During dinner, which was our last talking meal before the three-day silent retreat began, I happened to sit next to a woman who had come up from the city for the retreat, though not for the workshop. Her name was Stephanie Cowell, and our meeting would prove to change both our lives. As we talked, I thought to myself that no two women could have come from such different places and led such different lives as she and I had. Stephanie was an attractive woman in her late forties, a single mother with two grown sons. An opera singer and writer, she had lived in Manhattan all her life. We enjoyed hearing about each other's lives, and I looked forward to sharing the weekend with her, even in silence. We both hoped that we would have the chance to talk together more on Sunday. I had no idea then why I was so drawn to Stephanie, but I thank God that I was.

Madeleine's voice was the only one we heard for the next three days as she shared meditations with us from her book *The Glorious Impossible*. In one meditation she told us: "Christ became flesh and dwelt among us so that the flesh would be redeemed and glorified. He intended for us to *rejoice* and be *glad* in our bodies!" Suddenly it made sense! We had spent so many years denying our flesh as James had commanded us—making us afraid to enjoy "things of the flesh" like good food and wine, intimate friendships, and the beauty of our own bodies—when in fact our flesh had been redeemed in Christ. Amazing, I thought. Simply and wonderfully amazing.

By the end of the week, I found that the ritual of silence had become my friend. Sitting at breakfast, or with others in the library as we quietly read or wrote, I felt at peace and unified.

On the last day of the retreat, I met with Madeleine L'Engle for a private counseling session in her room. I had never experienced as much compassion as I did while we talked about fundamentalism and the fear of deception it had produced in me. Many times my pain seemed to show on her face. "Make yourself available to God," she said. "The fears will slowly subside, until, one day, they will be gone." I believed that her words were true; at least I hoped they were.

When I spoke to her about Michael, and my acute concerns for him, she encouraged me, "Be gentle with him."

When our talk was over, Madeleine said, "Why don't you come to the fall workshop and retreat, at a convent in Brewster in upstate New York, called St. Cuthbert's? Being with the nuns is a totally different experience from being here with the monks—and one that I believe you will also enjoy."

Sunday came, and after one more meal together it was time to go home—back to the "real world." Folding myself into Madeleine's outstretched arms one last time, I thanked her for her advice and kissed her on the cheek, then got into a car with the guest-master, who was driving Stephanie, another woman, and me to the train station.

On the train back to New York, Stephanie began to tell the other woman and me about a novel she had written and for which she was trying to find a publisher. It was called *Gentle Rebels*. "It's set in Edwardian times," she told us, "and is about two men—two gay men. It tells of their passionate love for one another, and for life."

For reasons I didn't fathom, I found myself saying, "I would like to read it, if you'll let me."

She laughed sweetly and said, "Well, yes, certainly you may. But I'm not sure you will like it. I write rather explicitly about homosexuality, and I fear you might find it offensive."

Feeling unusually fearless, I said to her, "But I *want* to try and understand about homosexuality. It will be a good stretch for me." Stephanie promised she would send the manuscript within the week.

When we parted in Grand Central Station, Stephanie turned to me and said, "Sally, I would love it if you would come a few days early for the workshop and retreat next fall and spend some time in the city with me."

I was ecstatic at the possibility of having a few days with Stephanie in New York City. "I'd love to!" I shouted.

My reentry into real life wasn't easy. For one thing, I could not convince the children that breakfast would be a more pleasant meal if it were eaten in silence. Michael, though interested in hearing about my time at Holy Cross, still seemed off in his own world—whatever world that was. I tried to be gentle with him, as Madeleine had suggested, but I was growing more and more exasperated with the fact that he was withdrawing further into himself and leaving me more and more out of his life.

Stephanie's manuscript of *Gentle Rebels* came within a week, as she had promised it would. I tore it open quickly.

"What's that?" Michael asked me when he saw the huge stack of paper.

"Oh, it's just a novel that a woman I met at Holy Cross wrote. I asked her to let me read it. It's nothing you would be interested in, I can assure you!" Actually I wasn't too sure what Michael would think about Stephanie's book. I decided to read a little before telling him what it was about.

And read it I did. For the next week I could hardly put *Gentle Rebels* down, though I did blink in surprise at the frank (and beautifully written) love scenes. One night I carried the bulky manuscript to bed with me. When I came to a part where the two men—one a good bit older than the other—were playfully wrestling and fell into each other's arms in a tender embrace, I began to cry.

Michael looked up from the book he was reading and gently asked, "What is it?"

"May I read this to you?" I asked a little nervously. He nodded. After reading aloud to him, I said, "Michael, these two men really love each other. I didn't know that homosexuals really loved one another like this." Suddenly embarrassed, I added, "I always thought it was— you know—all about sex."

Michael looked at me with a soft smile but said nothing, so I went on reading Stephanie's novel. After a moment, he returned to his own book as well.

I read the manuscript in its entirety, then wrote Stephanie to tell her how wonderful I thought it was, and how it had indeed helped me to better understand homosexual love. After that, we exchanged letters regularly.

My future, meanwhile, looked less and less hopeful to me. I had begun to wonder seriously whether I was losing my mind. Even my closest friends, Bonnie and Patty, along with my sister Camille, had begun to suggest that perhaps I did expect too much from my relationship with Michael. Sometimes I convinced myself that they were right. At other times I thought I would be driven completely mad by my knowledge that *something* was wrong—very wrong. And I began to have a new fear: that Michael knew what that something was and was choosing not to tell me.

Finally, one night in March, while we were talking in bed, I said, "I feel there is something definite you are withholding from me, and I think you know what it is."

At first Michael was furious. He shouted things I had heard too many times before: "The only problem with me is you! You would make any man crazy! Why don't you just leave me alone!"

His anger only fueled my own. I slapped him on the chest and cried, "You know you withhold yourself from me. And I *know* that you are keeping *something* from me! What is it? Tell me!"

Michael grabbed me—too roughly—and I could see that he had lost himself in his anger and despair. Though he had never raised a hand against me in his life, I was certain he was going to now.

"Go ahead—hit me! I'll scream for the boys and let them see how much you hate me!" Then I burst into tears.

Michael immediately dropped my arms and began to cry. "I *am* withholding something from you," he said, "and I need some time to think about what I have to tell you."

I tried to remain calm, so as not to frighten him back into himself. "Take the time you need to think about it, Michael."

Exhausted by our emotional ordeal, we moved to our own sides of the bed and fell asleep. In all the years of our marriage, Michael and I had never slept close to each other. I wondered now if it was because we instinctively respected each other's need for dream space—our dreams being, as they were, so very far apart.

The next weekend, which Michael spent away on a ski trip, was pure hell. I waited, sometimes feeling angry at Michael and constantly frightened of what I was going to find out when he returned. All the while I tried to prepare myself.

My sister was now convinced that it was another woman. "Come on, Sally. It has to be. All the signs are there. He's been working out and has a new hairstyle and new clothes. He looks great. But guess what? I hate to say it, but it hasn't been great for you, has it?" I tried to imagine that there might be another woman, but I remembered our past discussions in which Michael had told me that he was never attracted to other women. I remembered how safe that had made me feel.

On the night that Michael returned home, we settled the children into bed and sat down to talk in the little room off of our bedroom. He came out with a partial truth: "I'm just not happy, Sally. I'm not happy with any part of my life—well, except for the children. I'm unhappy with my job—and with our marriage."

I braced myself and asked, "Is there another woman?"

"No!" he answered emphatically.

Still hearing my sister's words in my mind, I asked again, "Are you *sure* you haven't slipped up and been with another woman—even once?"

Michael's face reddened and he lowered it before answering me again, "No. Never even once. I promise you that. There has never been another woman."

A thought struck me. "I bet you've come close, though. I bet you've been *tempted* to be with somebody else. With the way you've been feeling, I know it would only have been a matter of time before there would have been someone else." I can't say exactly why I pressed the issue; maybe, due to my own growing dissatisfaction, I was trying to nudge him to go ahead and say what it was I believed to be the truth—that he wanted out of our marriage. That is not, however, what happened.

"Okay, I guess I've been tempted to stray, and perhaps it *would* have been only a matter of time before I'd have given in to temptation. But that's not what this is all about, Sally."

"Why do you think you're so miserable, then? Why can't you be happy with your life—and with us?"

"It has everything to do with never having had choices in my life. First we *had* to get married," he said, "then I *had* to go to Georgia State rather than Tulane, then I *had* to work at a job that paid well but wasn't what I *wanted* to do. See—no choices. I guess this all sounds pretty selfish, doesn't it?"

"No, not really. It's not like I haven't had some of the same feelings." I was thinking that lately I had begun to believe that things would never be the way I wanted them to be with Michael and me, but that there was no other life for either of us except the one we shared together. Until this moment I had not allowed myself to see how trapped that made me feel. The thought gave me an unexpected surge of strength. "I can tell you one thing for sure, Michael. *I'm* at the place in *my* life where I have no desire to remain married if you don't. Frankly, I need to be chosen as much as you need to choose." Angry tears were stinging my eyes. I did not want to cry now and wiped them away furiously. "So," I continued, "you take the time you need to *choose* what it is that you want for your life—and that includes whether or not you want it to include me."

Michael needed to go away for however long it took him to decide what he wanted. Telling the children that he had to take a sudden business trip, I watched him drive away, hoping with all my heart that it would not take him very long and that when he returned he would have made the right decision. Michael looked thin and haggard when he left. I knew he had not been eating or sleeping well. I already missed him.

For Valentine's Day that year I had given Michael a copy of Robert Bly's book *Iron John*, hoping it might help him to understand his frustrations, which I assumed had something to do with his manhood. When he left, I noticed that the book was tucked under his arm along with his Bible and a notebook.

After a week of silence, Michael called and, in an unusually gentle voice, said he was ready to talk. We agreed to meet at the local ballpark, where one of the boys had a baseball game. As soon as he drove up, I could not help but notice how radiant he looked in comparison to the way he had looked a week ago. He smiled, lovingly, and handed me a letter, asked me to read it, and said that we would talk about it after the game.

His letter read, in part:

> These past few days have allowed me to see wounded parts of
> me that have never been attended to and those (hurts, questions,
> regrets, resentments) have had a tight hold on my true self. All
> of these things had made me position myself at a distance from
> the ones I really love, and the ones that really love me. I have re-
> alized that surely all I have is all I'll ever need. I'm not sure of all
> that is in me, but I know that in time it will all emerge. . . . I do
> love you and I do choose you.

That night we talked for hours. He told me that he had been going to a therapist for about six months and apologized for having kept it a secret. While I was surprised to learn that Michael had undergone therapy without telling me, I was also glad, especially since the therapy appeared to be bearing fruit. He seemed newly inspired, and it appeared that being able to choose had cured him of whatever doubts he had had.

The next day was Easter Sunday, the day of rebirth, and I did indeed feel reborn as Michael and I sat close together in church, holding hands tightly. Every now and then Michael gave my hand a squeeze. When he did, I looked at him—almost to make sure he was real. Halfway through the service he leaned over, kissed my cheek, and whispered, "Happy Easter."

Suddenly it seemed I had all the passion from my husband that I had ever imagined. For the next several weeks we were like honeymooners. Even the children noticed the change. On several mornings, after sending the last one out the door (Samuel was now in kindergarten), we rushed back to bed and made love—and it was the best ever.

I heard giggles behind us at church, which only made Michael smile and pull me closer to him. One friend told me that her daughter asked her why Michael and I always hugged so much. "I told her I didn't know, but it sure was great that y'all did!" Leaning closer to me, she added, "Whatever the reason is, I wish it'd rub off on my husband and me." I blushed and laughed, thinking maybe it *had* all been worth it after all.

It was not to last, however. And when Michael's tenseness returned about a month later, it was worse than ever.

Beside myself with worry, I finally found the nerve to ask Michael, "What's wrong with you lately? I mean—things aren't the same with us, you know?"

"It's just my job," he said. "I promise it has nothing to do with you, Sally. There's just a lot of pressure on me right now. It'll pass, I promise. Then things will be back the way they have been, okay?" He gave me a reassuring hug.

It did not pass, however, and as summer came, the fear that surely my sister had to be right grew within me. Whenever we talked, she begged me to ask him again. "I have," I cried. "He *swears* he has *not* been with another woman, Camille. I've asked so many times, I've almost made him mad."

"Hmm," she said. "Ask him again."

One afternoon shortly after that conversation, I drove to Coal Mountain to pick up the boys at school. Heading down the winding mountain road, I thought about how disturbed Michael seemed. "He really *does* act like a man might if he was having an affair with another woman," I said out loud. "But he swears he's not." Suddenly an absolutely absurd thought slipped into my mind.

What if Michael was attracted to other men? What a horrible, monstrous thing to even think about my own husband! I told myself. Still, for a minute I let my mind go. "Okay," I spoke out loud again, "there is *no way* Michael would have actually *been* with another man. But what if he's been *tempted* along those lines? *That* could definitely be what's been eating away at him." Immediately, the guilt returned. "That's awful, Sally. How can you even think about something as ludicrous as that?" I said.

Try as I did after that to push all thoughts of that sort aside, the question *what if?* occasionally nagged me. No matter, I chided myself, there was no way I could see myself ever accusing Michael of something like that, so I might as well go ahead and forget about it.

One night that spring, Michael and I met our friends Robbie and Patty at a restaurant in midtown Atlanta. There was a wait for a table, so we sat down at the bar to have a drink. The four of us were having a great time together that night—the sort of time that made me believe things would be fine with Michael and me if I could just hang in there.

Patty preferred to measure her own Scotch from an antique silver flask she carried with her. Somehow I managed to unscrew the stubborn top off of the flask after both men tried unsuccessfully to do so. It was one of those rare victorious moments, and when I was done, Patty and I burst out laughing and slipped off to the ladies' room together— leaving the men behind, smiling weakly. In the ladies' room, still laughing, I flipped my hair over to brush it out. When I came back up, Patty looked squarely at me and exclaimed gleefully, "*Your* husband is the most dapper, intelligent, and . . . either the dandiest . . . or the most *gay* man I know. Oh, for goodness sake, I don't know what I'm trying to say!" She trailed off laughing.

I caught her arm and held it. "*What* was that you said—about him being *gay?*"

"I don't know why I said that! I just meant—well, Michael is just so *stunning!*" For some reason, I let it go. Her comment stuck with me, though—right in my craw.

In July, it was time for our yearly vacation to St. Simons Island. I hoped that maybe a week together on the island would help Michael and me to return to the more loving place where we had been at Eastertime.

Camille and I had talked about Michael's and my marriage problems off and on all week. She still believed that Michael was seeing another woman. No one understood me—right down to my feelings of sexual unfulfillment—as my sister did. Not only did Camille know that I was feeling worse than ever about myself, but she also knew that it would be almost impossible for me to believe that I could ever have another life—much less one that included another man in it—if things did not work out between Michael and me. So, while she hoped for the best, she subtly helped prepare me for the worst.

One night, lounging in the same twin beds we had slept in as teenagers, she finally told me the truth about how she saw Michael's and my relationship. "I've listened patiently all these years while you raved on and on about your wonderful life together. I knew good and well that some of it was the way you *wanted* it to be, more than the way it really was. I've also heard you, especially these last few years, complain about the lack of desire you feel from Michael. I have to tell you the truth: Richard desires me to the point of distraction! You're *not wrong* to want more from Michael, Sally. In all honesty, I want the two of you to either get it right—or get out of each other's lives!"

Knowing that Camille was as adamantly opposed to divorce as I was, it surprised me to hear her speak that way. Sighing deeply, however, I said, "You're right—except for one thing. There's no way I'd ever leave Michael." She looked at me unhappily, knowing that it was probably true. Then, laughing, I pulled up my nightie to reveal the stretch marks on my tummy and said, "Besides, I would *die* if another man ever saw *these!*"

She didn't laugh along with me, as I had thought she would. Instead she addressed me firmly: "Stop saying that about yourself. Your figure is precious."

"Okay, well, I guess *somebody* doesn't seem to think so," I said, no longer laughing.

"That's *his* problem," she answered angrily.

Midway through the week, Michael and I and Camille and Richard decided to go out to dinner separately as couples, leaving two of the older boys to baby-sit the three youngest. Before Michael and I even made it out the door, we were arguing about something, and I threatened to stay home. I stood at the bathroom mirror putting makeup on my scowling face and grumbling to myself about Michael's continual bad mood. Suddenly, I thought to myself, What the hell—I'm going to ask him tonight. If I'm wrong, all he can do is be insulted!

Still angry with each other, Michael and I ended up at our favorite restaurant on the island, Blanche's Courtyard. Michael ordered a bottle of wine, and we both tried to relax.

Michael started the conversation off by saying, "I apologize for being in such a bad mood these last couple of days." My heart softened immediately; I still wanted so much for things to be good with us.

"I'm not doing so great," Michael admitted, "and I'm not sure why." Taking my hand, but not looking at me, he said, "It's not you, Sally, I promise."

"It's okay," I said. But of course we both knew it wasn't.

After dinner, Michael and I strolled slowly along the beach until we found ourselves back at the King and Prince Hotel, where, as a child, I had stayed every summer with my parents. Michael suggested we stop in the pub to have a drink. I agreed. I still had something on my mind, and one more drink might make it easier to bring it up. We ordered two Irish Creams on the rocks and took our drinks out to the swing with the best view of the ocean—the same one I had shared with Michael twenty-one years before on our first trip to St. Simons Island.

We sat in silence for a while, holding hands and listening to the music of the waves, and swinging slowly back and forth, very much together. I thought that I had loved Michael in too many ways and for too long to settle for less than the whole truth.

From somewhere came the rush of courage I needed. My heart pounding, I asked him, "You're still keeping something from me, aren't you?"

I felt him squeeze my hand slightly as he nodded his head.

"If I promise you I will not hurt you with the children and will tell no one unless you give me permission," I said, "does that help you tell me your secret?"

He said very softly, "Yes, it does."

After a few long moments, he finally spoke the truth to me. "It is not other women," he said slowly. "It *is* other men."

With that confession, the world as we knew it ceased to be.

chapter 10

Precious Pain

During those first numb moments after Michael told me his secret, I saw myself walking down, across the sand, and out into those steady, dependable waves, avoiding tomorrow and the next day and the next. But then, taking a deep breath, I realized that what I was feeling more than anything else was a deep sense of relief. When at last I looked at Michael, I saw it in his face too.

Slowly he began to unravel the details of his secret life to me. I listened, in horror, as first he told me about the nightmarish encounters he had had with the senior boys in high school. "It makes me sick to think about you carrying that kind of pain for so long," I said, choking back tears. "And it makes me furious that you couldn't tell anyone—especially your own parents!"

"I really couldn't, though," Michael said. "Even though I hated what they did, I was attracted to one of those guys—which confused the hell out of me. It also made it seem like it was my fault, so I figured my parents would somehow blame *me* if I told them. I couldn't bring myself to face their disappointment."

"I know. You always were their golden boy, weren't you?"

I had embarrassed him now, and he looked away. "Yeah, I guess so, something like that. Besides, those guys said they'd make life hell for me if I ever told anyone."

"I understand. I'm just so sorry."

Suddenly something hit me. "Michael, that was the scar you prayed about in James Smith's group, wasn't it?"

"Uh-huh," he said. "I asked God so many times to remove that scar. All those years I thought if He would just take it away, I'd be able to stop being tempted in my other life. But it never happened."

"I know," I answered weakly. Taking all of this in, I finally let my tears run freely.

After a while I asked him, "Do you think that maybe because those guys molested you at such an impressionable age, that's what made you *think* you were a homosexual?"

"Maybe. I guess sometimes I've wondered if that's what caused it. You know—until you, I was *not* comfortable with girls," he said sheepishly. "But after we got together, I figured I must be okay."

As we continued talking, Michael told me the truth about his double life over the last fifteen years and about the many attempts he had made to free himself from his struggles with homosexuality. As he worked his way up to the present, I tried to digest his words. Certain that his answer would be that he wanted a divorce, I finally asked him, "What do you want to do?"

His response surprised me. "Well, what I'm hoping is, now that everything's out on the table with us, maybe I really can change. I'd like to continue in counseling, and I'd like you to go to someone too."

"If that's what you really want, Michael. I'm willing to do whatever we can to try and fix this."

"That's what I want. Now, let's try to get some sleep. We can talk some more in the morning."

He was right. It was close to dawn, and we needed to sleep. He and I both knew that when the morning light came, our life of illusion would be forever left behind. It would be a whole new day for us.

We went to bed exhausted but wrapped in each other's arms—something we had never done before. As I lay thinking, I knew that for at least that one night I wanted to rest in the hope and love we both shared, because eventually the anger would come.

And come it did.

August 1, 1991, 5:30 A.M.: I'm wide awake after only two hours' sleep. Well, now I know. And it is good that I finally do. There really had been something dreadfully wrong with Michael all along. At least I know I'm not crazy. At this point I might be murderous—but I'm not crazy. While I wouldn't ever want to go back to the lies, the hell that lies ahead both terrifies and sickens me. I feel that I am entering into a world—an abyss?—that I cannot avoid. Neither can I embrace it. It is not my world—but it *is* Michael's. Please, God, be kinder to Michael than I fear I might be to him in the days to come. I love him, but I hope You love him more.

That afternoon, while the boys went to the beach with their cousins, Michael and I sat on the bedroom floor of our condo for several hours and I asked him question after question. I wanted details, which he patiently gave. "What exactly did you and another man do—sexually?" He told me and I listened.

Finally I said, "Michael, tell me exactly what it was you got from being with a man that you did not get from being with me."

"You probably won't believe this, but it was actually more the intimacy—the strong hugs and cuddling—that I needed from men. And I guess a sort of playfulness—wrestling around, stuff like that."

When I didn't say anything he gently said, "Sex was always better with you, Sally."

In those first few days, Michael and I were, for the most part, caught up in the freedom that living in the truth had already given us. We talked as often as we could. At one point I suggested, "Now that we can talk about all of this—can't you just tell me what your needs are and I can try to meet them? I can definitely give you more cuddling, and I'll even try wrestling if you want!"

For the first time in days we both laughed. Michael hugged me and said, "Yeah, that's what I *hope* will happen. Thanks for being so willing."

"Now that you're not carrying such a heavy secret, do you think you'll be able to be closer friends with Jeff and Robbie and that that might help?"

"I hope so," Michael said.

"Do you think you could tell them the truth?"

"I'll have to really think about that," he said dubiously. Frowning, he added, "Sally, I've got to ask you to do something. At least for now, and maybe forever, I don't want you to tell anyone about me without my permission." He paused before adding, "That includes your sister."

I hated the thought of keeping my first secret ever from my sister. Still, nothing was more important than saving our marriage. "Okay, I promise."

Sometime during the third night after Michael had divulged his secret to me, I suddenly awoke in a rage and found myself beating Michael awake with my fists and shouting, "What about AIDS? Damn you! You risked my life! And your children's!"

Groaning, he said, "I promise I was always safe, and I've been tested several times. Just to be sure, I planned to be retested when we got back from vacation. I'm sorry I've put you through all of this, Sally. Believe me—everything will be okay."

I tried to calm myself down and think rationally. He had said he was careful. I hoped that that was enough. I could not go back to sleep, however, for thinking about the fact that—safe sex or not—

Michael had played Russian roulette with our lives. I was furious now, and for the rest of the night I wondered who this man beside me really was. Did I even want to stay with someone who would risk his life without at least giving me the chance to get out first? How could I ever trust him again? In those hours, and in my hurt and anger, I hated Michael.

I prayed for God to have mercy on Michael, on me, and on our children, and for Michael not to have contracted AIDS. How would we ever explain to the boys something as horrible as their father having AIDS? I knew that in order to survive, I would somehow have to lay my worry aside. And if there was any chance at all of Michael and me staying together, I had to get a better handle on my feelings. I forced myself to curl up close to my sleeping husband. Soon the stronger desire that I had to love him and to try to understand what was still so painful and new overcame the anger and the hate.

After our return home from St. Simons Island, Michael allowed me to tell his secret to my friend Bonnie and said that she could discreetly discuss it with her husband, Jeff. Bonnie was shocked and distraught over what we were going through. Jeff was equally shocked, and angry at Michael's unfaithfulness to me. Still, he promised to be the best friend he could be.

In a few days, my very intuitive friend Patty called and said, "Michael thinks he's gay, doesn't he?" Since Michael had already told me he didn't mind if Patty and Robbie knew, I told her yes. "Robbie and I will do anything you want us to, Sally," she promised.

Now that our closest friends knew what Michael and I were dealing with, I counted on their support to help us stay together.

While Michael went to the Atlanta health department for the results of his AIDS test, I took a large bottle of wine and, along with Bonnie, went to Patty and Robbie's house. The four of us spent the afternoon drinking wine and talking as friends—trying to help each other understand Michael's battle with homosexuality. When I knew Michael would be home, I returned to our house. As soon as I saw his face I knew that he was not HIV-positive. Together we thanked God for His mercy and took the good news as confirmation that we were to fight hard for our marriage.

We held on to the belief that—with counseling and a lot of support, and even though it would be very hard at times—Michael could successfully choose to let go of his homosexual past.

One day I told him, "The only way I can handle this, Michael, is to admit that our old marriage, at least as we knew it—or didn't know it—is over. We have to begin all over again with each other. When you're ready to commit to that, let me know."

"Okay. I understand, and I will," he said.

One night a week later, Michael surprised me by asking me out to dinner. At the restaurant he presented me with a new set of wedding rings to signify the beginning of a new marriage commitment. As he slipped the rings on my finger, I was overcome with love for him, and with a hope that our "new" marriage would be what I had always longed for.

During the month of September we continued, for the most part, to be very hopeful about our future together. Michael said that his divulging of his secret, and my reaction, which he had feared would be one of rejection or retribution, had knocked down a huge wall of impossibility. While I shared his hope, and wanted to love him unconditionally, I began to worry silently whether *all* of the needs that had been met for him in homosexual activity could now be filled by me and a few close friends.

I also feared investing in our marriage everything I had emotionally—which was what I believed it would take—only to have Michael decide he couldn't change and, in the end, leave me. And would I become so consumed with trying to meet Michael's needs that I would completely lose myself in the process? All these questions began to plague me, along with the one that bothered me the most but that I would not discuss with Michael: could I ever trust him again? When he was away, how would I know for sure that he had not fallen back into temptation? Would he come home and tell me? Sadly, I thought not.

Michael had promptly resumed his therapy sessions, and I had begun mine. Already aware of his situation, Michael's counselor said that he would help him in his endeavor to live a heterosexual life. Michael hoped that through further counseling he might uncover the source of his "homosexual tendencies" and conquer them once and for all. Each week I waited anxiously to hear how his session went. I was so afraid that after one of them Michael would come home and tell me that he and his therapist had decided it was impossible for him to change.

As for me, my therapist, Ruth, likened my situation to living in the shadow of a volcano that had recently erupted.

One week, while listening to me, she said she often felt as though Michael, whom she had never met, were sitting right beside me.

"That's not okay," she added. "I need to be able to 'see' Sally—alone. My goal for you is going to be: 'Help Sally find Sally.'"

"I know you're right, and I do want to rediscover who I am. But I already believe I know two things: Michael *can* change, and he and I can make it."

"It's too soon to have sifted through the debris thoroughly enough to have possibly assessed all of the damage" she replied. "I'll help you find your own way in this, Sally, and I will never tell you what to do. You've had enough of being told what to do in your life. It's time that you learned to trust your own instincts and make your own decisions." While the thought of trusting my instincts still sounded very unsettling to me, I also knew that if I was going to survive in a world as precarious as I now knew this one could be, I had better learn how.

One week, I told Ruth that I felt as though my thoughts and questions never rested. "I only sleep for a few hours a night, and I think I'm having some slight panic attacks. Without warning, the recent events of my life seem to reach up and grab me in a vise of fear when, I assume, my guard's down—while cleaning the house, for instance, or changing a bed. My heart begins to pound so hard that mentally I try to find something secure to hold on to. But everything around me seems so unsteady. I just have to stop what I'm doing and breathe deeply until it passes."

Ruth explained her thoughts on this carefully. "I believe the reason for your feelings of panic is the result of your hiding something from yourself—something you need to allow yourself to deal with. Perhaps you're not allowing yourself to own up to some of your true feelings."

What I couldn't tell her yet was that I wasn't as certain that Michael and I could "fix" our problem as I said I was. Instead, I said, "You know something? I haven't made a decision on my own since I was sixteen years old. *That* makes me mad."

Michael and I finally decided to tell the oldest boys that there was a problem between us, but that we were going to work through it. We told them we were each in private counseling and that we would also need to devote all of the energy we could to our marriage. In order to do that, we had come to the difficult decision of letting Sarah, who was now eight, return to the state. Her caseworker, we told them, had already found a loving family who could care for her better than we could under the present circumstances.

On the day that Sarah left us to go to her new family, she hugged each of us good-bye and cheerfully said, "Don't be sad! I'm going to my new Mama and Daddy and my new sister!" In addition to the fact that her new family was thrilled to have her, Sarah's inability to form deep emotional attachments enabled her to make the transition easily.

For Michael and me, the loss of Sarah—although very sad—was quickly covered over by the threatening problems we were facing. For us it was a matter of survival, but the boys were terribly upset and angry with us, unable to understand how we could let her go.

"If you can give Sarah up because things are tough, how do we know you won't give one of us up one day, too?" Matthew asked. Even with our assurance that that would never happen, losing Sarah shook their world so much that I feared what would happen if, in the end, we had to tear it completely apart.

As soon as I could, with Michael's permission, I wrote to Madeleine L'Engle and told her about the situation he and I now faced. For some reason, I had a tremendous need to connect with her about what was happening in my life. Not only did I covet Madeleine's prayers, but I also hoped to have her guidance when, in November, I went to St. Cuthbert's for the writers' workshop and retreat.

I also wrote my new friend in New York, Stephanie Cowell. Though I did not tell her specifically what Michael had disclosed to me, I did tell her that he and I were working through a monumental problem in our marriage. And that, if the invitation was still open, I should very much like to go to New York a few days before Madeleine's workshop to spend time with her. I quickly received a letter back from her telling me that she was terribly sorry to hear about the problems that Michael and I were having and that she would pray for us. She also asked that I please come to New York and said that we would have plenty of time to talk. After discussing it with Michael—who thought a trip to New York would be very good for me—I made travel plans for the week before Thanksgiving.

As a result of my counseling, I slowly began to focus on my needs in addition to Michael's. Once I did, I had many questions. Could I expect a level of intimacy from my husband now that I had not expected before? I still needed to be romanced and desired; could he feel enough to do that now? I wanted to share all aspects of life with my husband—to be, in terms of what Madeleine had shared with us at Holy Cross, "cocreators" with him; could we be that together? And as he became more fully who he was—and as I did the same—would he be excited about who I was becoming, or would my changes be a threat to him? I had come up with the last question because I had realized that for so long I feared that if I was honest about what I needed or wanted, or about what I perceived as truth, I would be demanding too much from my husband. I did not want to live under those restraints any longer. I wondered how—despite his own evolution—my progression would affect Michael, who had been used to having a large measure of control over me.

Besides which, it seemed that every few days another small volcanic eruption would take place, leaving behind more debris to deal with.

September 17, 1991: All these years, the boys have unknowingly had a father with a destructive secret problem that left him tense and inconsistent. That, in turn, left them with a mother who thought she was losing her mind. A father in hiding plus a hysterical mother equal confused and angry children. What did I expect? Our children deserve to have two whole parents.

Well—I'm angry at God, at Michael, and at myself for being such a foolish coward—knowing for so long that our family was drowning, but never being strong enough to pull the plug. My guys—my babies—need for Michael and me to get ourselves together. Or—is it too late for that?

I did not yet know that in order to be whole, we needed to divide.

September 18, 1991: Bothering me more and more is the dark mystery I now see whenever I look at my husband. Just the fact of his "other life" gives me the feeling of having been married to a stranger for twenty-one years! *How* could he have lived like that and lied to me for all those years? I feel used and disrespected as a person. My feelings, my choices, and my needs—all were put aside for his own. How selfish! How cruel.

I asked Michael several times—because I could never fully understand it—how he had managed to live his double life for so long. Why did it not drive him mad? It was then that Michael told me about Don, the man he had become involved with in South Carolina, and of how he had thought about ending his life that night on the bridge. He told me, too, of other times when he felt so estranged from me, and from the life we shared that yet was not really a part of his other life either, that he had considered just driving away and never coming back. The love he had for me and for his children, he said with tears streaming down his face, was what had always brought him home.

I had learned a lot in one month about a different "world" and about a man who had tried everything—from deliverance from demons to Christian counseling to change. Now he hoped he could be what we both believed he had to be for his family's sake—a heterosexual man. No man ever wanted more than Michael did to change. No man ever tried harder or had more to lose if he failed. I was completely committed to "saving" our marriage, and I knew Michael was too, but sometimes I wondered if we had taken on something that was too big for us to conquer.

I told myself then that, no matter what the future held, I must never forget all that I knew to be true about Michael: that what had kept him from coming out to me sooner was the fear of losing what meant the most to him in all the world—his family.

After a while, I also began to wonder if Michael could remain "straight" without me. Suddenly I thought, If we were to divorce, would he then fully enter gay life? Maybe, just maybe, he might be happier. I could not let myself believe that! We had to remain strong and fight this thing together. Michael had to be victorious over his homosexuality—for the sake of us all.

As much as I had wanted Michael to desire me sexually, he now seemed almost frantic in his lovemaking. Rather than flattering me, his drive frightened me. I knew I could not be everything to Michael, no matter how I tried. I began to fear that I would never satisfy him enough, and I worried about how he would make up for the lack.

One morning at around 4 A.M., Michael woke me up by reaching over for me to make love. Afterward as I lay in his arms, he said sleepily, "I'd been dreaming about you all night." He then fell fast asleep. I remained awake with new thoughts pestering me. Who, I wondered, had Michael also dreamed of in the last fifteen years, while I slept by his side? Had he really been dreaming of me tonight—or of some man? Then I tried to brush these thoughts away and believe that Michael had indeed been dreaming of me, and only me.

Michael and I had used our liberation from his secret to explore and question areas we never had before. I stretched tremendously as my closest friend finally poured out his heart to me. Even though I had asked to know, now that the numbness had fully worn off, some things were very hard to hear.

"You actually *kissed* those men!" We were in the car en route to Jeff and Bonnie's house for dinner when one thing led to another, and suddenly I found myself fully tuned in to this fact. I had often wondered if my reaction would have been different had Michael had been with other women rather than men. This made me think not.

I didn't know why, but the idea that his lips had kissed my lips as well as another's sent me into a screaming rage. "How could you do that!" I shouted. "I never want you near me again!" With that, I grabbed the car-door handle, fully intending to jump out of the moving car. Michael grabbed me and, quickly pulling over to the side of the highway, once more let me beat my fists on his chest while I cried and continued to scream. By the time I finally stopped, he was crying too, and we held each other quietly.

One night in late September I said to Michael, "Tell me more about what it was like when you were with your gay friends." I saw a soft light begin to shine in my husband's face.

"Honestly, I felt truly alive—spiritually, emotionally, and physically. I could talk with them so easily about everything I was feeling. And we had so many things in common, whether it was literature or art, or whatever. I felt like I was in my element, I guess." His tone was somewhat apologetic.

I understood a little more, and it made me very sad. "It must be really hard for you to let go of all that, Michael."

"I'm sure I can change, Sally, but sometimes it hurts so bad, it feels as though I'm tearing the very skin off of my body." When he saw my face fall from the weight of his words, he quickly tried to lessen the impact by adding, "It will be okay, Sally. Just allow me some time to grieve over the loss, okay?"

My heart, however, had already broken and sunk within the reality of his words. I think I knew then that we were striving for the impossible. Still confused, I was beginning to see that somehow this wrenching, painful struggle to change was not right and did not ring as true as I had thought it would. But I did not know how to allow myself to let go, and Michael could not bring himself to do so either.

In mid-September, Michael and I went away to the mountains for some time by ourselves. While we were relaxing in the Jacuzzi, things naturally turned amorous, yet Michael was, for the first time ever, unable to make love to me. He was embarrassed, and I was crushed. Fears that this proved I was not woman enough to "keep him straight" rushed in even as he tried his best to alleviate them by assuring me it was fatigue or perhaps too much wine. Finally we dressed and went to dinner.

The possibility of Michael's impotency returning worried me. Had the reason really been what he said? I did not want to dwell on the true implications—that I was not satisfying him and perhaps never could.

Now I was feeling trapped and confused. What if, I wondered, in the end I was not happy with Michael? What if he still could not be what I needed in a husband? And—the worst fear of all—what if Michael was not able to detach himself fully from his homosexual emotions, but could only abstain from sex? He would remain forever frustrated and unhappy—which would leave us with a life I did not welcome.

The conflict within me grew more pronounced every day. I wanted our marriage to be healthy and alive and to last forever—yet I also yearned for my own pent-up passions and desire for creativity to be unleashed without the fear that they might not be compatible with Michael's life.

September 19, 1991: Am I with Michael by choice? Or do I hide in the life we have so that I won't know what I'm missing—or because I'm afraid that there is no other life for me—or, for that matter, for him either? I feel like I am either slowly coming to life or slowly dying. God—what is wrong with me? Did I "rise to the occasion" at first with Michael, only to want to bail out now? I can't let him down. He needs me to help him overcome his past. I have to stay. Besides which, I can't destroy six lives like that. I don't have that kind of courage.

"Well, what do you think?" I had decided to try on a new dress I had bought for my upcoming high school reunion, and now I wanted to see how Michael thought I looked. I wanted him to love not only the dress, but how I looked in it. As I stood in front of the full-length mirror and asked, I could tell immediately that he was not bowled over. "Tell me what you really think," I added.

"I like it, but I think you could find something even better." He was at the door now, ready to leave the room.

I was disappointed, but rather than get upset, I let the dress seductively slide off of me and onto the floor. I had nothing on underneath. "Michael!"

He smiled slightly and walked out the door.

"Thanks a lot!" I shouted behind him.

He came back then. "I'm sorry. I just wasn't tuned in to you at the moment. You should know by now that I want you—"

But his words were falling on totally deaf ears.

October 3, 1991: Michael has reverted back to some of his previous irritability and impatience. It's as though something is creeping back into him. When I approached him with what was wrong, he gave me some of the old answers—"You are demanding too much from me" or "I always have to react on your terms." The children have started asking me what's wrong. This time, of course—though I can't tell them—I know what it is. Seeing the tension returning, I have to wonder if denying himself that which made him feel so happy and the most himself is not making him totally miserable. What am I to do now?

Then something happened that, looking back, I know sealed our fate. Michael and I had an argument about something fairly insignificant. We had both gone about our day unhappy. That afternoon, Michael also had a counseling session. When he came home, I was in the kitchen fixing dinner, and he gently took my hand and pulled me back to the little room. I sat in a chair while Michael knelt on the floor in front of me. "Maybe I should leave, Sally," he began.

"Why?" I asked, and he began to cry.

Now I cried while he tearfully explained, "I am finding that I cannot love you the way you need and deserve. It is *not* your fault, Sally, I promise. The things that you want and need are everything that you should have from a husband. The problem is completely with me, and I am sorry I ever let you think it was anything else but me. I want to love you, Sally, and I do—just not the way I should."

"Why *can't* you love me like that, Michael? What is so difficult about it for you?"

He lowered his eyes. "I really don't know." We sat in silence for a while. Then once again I asked, "What do you want to do?"

He looked at me for a moment and then asked, "Can you hang in there with me for a while longer? I'm really working on all of this, and I still believe that the feelings will come."

I tried to smile. "Yes, I'll hang in there, Michael."

But in my heart I think I knew the truth then. Michael still didn't want to hurt me. He was so afraid that I could not live without him, and, of course, so was I. I was so afraid that one day our life would come crashing down around us. At this point I began to wish I only knew how to ease it down gracefully.

Michael left for the merchandise market in High Point, which gave us both a short reprieve from our efforts to save our fading marriage. One night while he was away and the children were asleep, I sat on the sofa flipping mindlessly through the TV channels. I stopped at a station that had a movie already in progress, and before I knew it I was engrossed in what was on the screen. The movie was about two very attractive men—a gay couple, I realized—one of whom had a father who was coming to visit. When the gay man sat down, nervously, to tell his father that he and the other man were a couple, the father surprised him by saying, "All I want to know is if you love each other." The son leaned forward to hug his father, and I fell apart. My God, I thought, that's all that matters.

All at once I had a realization so strong that I said it out loud: "I am depriving Michael of himself and of something else too—love. True love." What I had seen on TV between those two men, much like what I had read about in *Gentle Rebels*, was the very same love that I wanted so badly to have in my life. It was humbling to suddenly see so clearly that what I had assumed was the best life for Michael (that is to say, loving me) might not be best for him at all. I asked myself then: did I honestly believe anymore that gay love was wrong? I had to answer honestly that I did not. So, how then could I continue to deprive Michael of what might be true love?

Coming to understand that the gay life was a viable way of living and of loving was still a slow process for me, but once I began that process, there was no turning back. I had prayed for years for Michael's wholeness. Begged him to find what he had been created to be and then be it. Maybe, I thought to myself now, he had found out and it was our fears that were holding us together.

As soon as Michael called, I shared with him the place of understanding I had come to. He was grateful but still not ready to call it quits. We had a trip planned to, ironically, San Francisco. "Let's try to make it a good one, okay?" he asked.

At first Michael and I had so much fun together driving into the wine country of the Napa Valley and Sonoma—tasting wine, eating wonderful food, and shopping—that I thought maybe we could still make it work. It wasn't until our second night that things took a different turn.

All day I had felt Michael slipping away from me. That night, when we tried to make love, it was hopeless. Michael cried and said, "I'm sorry, Sally. I just don't know if I can tear myself away from my old life. It's killing me. I seriously wish I had two lives. But I don't. I've made a decision to make this one work, and I will."

His final words did not sound even remotely hopeful to me. What Michael was attempting to do was killing me too. In fact, I already felt dead inside.

Our trip was cut short when we received word that Daniel and Matthew had been in a car wreck and we decided to return home. Once we were back, we found that the boys' injuries were slight. Though we both had hated leaving California early, I couldn't help but wonder if it had not been just as well that we did leave. As far as I was concerned, our trip had really ended even before we heard about the accident.

Finally, seeing that I was becoming frayed around the edges and really needed my sister, Michael gave me permission to talk to Camille about him and our situation. When I arrived at my sister's house, she spoke to me as directly as she ever had in her life. First she asked, "Are you staying with Michael because you're afraid of being on your own? Do you really still love him, Sally, or are you so emotionally attached that you can't let go?"

"I don't think I'm as afraid as I used to be of being on my own. And, yes, I do still love Michael," I answered, though I doubted both of my answers.

"Okay, let me ask you this. Do you honestly believe Michael is the man for *you,* or is it that you still think there could not *possibly* ever be another man in your future?"

To that I had to say, "I don't know, Camille."

"Well, I do!" she retorted. "And I'm telling you this, Sally. You will be *fine* on your own, and there *will* be another life and another man for you. I'm sorry, but I don't want you to settle for barely making it with Michael. I want you to be really happy. Please . . . try to open yourself up to hearing that!"

As I drove away the next day, as so often happened with my older sister, her words gave me courage—in this case, the courage I needed to begin one of the most painful processes of my life: letting go.

November 11, 1991: Is it fair to consider this week as a mini-separation time for Michael and me? Could it be—for just this period of time—I could just be *me?* Not anyone's wife. Not anyone's mother? Just me.

I flew to New York City, then taxied to my friend Stephanie's apartment. I had nervously prayed and asked God to orchestrate my time away. After that prayer, I had the strangest sensation of being *carried.* As though a gentle but firm hand had given me a push and said, "Go on. It is all right. Walk ahead."

Stephanie rushed out from the apartment to greet me and, after we had talked for a while, took me on my first subway ride—to Greenwich Village to look around. Afterward we went to the Metropolitan Museum of Art, and then to dinner. I loved the city immediately and envied Stephanie the opportunity to enjoy its energy every day of her life.

Later that night, Stephanie and I talked at great length about Michael and about his homosexuality. Just as I expected, Stephanie had a great deal of compassion both for all that Michael had suffered and for the decisions we faced about our marriage.

"Michael's working hard to try to change," I said.

Stephanie suddenly looked very puzzled. "What do you mean?" she asked.

"He wants to be heterosexual so that we can continue in our relationship and keep our family together. It is very hard, but he is trying," I said, knowing full well that I did not sound all that convincing.

"Well, yes," she said slowly. "I should think that that would be quite a difficult—if not impossible—thing for a gay man to do."

The next morning Stephanie and I taxied to St. Thomas Episcopal Church, where we attended the eleven o'clock worship service and I heard the church's magnificent choir of boys and men for the first time. Afterward she suggested we have brunch with a few of her friends at an Irish pub called Parnell's. It was then that I met Bruce, who would come to be one of my dearest male friends. As I sat across from him during brunch, I thought to myself how handsome he was, with his gorgeous eyes, cute dimples, and sweet smile.

After lunch, while Stephanie and I were walking, I said, "Bruce is quite attractive."

"He certainly is," she agreed. "He's also very sensitive, and caring, too. And so is his companion, Chris."

"His companion?" I asked.

"Oh, didn't I mention that Bruce is gay?"

I laughed and said, "It figures I'd come to New York and be attracted to another good-looking gay man!"

Stephanie insisted that we have dinner at the "city convent," St. Hilda's, so that I could meet the sisters there before I went to the "country convent," St. Cuthbert's, for Madeleine L'Engle's workshop and retreat. As soon as we entered the bright red door of the lovely white brownstone, I was glad we had come. The sisters were quiet, but warm and gracious, as they ushered us downstairs to the refectory, where a light supper was about to be served.

During dinner, I sat between a female priest who was also visiting from Georgia and a very tall, handsome man. Stephanie sat across from us. While I chatted with the priest, I could hear the man's rich bass voice as he said to Stephanie, "I guess I lead about as close to a gay life as a person can lead without being gay."

With those words, I whirled around so fast that I startled him. "Hey!" he said, throwing back his hands, "I was just telling your friend, Stephanie, that because of my work, I'm close with a lot of gay men and really believe they understand the meaning of friendship. In fact, my two closest friends are gay. But—listen—I'm one hundred percent heterosexual myself!"

Stephanie laughed and introduced me. "Sally, this is Mel. He's an opera singer from California, and he's staying in the convent guest house for a month of auditions."

"Hello. I'm sorry I reacted that way. I was just terribly interested in what I heard you saying."

The three of us left the table and went into the parlor to talk. Mel continued from where he had left off: "My gay friends are much more open to having intimate friendships than my heterosexual friends are. Too homophobic, I guess."

I had never even heard the term *homophobic* before, but what he was saying sounded so much like what Michael had described about his gay friendships. Assuming I would never see this man from California again, I gave him a brief account of Michael's situation and our marriage and our six children, all as a way of explaining my intense interest in gay-related matters. He was amazed. When I told him how Michael was struggling to stop being homosexual, he gave me the same puzzled look I had seen on Stephanie's face the night before. The three of us talked for a while longer, and when at last it was time for us to leave, Mel walked us to the door, where he very gently said to me, "Sally, it sounds like you and Michael have a very special relationship, and, while I admire what you are trying to do, I have to tell you something."

"What's that?" I asked.

"If Michael is gay—and I believe he is—nothing you can do will ever change that fact. Michael didn't *choose* to be gay, Sally. God made him that way. He can't change the way he was made—and neither can you."

From beside Mel's six-foot-six frame came Stephanie's soft voice: "Sally, sweetheart, that's what I've been trying to tell you as well. If Michael is gay, he cannot change. You can only love him as he really is."

Close to tears, I thanked Mel for our talk and turned quickly to leave. Once Stephanie and I were on the street, I said, "Michael *is* gay—I know that. He really can't *choose* to be heterosexual, can he?"

Stephanie wrapped her arms around me. "No, honey, he can't."

Stephanie had invited Mel to join us on our tour of the city the next day. In the afternoon, she had to return to work, leaving me alone with Mel. He and I had so much fun together that day. He teased me and I teased him back. We talked about our families and a little about our dreams. His were to further his opera career; mine were not so definite. "So much depends on what happens when I get back," I said.

As the afternoon progressed, I grew keenly aware of a pleasant sensation every time Mel's hand touched the small of my back as he guided me protectively across busy streets or moved me to the inside of the sidewalk. On the lurching subway rides when he was forced to hold on to me tightly, I was close enough to feel his muscular body and smell his cologne. And his gorgeous blue eyes had begun to make me feel a little too lightheaded for what I thought was my own good.

Close to dusk, we found our way to Rockefeller Center. Mel bought a bag of hot roasted chestnuts and two lukewarm Diet Cokes. We sat together on the curb watching the ice-skaters, all of whom I noticed were smiling, while Mel shelled the chestnuts and fed them to me one by one. This would be a perfect place to fall in love, I mused. Then I laughed out loud at the ridiculousness of that thought. Mel gave me a quick squeeze, as though he had read my mind.

By the time Mel and I finally returned to Stephanie's apartment, there was an obvious unspoken attraction between the two of us. We had unquestionably indulged in some flirting—and I had loved every minute of it.

Sure that I was blushing madly, I hoped that Stephanie wouldn't notice my face when I tried to slip down the hall and into my room. She did, of course, and, following me into my room, she said in mock horror, "What on earth has happened to you? I left you with that man for only four hours, and look at you! My God—look at that smile!"

Looking at myself in the mirror, I fibbed, "Nothing happened! I promise. We just had a good time together; that's all. After tomorrow I'll probably never see him again. It's harmless—right?" Stephanie laughed and said she guessed it was.

The next morning I was on a train bound for Brewster and starting to prepare myself for the next part of my journey—the writers' workshop and retreat. I took out my journal and tried to catch up on all that had happened in the last few days.

November 20, 1991: God—I don't really know where you are at this point. Maybe for a moment, in your mercy and compassion, you turned your head and just let all of this be. Do I dare thank you for Mel and for these last few days? I certainly have not ever felt your displeasure. Am I deceiving myself about all that I have come to about Michael? I don't think so. Rather I think that all of this is you.

My first impression of the convent was of how different it was from the monastery. First of all, it was a lovely old white farmhouse, and the atmosphere felt less cloistered. I decided that I liked both places. The first thing I wanted to do was counsel with Madeleine. When at last I found her out walking her golden retriever, she welcomed me warmly and together we planned a time to meet later that day.

Madeleine listened as I detailed Michael's story for her. Now I saw on her face not only my pain, but his as well. This time her counsel was for me to be gentle not only to him, but to myself.

"In spite of how much I love and care about Michael," I told her, "I'm still very angry at him—and at God too! And I don't know what to do about that."

"Don't do anything about it. Just let God do His own work."

When I shyly told her about Mel, and how he had affirmed me as a woman, she said, "I think that was very good. Just be a little careful, Sally. Take it all very slowly."

"I will," I assured her—hoping it was possible.

Madeleine asked, "Is your mother alive?"

"No," I answered.

"Come here," she said. "You need a lap to sit in."

So for the next few minutes I sat in Madeleine's lap, put my arms around her neck, and wept out my anger, and bitterness, and loss—safely held like a child.

November 21, 1991: Being with Mel brought out what I have been searching for—*me*. He only knows me as Sally Lowe and it makes me feel so alive. I think maybe I understand better how Michael must have felt as truly *himself* in his other life! *But*—in no way do I want a relationship with Mel. What we shared together was safe—and probably quite enough.

The workshop and silent retreat seemed to be designed with my specific need in mind. Madeleine's meditations centered around allowing joy to be in one's Christian walk. "We have so little say in the story of our lives," Madeleine told the group one morning. "God is truly the author and the finisher of our faith and lives."

During another meditation she said, "When you love someone, it should be an act of freeing them—not trampling them." I thought of Michael. I had wanted so much to truly love Michael. Now I knew that to do so would have to mean setting him free.

When I returned home, Michael was strangely aloof, and we were both uncomfortable around one another. Finally, a few days before Thanksgiving Day, we sat down to talk. I began, and I told him all that I had discovered about both myself and, I believed, about him while I was away on my recent trip. I had already told him a bit about Mel when I had called him from Stephanie's, and now I told him the rest.

The peace and confidence that Michael saw in me as I spoke, coupled with the fact that missing from me was much of the anger and fear he had seen in me before my trip to New York, now allowed him the freedom to be more relaxed and open with me as well.

"I've done a lot of thinking, too," he said, "as well as spending some time with some gay friends in Atlanta." He looked at me then to see if that bothered me, and, seeing that it did not, he continued, "I know now that the fact is, I'm gay and will never be otherwise—no matter how much I try. I don't guess I'll ever be completely happy unless I can experience gay life one hundred percent."

"I really do understand, Michael," I told him. Then, looking at him, I asked him very calmly and with all of the love I felt, "Michael—you can't be a husband to me, can you?"

"No," he said, "I can't." We were both crying.

"But you can still be my closest friend in the world, can't you?" I said, trying to smile through my tears.

Michael and I embraced then, and, while clinging tightly for a long time, we talked about how we had loved each other and had done so, out of mutual protectiveness, even to the point of denying ourselves true happiness.

"I was so afraid," he said, "that if I admitted I couldn't change, you would totally reject me, Sally. And losing you completely would have been more than I could bear."

"I know—me too. I don't ever want to not have you in my life, Michael."

"Also, I was terrified that if we didn't make it together, you might retaliate against me with the boys. I could not stand to lose them, Sally."

"Michael, you are a wonderful father. The fact that you cannot be my husband does nothing to change that."

"I'm afraid of what's ahead," he said.

"I understand. We'll go all the way through the pain that lies ahead—together—until we finally get to the other side. We both deserve some measure of true happiness in this life, Michael."

"I promise I'll do whatever I can to ensure that you have yours, Sally."

"I promise I'll do the same," I assured him.

Michael was very grateful that I was ready to begin this chapter of our lives and that we would enter it together. We began now to prepare for our immediate future. For the next few days, we stayed very close to each other. We laughed and cried a lot as we tried to imagine a world where, divorced, we could lead new lives, have new life companions, and somehow share our six sons. We promised each other over and over that we would stay close.

"We will never stop needing each other, Sally."

"Never."

One night Michael said, "You are so naive, Sally! You are going to have to be really careful about men."

"Oh, thanks. Maybe you can check them out for me!" I replied, blushing and laughing.

In those days toward the end of 1991, our relationship was beginning to undergo a shift from a gallant but futile effort at married love to a stronger love between friends than most people would ever know. In the months and years ahead that love would be challenged, and at times I would fear that we could not keep the promises we had made. Michael would have trouble relinquishing his control over my decisions and learning to value and respect my capabilities. For my part, I would have a difficult time not seeking and needing his approval. But even when it felt strange and painful and even impossible, we always returned to the promise we had made to work through the pain until we got to the other side. Every time, in the end, we would be glad that we had.

Shortly after I arrived home from New York I called Camille and told her about the painful conclusions Michael and I had come to about our marriage. Though it broke her heart to know that a divorce was in the making, she was also relieved.

"Something else happened in New York," I began.

She interrupted me with "You met a man."

"Well, yes, but . . ." I stammered.

"Good," she said firmly. "That's exactly what I asked God to do—send you a man. I just didn't believe He'd really do it!" she laughed.

While I had been away, Michael had sought counsel from our priest, Sam Candler, and had told him that he was gay and had finally come to the realization that he could not change. Sam had been understanding and supportive and had encouraged Michael to move forward in the truth. Now I needed to talk to Sam as well.

"I'm so glad that Michael came to talk with me, Sally," Sam said. "He is a very courageous man. And you are also very courageous. In fact, I'm really amazed. As far as I'm concerned, you would have every reason and right to hate God, and church, and pastors. Men in general, for that matter!"

"There are many times when I don't feel courageous," I told him. "And at one time or another I have probably hated every man in my life—along with God! But I've always sought the truth. Once I found out the truth about Michael, I couldn't then turn my back on him. That would not be being true to truth. And now that I understand and have, for the most part, made peace with it, I am actually free to love him in that truth. Besides, Sam, for years I've watched what hate and unforgivingness do to people. I don't want to end up a bitter old woman!"

Two fears still nagged at me that I needed Sam's help with. Though I no longer believed homosexuality was a sin, I had no idea what God would do with homosexuality in the final judgment. I had decided, however, that if being gay was not a choice, then God definitely had a plan for figuring out the rest. Still, considering how important Michael was to me, I needed to be set free from my self-assumed responsibility of keeping him safe, spiritually speaking.

"What if—without me—Michael would fall completely away from God?" I asked Sam. "And how can I be sure that God has given His consent for us to divorce? Will He really bless our new lives?"

"Sally, you and Michael were married under pretense. Michael did not have the courage, then, to be real about who he really was. To tell you the truth, your marriage was actually formed on a lie. God in His mercy and grace has nonetheless richly blessed it by giving you and Michael a remarkable love for one another and six fantastic sons. I see you both as ready to be set free from that lie now. And God is more than ready to set you both free to walk in truth. It's time to let go, Sally.

"And I promise you this: you and Michael are about to witness God's finest act of redemption *ever* in your lives!"

chapter 11

A New Beginning

Michael and I had decided to wait until after Christmas to tell his parents and the boys that we were getting a divorce. Saying that he could handle only so much pain at one time, Michael had decided to tell only the two oldest that he was gay, then tell the next three during the summer. It would be a couple of years, he felt, before Samuel would be old enough to be told. In a way, I dreaded beyond belief what lay ahead—and in another way, I thought I would be glad when things were finally out in the open.

Christmas was very bittersweet that year. Every tradition that Michael and I and the children normally enjoyed seemed to be shrouded in gray. Still, knowing it would be the last Christmas we would share as husband and wife, we were doing our best to take as much pleasure from the holiday as possible. While the boys and their father were out cutting down a tree, Michael Jr.'s new fiancée and I stayed at home making our family's traditional hot chocolate and doughnuts. While she talked happily to me about wedding plans, I found myself worrying whether she would still want to be a part of this family once the truth about Michael was out. Also, would she be able to endure the anger and sorrow that I knew Michael Jr. would experience?

As Christmas Day approached, I began to worry tremendously about Michael's ability to bear the guilt and the responsibility for the hurt he would soon inflict on his parents and, especially, on his sons. What if it all proved to be too much for him? And would a new life really be possible for us after all this was finally over?

Michael and I had become increasingly tense with each other. Living together, though not as husband and wife, was hard on us both. By Christmas Eve he was hardly speaking to me; when he did, he was not very civil. Finally I asked, "Why are you pushing me away like this?"

"I'm sorry," he said. "You're right . . . I have been pushing you away. I think maybe I've been purposely detaching myself from you so that it will be easier on us both when I move out in January. I don't know how to do this, Sally."

"I know," I said. "I don't either."

We agreed then that we didn't need to push one another away. Our independence would come—though never completely, because we would always need one another.

"We especially need each other now, Michael," I said.

"Yeah, you're right, we do." We hugged tightly and promised we would be kinder to each other and more considerate of how fragile we both felt.

On Christmas morning, Michael gave me a framed print called *The Promise,* with a note taped to the back. It read, in part: "A promise and a reminder of all that was, is, and is to come. . . . It is strange today, but next year will be new. . . . I will treasure you in my heart always. Merry Christmas. Love, Michael." Looking at him after I finished reading it, and seeing the same pain on his face that I felt in my heart, I could only hope that what he wrote would be true for us both.

The Sunday after Christmas, Michael called his parents and asked if he could come over to talk. Michael had told me that he would like to talk to them alone first, and that he would like me to join them after an hour.

It was dark when I drove into the driveway. The first thing I saw was Virginia standing in the yard. As soon as I got out of the car she came over to me. Her first words were: "Sally, I am so sorry. This must have been awful for you."

"Right now, I am so sorry for you," I said. "It *has* been awful—but I really will be okay. Right now Michael needs you more than he ever has—more than he does me from now on."

She seemed surprised. "I doubt that's true."

But I knew that it was. "How are Riley and Michael?" I asked.

"Well," she said, "he hasn't thrown him out of the house yet. They're talking, so I guess that's good. I don't know, Sally. Do you understand any of this? Because I don't."

"Yes, I do," I said, putting my arm around her shoulder. "And I promise I'll tell you everything I can to help you understand. Do you think we should go in now?"

"I suppose we should." Virginia looked, however, as though she would rather go anywhere else but back into the house. Remembering how I had first felt on the swing at St. Simons, I understood.

When I saw Michael, sitting in a chair, he looked completely worn out but somewhat relieved. Across from him, also in a chair, Riley looked frantic.

As soon as he saw me, Riley said, "I love you like my own child. I can't believe any of this. In fact—I *don't* believe it."

For some reason, I had not anticipated this reaction. Riley was going to have to be convinced of the truth! Now *I* felt worn out.

I sat as quietly as Michael did while Riley ranted and raved about the possibility of shock treatments and the suggestion that Michael be a eunuch. Suddenly he turned to his son and blurted out, "Why don't you just go away?"

With that, Virginia jumped up out of her chair. "Riley!" she shouted. "You don't meant it!"

"No, I don't," he said quietly. I found myself feeling sorry for him. He's so caught up in his fears and ignorance, I thought, just as I was not so long ago.

"Can you just hang in there until we get Michael the help that he needs?" Riley asked me. "No—of course you can't. How have you done so for this long? Why the hell is he willing to give you up?"

I knew Michael was mortified by now and had to be feeling like a specimen under glass. When I looked at him, his hollow face said one word: *help.*

Riley brought up the senior boys who, Michael had finally told them, had molested him in high school. "Why didn't you tell us when those guys hurt you?" Riley said. "I'd like to find them now and—"

"Because, Dad," Michael interrupted, "I just couldn't face disappointing you. I was . . . "

His father finished his son's sentence: ". . . our golden boy."

Michael said, "Yeah."

Both of Michael's parents were furious at him about his years of infidelity. When, at their request, I went alone to see them a few nights later, Riley said, "Michael should have just kept his secret for ten or twenty more years like other men who have affairs—until the children were raised—and then told you if he thought he had to."

Seething, I glared at him and said, "Really, Riley? Well, then you would have had murder to deal with—because after all those years, I would have killed him!"

Virginia said, "I think she means it."

"You're damn right I mean it! I believe I deserve a life—perhaps one day with a man who wants me!"

"I'm sorry, Sally," Riley said. "I just hate what's happening so much."

Just as my heart softened a little, he added, "But—come on—what man in his right mind is going to want to go out with a woman when he hears she has six kids?"

Virginia shouted, "Oh, Riley—shut up! You don't mean a word you are saying now. And you won't make her stay by saying ridiculous things like that!"

"Nothing will *make* me stay," I said. "Can't the two of you understand that Michael and I no longer have a marriage?"

The words stunned me as much as they did Virginia and Riley.

For the next few weeks—while feeling my way down a dark and unknown hall—I tried to help Michael's parents understand as best I could. I explained to both of them how wounded Michael had been for so long by his inability to come to them for the comfort and protection a child needs when he or she has been hurt. "That's why," I said to Virginia, "I told you it was *you* he needed now." Over and over, I begged both of them to love and accept him.

Now that Michael had told his parents, we began to prepare ourselves to tell the boys. Nothing, however, could have prepared us for what sorrow was ahead.

On the rainy night of January 2, 1992, Michael sat down with Michael Jr., twenty, and Daniel, sixteen, and told them gently that he was gay and that we would soon divorce. As he tried to explain his secret past, they crumbled into pieces. Michael Jr. slammed his fist into the wall. Daniel ran from the house and drove his truck down winding, slippery roads. His older brother drove off in his truck behind him.

I walked into the room where they had been talking and found Michael pacing back and forth frantically. "I can't do this, Sally. It's killing them—and it's killing me! Oh God—why? Why?" I held him tightly and felt as though I were literally holding him together.

"It'll be okay," I said, though I was absolutely terrified that one or both of our sons might have crashed into a tree—or would just never come back home. "We agreed we would have to go all the way through the pain, remember? Before we could get to the other side. We'll make it," I said. But Michael was inconsolable.

Suddenly I became angry. "Stop it, Michael!" I yelled and shook his shoulders. "You *cannot* fall apart now. You have got to hold yourself together for them. Do not quit! You have got to be true to yourself!"

With that, Michael pulled himself somewhat together and went to look for the boys. In a few minutes, all three returned to the house. While Michael Jr. stood in his bedroom with his face against the wall and his bleeding hand, which he had slammed into it earlier, dangling at his side, Daniel sat on his brother's bed and rocked back and forth like a baby, repeating, "No, Daddy . . . no . . . no . . ." I moved from one son to the other, trying to console where no consolation was possible. Their father collapsed into a heap of tears then, and I had never felt so alone. Surely this is hell, I thought. And if it is—God, please deliver us before we perish.

My babies were being destroyed, I thought. For me, panic was setting in. Suddenly I realized I was crazy to have thought that I could handle this night alone. My God, I had not imagined that the boys would be so shocked! I had to admit to myself now that if I'd had any idea of the anguish I would see on my sons' faces, I'd never have been able to go through with this. And I knew the same was true for Michael. I had to believe that there was good in it somewhere. But now I was frightened.

I phoned Sam Candler. He was not home. Then I called my sister and brother-in-law, who drove the ninety miles to our house in record time. I hoped that the presence of their aunt and uncle would give the boys a sense of stability and hope. By the time they arrived, Michael and I had somehow managed to calm them a little. Richard and Camille spoke to them, letting them know that we would all help each other through this horrible time. Though I hated how uncomfortable it made Michael, I was grateful to have them there.

The next day we told the other four boys that Michael had "personal problems" that made it impossible for us to remain married. They didn't understand; we couldn't blame them. They were also full of anger, and I was finding that the more hurt I saw on my boys' faces, the more anger I felt as well. Sometimes I had to escape from the house to find any relief from the oppressiveness that filled it and was making it a place of almost unbearable sadness.

It was at this point that I made an important decision. I saw clearly that the tone I set would be the one that the boys would now follow. Though I certainly had anger to deal with, I loved Michael and understood why he had lived his secret life. I decided I could let them know that I was hurt and even angry. But I did not want the children to consider me the "victim" to the extent that they overprotected me to the detriment of their father. I hoped too that by observing my actions, Michael Jr. and Daniel would eventually regain the respect and understanding they had temporarily lost for their father on the night he told them the truth.

The truth—that was what I wanted to be true to. Unfortunately, I did so to a fault. Somehow I hid my feelings too well, which in turn caused the boys to acquire the false notion that "if mom's okay, then we should be too," whether in fact they actually were fine or not. It felt as if Michael and I were forging new territory. And sometimes we both made some costly mistakes.

Soon we began to hear from Michael's siblings and their spouses, all of whom were surprised to learn that their brother was gay. Their reactions to the news varied tremendously. Mac, the oldest, and his wife, Carolyn, were equally compassionate and supportive of us both. Dick and Anne were the same. Helen and her husband, Thomas, a Baptist minister, were terribly upset. One afternoon Thomas came to see me.

He expressed his sorrow and deep concern that Michael and I were divorcing. "God could still change Michael if you could just hang in there long enough to let Him," he said.

Eternity? I mused to myself, then tried to explain just how impossible that was in my view. He still thought we were wrong to "give up."

"Well, Sally, how are you with the Lord?" he asked.

For some reason, I suddenly wanted to laugh. "Well, Thomas," I said, "I'm fine with the Lord. In fact—come to think of it—I'm great with Him. God has taken me places lately that I didn't even know He went! Years ago, I would have thought them too 'fleshly' or 'dirty' for Him to touch. But now I know there is nowhere God hasn't been and won't go."

Thomas rose then to leave. "Yes, well, I know it's been hard, and it is certainly true that God can only work with a willing vessel."

That was when I had had enough. I said, "I know that this will go against all of your theology, Thomas, but I have to tell you something. There has *never, ever* been a more willing vessel than Michael for God to 'work with.' No man has ever had more reason to change or more to possibly lose if he could not. I lived with him, Thomas! I know that it's true, and it's enabled me to understand that God made Michael gay and God chose to leave him that way! As to what that all means theologically—I have no idea. And you know what? I leave that up to God!"

With a completely deadpan look, Thomas replied only that he had a tape he wanted me to listen to and left. When the tape arrived the next week, I threw it in the trash.

Michael's youngest brother and his wife, who were Christian fundamentalists, were crushed when they heard the news about Michael. They had always looked to us and to our family as models. He also came to talk to me, but he cried rather than preached. "Even though I wish with all my heart that you and Michael could stay together," he said, "I understand why you can't."

I knew that it would be difficult for him to accept Michael's gay life. Yet I also knew that because he loved his brother with a truly unconditional love, he would always find a common ground for them to meet on.

January 14, 1992: I worry now that the horrible feelings of judgment and rejection that Michael suffered through have taken a dreadful toll on him. He looks awful. I hope this will all be worth it for him. The constant look of anguish I see on his face nowhere near resembles the happiness I pray he will one day have in his life. I hope to God he does not doubt or regret his decision—the way back would be an impossible one for him.

Michael was, however, suffering with much doubt and despair in those early days of 1992, often wondering if he had traded one misery for another.

February 2, 1992: The other day Michael told me that now he is free, he has met no one who really interests him and he is both sad and lonely. He thinks that at this point I am experiencing more joy and release than he is. I think he's right and can only imagine how much that confuses him and hurts him. I'm so glad he joined the support group for gay and bisexual men. I hope happiness will soon follow.

On the night of the first support group meeting Michael openly shared his pain and touched the heart of one man in particular who was struggling then with his own sexuality and a marriage of eight years. On the night of the second meeting the two went out for coffee and began a friendship that would eventually lead to a permanent and loving relationship.

February 26, 1992: Tomorrow Michael and a "friend" will come and move the heavy things to Michael's new house— things like the desk we bought for him to study on when we were first married. This morning I passed by it on my way to do laundry and noticed a note stuck to the top of Michael's calendar: "THIS SUX DAD!!—Michael Jr." I quickly snatched it off to prevent Michael from seeing it and when I did I saw a note underneath that Timothy had written several months before:

"Smile Dad—God loves you!" Both notes are true. Thank God the second one holds the larger truth. Much larger.

The day that the judge in Cumming signed the papers making our divorce final, Michael came over to the house. The finality of the day was very real to us, and we were both emotional. Before he left, Michael handed me a tape and a letter.

In his letter he wrote:

These songs are for you from me and somehow they express a menagerie of my feelings about us . . . the last few months . . . a lifetime. We've shared a lot over time, mostly a love that goes so deep . . . please know that I am so sorry for all the pain . . . I truly want your life to be redeemed and happiness to once again reign in your heart and soul. Our lives will go in two different directions, but I hope our hearts will somehow, somewhere remain joined. A piece of my soul and whole life will always remain with you . . . the letting go seems almost unbearable . . . but as you said, we have to go through the pain to get to the other side and I do believe that now. You're always in my heart. Love—Michael.

After reading Michael's letter and listening to the songs on the tape, I cried for a very long time. Each song reflected something of the life and love we had shared together for twenty years. Today our marriage was over, yet at the same time our new life—together, yet apart—was just beginning. Michael did not have to worry; our hearts would remain forever joined.

Mel and I wrote each other almost daily. I had managed to make two more trips to New York when Mel was there for auditions, and he had come to Atlanta once. Our relationship was clearly "going someplace" now—though we were still unsure where. What we did know was that we despised the long distance between us.

Once, before I left to see Mel, Michael, who had come over to stay with the boys, gave me some advice: "You know how you are, Sally. You give all of yourself to a relationship. Please be careful."

We laughed then and hugged each other before I left to see the man I was sure I was falling in love with.

I found that trust, however, would not return easily to me. Though Mel had never done anything to warrant my distrust, as our relationship grew, I found that my scars were deep. It took time, but, fortunately, Mel was wonderfully patient and eventually led me back to the place where I could fully trust again.

One day while Mel and I were in Stephanie's apartment on one of my trips to New York, the phone rang. It was Michael. I went into the other room so that we could speak privately. It was then that I realized he was crying. Michael was at the merchandise market in High Point, where I knew he had planned to see our old friend Chuck, from Lambs' Chapel, who was attending the market on business as well. Several week before, Michael had found the courage to tell Chuck about his gay life, how he had hidden it for so many years and how he had suffered because of his secret. Chuck had been so shocked that he had finally asked Michael to give him a little time to sort things out. Now they had spoken, and it had not gone well. Michael sounded completely spent as he told me what Chuck had said. Chuck had told him that, while he still loved and cared for Michael, he would have to "break fellowship" with Michael until he "turned from his sin." As far as Chuck was concerned, Michael had made a terrible choice, one that Chuck could not tolerate if he cared for the salvation of his brother Michael's soul. And so it was Michael's turn to be shocked. He had hoped that because the four of us had gone through so many trials and tribulations together over the years, and had always been a help to each other, our friendship might still be a strength to us all in this trying time as well, even if we did not agree in all areas. Instead, it was just the opposite.

Michael was clearly devastated and cried as he continued to tell me that Chuck refused to share a room with him or even have dinner together until Michael chose to change. We both sadly recognized Chuck's firm stand as the purely fundamentalist way of "dealing with a brother in sin." I cried on the phone with Michael as I tried to make sense of the nonsense of Chuck's cruel rejection. I wondered if he would ever understand that Michael had made no choice—that the choice had been made by the same God we had loved and worshiped together at Lambs' Chapel.

The Shores' reaction was similar to Chuck's, though not quite so verbal. From the time that Michael told Stu of our decision, Stu avoided Michael. Becky, on the other hand, remained warm and friendly, even though Michael and I knew that she did not accept Michael's gay life as valid. She was good to come and talk with me often, just to see how I was. Our friendship actually seemed to have mellowed into a gentle place of acceptance in spite of our differences. Their children were terribly upset about the divorce and tried to comfort our boys. Our house was up for sale now, and it was hard to think of not living next door to one another after all these years.

Michael was living a quiet life in Cumming. Still heavily involved with commissioning, he had to be very discreet about his gay life. However, I knew that he had met someone special. Recently Michael had met Mel. Now I told him I wanted very much to meet Craig.

That finally happened in early May. Driving to a restaurant in Buckhead to meet Michael and Craig, I was excited, nervous, and very curious. I was late as usual. I knew they would be waiting for me.

They were.

Seated across from each other, both rose to their feet when I joined them. Michael pulled out the chair next to him for me to sit in and then—his attempt to be cool belied by his obvious proud blush—introduced me to Craig. I could easily understand why he was so clearly pleased with himself. Craig was a good-looking man in his early thirties with light brown hair. Not tall, but very well built, and quite handsome. In fact, I realized that these two impeccably (almost identically) dressed men made a head-turning couple.

During lunch, after an initial shyness had passed, I was pleased to find that conversation with Craig was easy. He was very interested in my writing, and we discussed books and certain authors that I had met in New York. As we became more comfortable with one another, we talked a little about what a difficult time Craig's former wife was having adjusting to Craig's new life and to her own.

"I'd really like to meet her one day if that's ever possible," I said.

"I'd like that," Craig said.

After we rose to leave, Craig surprised me by asking whether I had ever thought to write my life's story. As Michael and I had just briefly touched on the idea a time or two, I shyly said, "Well, maybe—someday."

"Would you write it as fiction or nonfiction?"

Looking at the two of them standing there, I said immediately, "Fiction."

To my even greater surprise, the men glanced at each other briefly and Craig said, "Why don't you write a memoir?"

"The biggest reason would be to protect the two of you," I answered.

Looking at Michael again, Craig firmly said, "We want you to tell it straight. Write it just as it happened, so that people will hear the truth—and maybe understand."

I was amazed—both at their courage and at their vision. And I was challenged. "Okay," I promised. "I'll do what Madeleine always says—I'll just tell the story." After telling Craig how glad I was to have finally met him, I hugged them both and, crying most of the way, drove home.

The hardest part of Michael's struggle for acceptance continued to be with the boys. Michael Jr. and Daniel were still trying to accept and adjust to a "new father." As far as they were concerned, Michael was "suddenly gay." For a while I had encouraged them to express every ugly thought and feeling that they needed to express. I had thought a lot about what it meant to be the victim in a painful situation, however, and had decided that if one remains the victim for too long, one eventually becomes the victimizer. "When we've been hurt," says the Reverend Murphy Davis, a female priest who ministers to death-row inmates, "revenge is a very natural human emotion. But if you don't at some point move beyond that, you cannot heal."

Fearing that Daniel was nearing this dangerous place in regard to his father, I suggested that we have a talk. "Daniel," I said, "do you not know that this whole thing could be so much worse? Think about it. Your father could have been horribly abusive; he could have abandoned you; he could also have been killed or wounded in a way that really would have prevented him from being the father you once knew. But *none* of those things happened. To be honest, the only thing that has changed is that he cannot be my husband. He is still your father. And you and I both know that he is a wonderful, caring, and very involved father who loves you very much."

I also told Daniel something I would eventually tell each of my sons: "Your father did not choose to be gay. If he had, that would make him a very cruel man to have allowed his wife and children to suffer so much pain. He wouldn't deserve either your forgiveness or your acceptance. But because his being gay is not a choice, he deserves both."

Daniel broke down and cried, and I could see that at last his tears were ones of healing, not retribution.

Michael had made a difficult decision not to run for commissioner again, and his term would be up the following January. Until then, he would keep a residency in Forsyth County, while sometimes staying in

Atlanta with Craig and his good friend and roommate, Gregg, who, as the boys got to know him, would become Uncle Gregg. As soon as the next school year was over, in the spring of 1993, Michael would move to Atlanta, and Gregg would move in with a nearby friend, creating an extra room for the boys. Michael was excited about his plans, though I knew he wished he could move to Atlanta sooner. The only thing left then would be deciding about the children. And about me—what *I* was going to do.

As much as I loved the South, I knew that I was badly in need of a change. Over the last year, I had become increasingly close to a small group of writers in New York, including Stephanie. Mel had made a major decision to move himself and his career from California to New York in August. All things considered, I began to wonder if New York might not be a viable option for me as well. He and I both knew that we could not continue a long-distance romance forever. It was beginning to make sense that I should be the one to move. My biggest concern was what that would do to Michael's and my promise to share the boys.

Michael and I began to discuss how it might work. Though he understood my reasoning and my need to move, he was not at all pleased at the prospect of my taking the boys so far away. At the same time, we both remembered our promise to do all we could to help ensure each other's chance for true happiness. For now, moving to New York seemed to be the way for me to find mine. Michael Jr. would be married in the summer, and Daniel would go away to college in the fall. Finally we decided that Matthew would stay with his father and Timothy and Josiah would live in New York with me.

That left Samuel. It was the toughest decision of all. Though I wanted my youngest child with me, I knew that it would break Michael's heart for me to take him away. I also knew how attached Samuel was to his father. In the end, we listened to Samuel, who said, "I want to *visit* you in New York, Mama, but I want to *live* with Daddy." As much as it hurt, I agreed to let him stay with Michael.

Having two sons aged eighteen and eight living with their gay father and his companion challenged me to face up to even the smallest degree of fear and prejudice that I might still be feeling. My issues—which in essence were how it would affect them sexually—were no doubt influenced by some other family members and some "well-meaning" friends, who were not at all sure it was a good idea. Finally I confronted the matter head-on. If I really believed that homosexuality was, for one thing, not a choice and, for another, a completely valid way of being and of loving, then what was I afraid of?

I thought long and hard and decided that it was not the possibility that a son of mine might be gay that frightened me; rather, it was any distress that he might experience in his life if he was. That realization only made me want to work all the harder to create an environment where there was as much love and acceptance as possible—in both of our homes.

Michael was shocked and hurt to discover that I had any doubts whatsoever. "I can't believe you would question Samuel and Matthew living with me at all!" he said.

"I apologize for my ignorance, Michael," I said, "but you have to allow me to continue to become educated about gay parenting, as well as other issues that might come up as we go along. I can't know and understand everything at once!"

"You're right . . . I'm sorry. I promise I'll try not to be so defensive in the future."

Michael and I were still evolving in our new relationship, and I still hated to ever be at odds with him. But more and more I was beginning to speak my mind—and he was beginning to respect me for the more independent woman I was fast becoming.

One afternoon I received a call from the local hospital saying I should come right away. Michael had suffered a possible heart attack. All the way there, I cried out loud, "God, *no!* Not now. Please. Not now that we've come so far. Please, *no!*"

Once I arrived, I was led into the emergency room, where Michael lay on a bed looking pale and frightened. The doctor told me that as yet they were not sure why Michael's heart was showing "unusual activity." I held Michael's hand, trying to keep him calm while he explained that after jogging he had been in such terrific pain that Craig had insisted he go to the hospital. Suddenly Michael grabbed my hand. "Sally," he said, "will you take care of Craig?"

My God, I thought, you're not going to die!

Michael continued, "He's on his way over here—and so are Mom and Dad."

Then I understood: Michael's parents had never met Craig. "Sure I will. I promise I'll protect him!" I said and squeezed his hand.

"Thanks," he said, closing his eyes.

I guessed that Michael had forgotten that his oldest sons were also on their way. As soon as Craig arrived—looking white as a sheet himself—I hugged him and told him that Michael seemed okay. "But," I warned him, "you might not be. His parents and some of the boys are headed over here."

As it turned out, the boys were so concerned about their daddy that it took the edge off their seeing Craig. In fact, it appeared to be a good thing for Craig and them to share their concern. Michael's parents arrived in a flurry of anxiety. I watched them hug their grandsons, then saw their eyes fall upon the stranger in our midst—Craig. That's when I took a deep breath and stepped in.

"Virginia and Riley, this is Craig. Michael's . . . friend," I said as though it were the most normal thing to say on earth.

"Well, hello, Craig . . . nice to meet you," Virginia said with all the southern hospitality she could muster—and sincerely so, I mused.

"Hello," Riley said with no smile, no expression whatsoever. He did shake Craig's hand.

I felt sorry for Craig. Here his companion was seriously ill, and he had to worry about how everyone felt about his being there. I watched as he held back for the rest of the night like an outsider. The wrongness of the entire scene had a profound impact on me. I didn't even know then that Craig and I would become very close friends; I knew only that to be treated as he was treated that night was inexcusable and that I was going to do everything in my power to stop it from happening again.

By late that night we were told that Michael had not had a heart attack but still needed to rest for at least one more day. Everyone but Craig went home for the night.

Michael and I had believed that there was no valid reason why we should not work toward having a friendship—and one that would only get better with time. Despite our best intentions, however, things sometimes moved along in both of our lives faster than the evolution of the relationship could handle. For instance, though he knew it was irrational, Michael found it difficult to deal with the fact that Mel was visiting me in *his* house, around *his* children. At times like those, we would try to talk about it honestly—again working through the pain to get to the other side. Usually we managed to help one another better understand. But then there were times when what would happen would catch one of us completely off guard.

There was, for example, the time that Mel was visiting in Georgia, and Michael and Craig asked him and me over for dinner. I was a little nervous as we drove to their house in Atlanta, but both Mel and I were looking forward to the evening. I thought it would be great for the four of us to have a night together just to relax and get to know one another.

First there was driving through Midtown—a part of Atlanta that Michael and I had at one time talked about moving to ourselves. Now he was there with another man. And was much happier, I reminded myself, than he had been with me. It felt odd. Then there were the photos on the mantel—some of the children, and some of Craig and Michael, both together and with friends that I didn't know. It was emotionally overwhelming to be confronted with these evidences that Michael had a whole life that I was not privy to. The house itself was lovely and decorated with furniture that I knew he and Craig had chosen together. It was so obviously their home, and that hurt me in a way I hadn't expected.

The last straw was dinner itself. Not only had Michael done a spectacular job of cooking and presenting the food, but throughout the meal he and Craig teased and were mildly affectionate with one another. Much to my dismay, I found I was not ready for that.

Mel was driving us back to Cumming on I-75 when I suddenly burst into such hard tears that he had to pull off the highway and hold me while I sobbed and sobbed.

"What's wrong with me?" I cried. "Why am I reacting this way?" I was disappointed with myself and felt that it was somehow wrong of me to have such an outburst.

Mel held me firmly and surprised me by saying, "You know—I was actually wondering how you were handling it all so well. Sally, come on, you're way too hard on yourself. Give it some time, darling." If his words gave me the permission I needed then to express the feeling of being displaced in Michael's life, his embrace helped me to get over that feeling.

That was over four years ago. Since then, our sons and daughter-in-law have gone through every possible reaction. So have our family and friends. A whole small-town community discovered that a trusted and respected political figure was gay. Each son has come into his own respectful and loving relationship with Michael and, in time, with Craig. Learning new ways to support one another, we moved through a painful but determined process of rebuilding our lives.

An important step in that rebuilding was my move to New York in January. Mel and my niece helped to move me, then settle me and the boys, into my new apartment on Central Park West—on the edge of Harlem. The neighborhood unnerved me a bit, but Mel insisted I'd be fine there, and as it turned out I was; Mel, however, was held up at gunpoint one afternoon in broad daylight while on his way back from the store across the street. One day while Josiah, twelve, was playing out on the sidewalk with the other children, our Hispanic "super" said to me, "Your son looks like a piece of white rice in a big bowl of black soup!" Six months after we moved in, one of our neighbors went to jail for attempting to murder his ex-boss by burying him alive for two weeks, and we went two days without electricity. We soon moved out. But none of us would have exchanged our experiences living there for anything.

I visited Matt and Samuel in Atlanta as often as I could. Usually I stayed at Michael and Craig's house in order to spend as much time with the boys as possible.

> May 20, 1993: This morning while I lay in bed waiting for the boys to get up, I heard Michael and Craig kiss good-bye! While it made me blush, it also made me smile. Yesterday I watched Michael's face while he cooked dinner and realized that the look of inner conflict he had on it for so long is now completely gone. Instead he has a genuine look of inner peace and joy. I'm so glad.

Meanwhile, Mel lived at the convent—though the mother superior often found him at my apartment when she called. I began to develop a close relationship with all the sisters, just as I had hoped I would.

I called Mel my new love and my only love because he really was both. Though I had loved Michael with a love so strong that it had kept him in bondage far longer than it should have, I was never able to love him fully, in the way that I could now love Mel. Mel's love completed me as a woman and also allowed me the joy of completing him as a man.

Though we had discussed marriage, Mel had let me know that it would be very important to him to surprise me with a marriage proposal when he was ready. Finally he asked and I said yes. We planned a wedding for February 5, 1994.

Mother Madeleine Mary and the sisters surprised us by giving us, as their wedding present, not only the convent's beautiful chapel to be married in, but all of the guest rooms for our out-of-town guests to stay in. Sister Catherine Grace directed the wedding, and Sister Helena Marie, along with Mel, prepared the music. The result was what was affectionately called the *Sound of Music* wedding. One reason was that the bride and groom, as in the Julie Andrews movie, came already equipped with a large family of children, all of whom participated in the wedding. And another reason was that the chapel almost washed away with tears when Mel—as a complete surprise to me—sang to me, from *The Sound of Music,* "I Must Have Done Something Good."

One of the greatest blessings of the day was having Madeleine L'Engle present me to Mel. Stephanie and Bonnie were my bridesmaids, and my sister Camille was my maid of honor. Daniel and Matthew preceded me into the church, followed by Samuel as ring bearer. Josiah and Timothy served as acolytes. Mel had his father, Don, who came out from California, as his best man and Camille's husband, Richard, and Michael Jr. as groomsmen. Our friend Bruce and his companion, Chris, read the prayers. Russell and Jeff did the scripture readings. Another very special blessing was that the Reverend Sam Candler flew to New York to marry us. Sam helped us create a very inclusive service that celebrated *all* unions—same sex or otherwise.

Michael and Craig had decided not to come to the wedding because at the time Michael felt that it might detract from what was important—Mel and me—and might cause the boys unnecessary anxiety. Though I understood his decision and appreciated his sensitivity toward me and Mel, I regretted his decision as well.

Sadly, my good friends Russell and Scarlett divorced. For Russell, however, something close to a miracle happened at our wedding reception. But, then, miracles often do happen at St. Hilda's. He met and became very attracted to Stephanie. After a yearlong romance, in December 1995, with many of the same people in attendance, they were happily married at St. Thomas Church.

My marriage to Mel completed me, and his love gloriously fulfilled my lifelong wish to be desired. We began then—and continue today— to enjoy a marriage of mutual respect and devotion that is happily devoid of control and submission. It has not always been an easy road, but we strive together to seek the truth and be faithful to it.

Though Mel and I were immensely happy together in New York, my longing to be with my sons in Georgia became unbearable. My father's death a month after our wedding only made me all the more homesick. Finally one day Mel came to me and said, "Sally, it's simple. We have to go back to Georgia."

Michael and Craig were ecstatic about our decision, as were the boys, who would live in each household according to their individual needs but with the advantage of an easier flow back and forth between the two homes. Now we would all learn to share our new lives on a closer day-to-day basis.

The experiences of the past twenty-six years span the time from when I couldn't say *homosexual* without an embarrassed giggle to now, when my life is blessed by a rich diversity of people and their lifestyles. My life and the lives of my children have all been strengthened by and have more than benefited from not just Michael and Craig but our many other gay and lesbian friends.

Our move back to Georgia took place over two years ago. One chilly day in March 1996, Timothy, sixteen, came home from playing a high school soccer game and told me a story that wonderfully reflects the new life we enjoy today. Craig and Michael had been at the game, and they sat in the stands huddled together under a blanket. Tim and another boy were down on the field warming up before the game when the other boy said, "Hey, Tim, I probably shouldn't say this to you—knowing how you are about people judging people—but see those two guys sitting together up there in the stands?"

"Yeah," Tim said.

"Okay, well, they look gay to me."

"You're right," Tim said, "that is a very judgmental thing to say. But, in this case, I'd say you're probably right."

He and his teammate kicked the ball back and forth for a minute. Then Tim added, "By the way—the guy on the right?"

"Yeah?"

Tim grinned. "He's my dad."

Mel and I grow stronger in our relationship every day. Still, memories of the life Michael and I shared occupy a place within me that rightfully defies time and healing, a precious ache that is just understood.

Sometimes my husband says he knows that if Michael were not gay, I would still be married to him. As secure as Mel is in our wondrous love, that is hard for him. His first marriage did not have such a specific reason for ending, and he and his former spouse do not share friendly dinners with Mel and me, as we now do comfortably with Michael and Craig. I have to remind him that we are breaking new ground here—sometimes strange new ground. The process of moving from ignorance and prejudice to knowledge and love has strengthened all of our lives and will, we trust, help leave the world in better shape for our children.

"Can you really handle all of this?" I sometimes ask Mel.

"Yes," he says. "Breaking out of old thought patterns that no longer fit is difficult—but very, very good."

As I complete the writing of this book, it is the fall of 1996. Last fall, for the first time, everyone was invited to Michael's parents' house for Thanksgiving dinner—including Craig and Mel and me. As I stood and watched the family that I still claim as my own, I thought how proud I was of them.

From Michael's father, Michael and I have both had to learn that "tolerance works both ways." I hope Riley and Virginia have learned that love truly is the greatest force on the earth. And that a family is one of life's greatest treasures.

This summer our lives came full circle. Once again Michael and I returned to St. Simons Island. This time we shared a rental house with our children; Mel's daughter, Leah; several friends and girlfriends—and our new partners, Craig and Mel.

Late one night, Michael and Craig and Mel and I took a walk down to the swing that overlooks the ocean at the King and Prince Hotel. We stood there for a long time, each of us lost in our own thoughts. The steady old waves rushed up to greet us, saying, I'm sure, that they were glad we were all there together. Thanks be to God.

Michael

*The memories of the past triumph through my mind,
and it is those that filter and shape the past into an
acceptable package of events that becomes palatable to
remember.*

Fenton Johnson, *Geography of the Heart*

Throughout my marriage, the struggle to come to terms with my sexuality led me on a tenuous course of survival. As a confused eighteen-year-old, I made a commitment to ignore my homosexual desires and thrust forward into marriage and fatherhood. Always thinking that I could control my feelings for other men, I attempted to live a life that ultimately crisscrossed the worlds of heterosexuality and homosexuality. I anguished over the guilt and shame that a possible confession might bring to my life. The stark realization was that if I came out, life as I knew it would crumble and disappear. So the threat of this happening continued to hold me emotionally and spiritually captive.

Turning to numerous diversionary outlets—foster children, social causes, and a lengthy journey through fundamentalist Christianity—I began to understand that I couldn't discard my sexuality like a bad habit. I slowly began to contemplate what would become the most critical decision in my life. Unsuccessful in my attempts to change or to reach a point of equilibrium in my struggle, I set out to understand myself through therapy. This understanding led me to the initial point of acceptance, but still staring me in the face was the question of what I was to do now.

The painful answer to this question came a few months later. After years of tension and unresolved anger had taken their toll on our marriage, I realized I could no longer bear to let Sally feel so much personal fault in our relationship. My acceptance of my sexuality led me to the belief that everyone deserves their personal happiness, and this applied not only to me but also to Sally. On that cloudy night on St. Simons Island, years of confusion and mystery began to clear, and a new, uncharted course was set in motion.

When I came out to Sally in 1991, I immediately felt a sense of relief and freedom. Those feelings soon turned to fear of the next step and thoughts of trying to change, though I wondered if I "would" or "could." But from the moment I finished telling her my secret, my anguish was dispelled by her extraordinary love and acceptance. When I think of how compassionate Sally was toward me back then—even as she was emotionally rocked by my revelation and was struggling to come to terms with her own pain—my heart is filled with awe and gratitude.

In the years since, she has continued to express to me the same sensitivity and tenderness that shines in the book that you—and I—have just finished reading. During the writing of the book she constantly consulted with me on how she should describe my feelings so the book could reflect my perspective as accurately as possible. Thanks to the extraordinary gift for love that first drew me to her, Sally has made it possible for us to develop a remarkable relationship that I could never have imagined and that few people fully appreciate or understand. In a way, she and I are closer to each other than ever. Certainly we know each other infinitely better. And we love each other no less.

I must confess that over the past few years, as Sally has contemplated this book, discussed it with friends and family, and gone through the intense process of actually writing it, I've had conflicting feelings about it. "Whose story is this?" I wondered. At first I took it for granted that it was my story—or Sally's story about me. But through the actual yearlong writing process, I realized that this book is the story of not just one person but many people whose lives cannot be separated from one another. These lives—of our children, our friends, and our parents—were torn apart by a secret revealed in utter desperation and were then carefully sewn back together again with threads of truth, pain, and love.

Those feelings of pain and love remain a part of our day-to-day life as a family and probably always will. I ache when I think of the anguish that I caused my family and the challenge my revelation presented to them. Yet at the same time my heart soars with joy when I behold the wholeness and honesty that now characterize our life. Every time I look at one of my six sons, I'm reminded of the strength and courage that they've all displayed in the past few years. All my boys took on the challenge of dealing with our dramatically altered family situation and all of them have grown into young men with a maturity well beyond their years. Each has excelled in his particular field of interest (drama, home renovation, business), and I continually feel an overwhelming sense of pride in their triumphs. Though I was always close to my sons, our relationship has grown since my coming out into something even deeper and more meaningful. Our love has been tested and strengthened by adversity; we all know now that whatever happens to any of us, we will go through it together. One way or another, this transformation has produced a greater sense of being there for one another, and I'm unsure if this could have occurred in a traditional setting. Many of the boys have participated in the Atlanta AIDS Walk and have used their firsthand understanding of gay issues to combat prejudice and ignorance on a local level. About three years ago Matthew came to me and asked if I would be willing to talk to a fifteen-year-old gay friend who had asked for my help. I was very enthusiastic about the opportunity to help this young man, but even more encouraged that Matthew felt he could come to me with this request.

Many people who are close to Sally and me have wondered aloud why, after our family has "already been through so much," we should want to set before the world some of the most intimate and painful details of our lives. All I can say is this: Years ago, when Sally and I first went looking for a church, we wanted above all to find a place where we could help other people. It is for this same reason that all of us—Sally and Mel, Craig and I—view this book as an attempt to offer our experience to help other people. Though it has been uncomfortable for me to read parts of it, I know that our way of dealing with the story is the right one: be honest about it, be open about it, and make an offering of it to the world. Not long ago, after some particularly trying circumstances surrounding the book, Craig had a dream about Sally having a baby. In the dream, I was the father of the baby, yet we had all agreed to jointly raise this child. As that dream reveals, we have all agreed to be on this journey toward reenvisioning faith, family, and love.

This book is principally concerned with my twenty-year marriage to Sally, but I would be remiss if I did not comment about my relationship with Craig, which is now in its fifth year. For a long time I dreamed of a life that I couldn't imagine ever really experiencing and looked for someone whom I couldn't believe actually existed. Even after I came out, the search seemed hopeless.

Then, one day when I wasn't even looking, that man walked into my life and I fell hard in love. In the past five years, that love has been the sustaining force and the wonder of our lives. Together, Craig and I have made a home and a life that neither of us ever thought we would have. He has taken my sons into his life and has sustained me through difficult times with his strong, solid love, his sensitivity, and his understanding.

As much as we might like, we can't write scripts for our lives. If someone had told me twenty-five years ago about the course my life would take, I would never have believed it. I have learned from my years with Sally and Craig the importance of honesty and the redeeming power of love. From my more recent experiences with her and Mel and Craig and the boys, I have learned that a shattering upheaval can lead to a new wholeness. The memories of the past could have resulted in an insurmountable obstacle to overcome. I have chosen to cherish the past and allow God's grace to give me continual hope for a better future. Truly, this occurrence has become "memory's triumph" over the seeming "tragic" events of the years gone by. God replaced the despair and doubt that I experienced for so long with a deep sense of inner peace and a conviction that however brutal life may seem, such times, when faced with honesty and love, can lead to a fuller, more abundant life. In my own life, it has become quite evident to me that God took me the only way I knew to go.

The story as you have read it could have happened no other way. I am at last at peace and I have no regrets.

Acknowledgments

Writing a book turned out to be much like another experience—one I am much more familiar with—that of conceiving, carrying, laboring, and delivering a baby. The major difference was, however, that this time I felt like a surrogate mother who, after a long and difficult delivery, immediately and carefully wrapped the still warm thing up in swaddling clothing (actually a Fed Ex box) and entrusted it (via overnight air) into the waiting hands of Harper San Francisco, who eventually placed it into the arms of its new mother—the reader. I could only hope and pray then that it would be understood and appreciated in the way it was intended. The entire process was miraculous to me and clearly one I could not have accomplished by myself.

So, with a very full and thankful heart, I now ask Divinity's richest blessings on all those who lovingly succored the happy event. Bless Michael for all that he truly is, for our life together, especially the sons we share, and for the tremendous courage it takes to live in truth. Bless our sons, Michael, Daniel, Matthew, Timothy, Josiah, and Samuel, for being (mostly) willing to share their personal lives with others, for enduring the occasional absence of their mother—in both mind and body—during the last two years of writing, and for one or more of you asking daily, "How's the book, Mom?" and then adding, "Hang in there, we're doing fine." You guys are the very best, I love you. Bless my lovely daughter-in-law for well-timed words of encouragement too. Bless you big-time, Mel, for keeping the good faith (that surely I *would* soon return to you!), for sublime comfort whenever my mind and memory were simply "gone," and most of all, darling, for your calming presence, patience, and love ever since the day we met. Bless Craig for rescuing me from all manner of computer calamities, for having the neatest dreams, and for the many phone calls just to be sure I was writing! Bless my precious sister Camille for her selfless celebration of this work and for daring to be the the person who knows me best and yet loves me no matter what. Bless her ever-so-willing husband, Richard, and their awesome kids too.

In magical, mystical New York City, blessings galore to Madeleine L'Engle, my wonderful mentor and friend with whom the heavenly chain of serendipity began; Stephanie Cowell-Clay for intuitively accepting our divinely appointed friendship and extending great writer's support; Russell Clay, Bruce Bawer, and Chris Davenport for knowing and honoring the true meaning of friendship. Bless Bruce all over again for invaluable assistance and attendance during all the marvelous stages of "birth." Bless the very warm and nurturing Elaine Pfefferblit, whose original commitment to the charity and truth of this story set everything else in motion—especially my relationship with Anne Edelsteine, who as far as I am concerned is the finest, most considerate, and most caring literary agent a writer could ever be privileged to work with. You are *truly* extraordinary, Anne—bless you and yours! Bless both NYC writers' groups, including Stephanie Cowell-Clay, Casey Kelly, Elsa Rael, Katherine Kirkpatrick, Judy Lindberg, Ruth Henderson, Isabelle Holland, Peggy Harrington, Sanna Stanley, Pat MacMahon, Pamella Leggett, and a host of talented others for gingerly listening to the earliest draft. Bless Mother Madeleine Mary and all of the sisters at St. Hilda's and St. Cuthbert's for their prayers and support and especially Sister Catherine Grace for generously typing and editing the book's proposal. Bless Barry and Evelyn, Sandy Hudson, Sheryl and Malik—you believed and it was so!

In Georgia, abundant blessings to Bonnie and Jeff, who—from the lunatic fringe to the inclusive circle—have remained fabulous, devoted friends and genuine supporters (along with your terrific family) of my whole gang; Patty and Robbie for limitless untethered love, strength, and inspiration; and Rosita for true friendship and the courage to survive your own remarkable story. Bless the Episcopal Church of the Holy Spirit in Cumming—especially my good friends Reverend Dwight and Babs Ogier, Sharon, Nancy, Mark, Russ, and Janice, and all who prayed for me while I labored. May the awareness of truth set the Episcopal church and its spiritual leaders free to love and serve the Lord. Bless Sisters June Racicott and Katherine Cliatt, who so graciously shared the tranquillity of Cedar Hill Enrichment Center with me, specifically for your gentle protection and hearty encouragement while I retreated and wrote in "my trailer." Bless Linda Purdy for first helping me to embrace the freeing power of truth. Bless Nita, Charlie, Kelli, Eli, Yatsey, Kevin, Lenore, and the FCHS drama group for star-quality support! Bless Bill Bagwell for enjoying the magic of St. Simons

Island with me and my aunt and uncle, Tom and Clotie, for the use of their home on the island to peacefully write and reflect in. Bless Tiffany, Bonnie S., Don and Tucker, Debra, Janice, Fran (for the gift of my talisman), and Nick and Brian for all sorts of encouraging words.

A bouquet of blessings goes to the entire "community of believers" at Harper San Francisco. Bless Tom Grady, who believed in the book initially and thankfully passed it on to senior editor Lisa Bach, who provided me with all-round caring and supportive editing and whose amazingly sharp eye for integrity consistently enabled me to better serve the story. As a result, I learned a lot—not only from Lisa, but also from her skillful assistant Laura Harger. Bless both of you, along with my excellent production editor, Rosana Francescato, my diligent marketing manager, Margery Buchanan, and my publicist, Amy Durgan—all three of whom served and guided this book along so well.

Generously bless the Very Reverend Sam Candler and Boog Candler, whose model of authentic love and community is what I call true church. Bless Dick and Sydney, Bill and David, Mel's mom, Adele, his dad, Don, and Laura, whose kind inquiries about how the book was coming meant so much. Extra sweet blessings to Mel's beautiful daughter, Leah, whose innocent example of an open, loving, and forgiving spirit should encourage us all to walk lovingly and responsibly into the next millennium. Bless Gregg for a burst of energy and courage every time we spoke. And, finally, with eternally burning candles and heavenly bouquets of roses—bless Jeffrey, who had to depart from his true love, Gregg, and the rest of us who knew and loved him because of death from AIDS. Shalom.